Dialogue and Dialectic

HANS-GEORG GADAMER

Dialogue and Dialectic:

Eight Hermeneutical Studies on Plato

TRANSLATED AND WITH AN INTRODUCTION BY
P. CHRISTOPHER SMITH

YALE UNIVERSITY PRESS
NEW HAVEN AND LONDON

The preparation of this volume was made possible in part by a grant from the Program for Translations of the National Endowment for the Humanities, an independent Federal Agency.

Designed by John O. C. McCrillis and set in VIP Baskerville type by United Printing Services, Inc., New Haven, Conn. Printed in the United States of America by The Vail-Ballou Press, Binghamton, N.Y.

The essays in this volume were originally published in German by the following:

"*Logos* and *Ergon* in Plato's *Lysis*," © 1972 by J. C. B. Mohr, Tübingen; "The Proofs of Immortality in Plato's *Phaedo*," © 1973 by Neske, Pfullingen; "Plato and the Poets," © 1934 by Vittorio Klosterman, Frankfurt; "Plato's Education State," © 1942 by Koehler & Amelang, Leipzig; "Dialectic and Sophism in Plato's *Seventh Letter*," © 1962 by Hans-Georg Gadamer, Heidelberg; "Plato's Unwritten Dialectic," © 1968 and "Idea and Reality in Plato's *Timaeus*," © 1974 by Carl Winter, Heidelberg; "*Amicus Plato Magis Amica Veritas*," © 1968 by Felix Meiner Verlag, Hamburg.

Library of Congress Cataloging in Publication Data

Gadamer, Hans Georg, 1900–
    Dialogue and dialectic.

    Includes index.
    1. Plato—Addresses, essays, lectures.
I. Title.
B395.G15   184   79-18887
ISBN 0–300–02126–7 (cloth)
        0–300–02983–7 (paper)

11   10   9   8   7   6   5   4   3

Contents

Glossary

agathon	the Good
aisthēsis	sense perception
aitia, pl. aitiai	cause
alētheia	truth
amathia	ignorance
anankē	necessity
anamnēsis	recollection
apeiron	the unlimited
apodeixis	demonstration
aporia, pl. aporiai	insoluble puzzle, "dead end"
archē	first principle
aretē, pl. aretai	excellence, virtue
arithmos	number
autokinēsis	self-movement
chōra	space
chōrismos	split, division
dihairēsis	division, separation
dikaiosynē	justice
doxa, pl. doxai	opinion
dyas	the Two
dynamis	potential
eidōlon, pl. eidōla	copy, image
eidos, pl. eidē	form, essence
eikōn	image
eikōs logos	probable account
elenchos	refutation
energeia	actuality
entelecheia	fulfillment
enhylon eidos	embodied form, form in matter
epistēmē	science, knowledge
ergon	deed
euporia	felicitous resolution of a problem, the "way out"
hen	the One
heteron	different

heterotēs	difference
hylē	matter
hypokeimenon	underlying substance
idiopragein	doing what pertains to one
kinēsis	motion
koinōnia	blending
logos, pl. logoi	account, statement; pl. all that can be stated, language as a whole
methexis	participation
mimēsis	imitation
mythos	story
nous	mind, reason, intelligence
on	Being
onoma	name
ousia	substance, essence, reality
paideia	education
parousia	presence
peras	limit
phronēsis	prudence, wisdom
physei on, pl. physei onta	what is by or through nature
physis	nature
polloi	the crowd, mass of men
pseudos	falsity
psychē	soul
sophia	wisdom
sōphrosynē	temperance
symplokē	interweaving
synagōgē	collection
technē	craft, art of making something
ti ēn einai	the being which it was, essence
ti esti	what it is
tode ti	the "this something"

Translator's Introduction

This book contains translations of eight of Hans-Georg Gadamer's best known studies on Plato. Although they all display the interpretive art for which Gadamer is so well known and may be said to exemplify the hermeneutical theory which he elaborated in his magnum opus, *Truth and Method* (*Wahrheit und Methode* [Tübingen, 1965], henceforth *WM*), they come from different periods in his development, and consequently the emphases are somewhat different in each of them. The first two studies are later works, "*Logos* and *Ergon* in Plato's *Lysis*" (*Logos* und *Ergon* im platonischen 'Lysis,' Gadamer, *Kleine Schriften III* [Tübingen, 1972], pp. 50–63) and "The Proofs of Immortality in Plato's *Phaedo*" (Die Unsterblichkeitsbeweise in Platons 'Phaidon,' *Wirklichkeit und Reflexion–Walter Schulz zum 60. Geburtstag* [Pfullingen, 1973], pp. 145–61). These were chosen to begin this volume because they most clearly illustrate Gadamer's hermeneutical approach to Plato, an approach rather different from that with which the English-speaking world is familiar, although one which should make good sense to us now, given the development in our philosophy of language from the later Wittgenstein to Austin. Gadamer maintains that each of Plato's dialogues must be understood as spoken language, as a developing discussion. Accordingly they must be interpreted not only with regard to the objective or locutionary meaning of the statements made but also, and even primarily, with regard to the illocutionary and perlocutionary meanings which they contain. In each case, that of the *Lysis* and that of the *Phaedo*, we are dealing with a specific situation in which Socrates speaks to individuals who have special concerns and who, being the people they are and having the perspectives they do, define the horizons of what Socrates wants to say and can say. Thus it is one thing to find the obvious faults in the deductive logic of Socrates' arguments—faults of which Plato himself was well aware and with which, if Gadamer is correct, he deliberately confronts the reader—and quite another to perceive the pedagogical effect of what Socrates is saying. In live discussion, Gadamer tells us, we do not proceed *more geometrico*; instead we move back and forth, often illogically, from one aspect of the thing to another, within a given context or situation which defines the limits of what we say to each other. And the success of such a live discussion is not at all to be measured by its logical rigor but by its effectiveness in bringing the essence of the subject matter to light to the extent that the limited conditions of any discussion permit. Two young boys, one of whom is being pursued by an ardent lover whose love he rejects, can be led only so far in coming to see what friendship and love are, and similarly Cebes and Simmias, two "Pythagoreans" for whom, however, the religious content of Pythagoreanism has lost its significance, can grasp only as much of the reality of the soul as their knowledge of mathematical realities makes accessible for them. Furthermore we should not be misled when each of these dialogues ends in an *aporia* and a puzzlement (which Socrates often sophistically induces) rather than in a clear answer deduced with cogent reasoning. As opposed to methodical deduction, in discussion the question as such prevails over the answer. Good discussions are provocations to think further and precisely therein lies the pedagogical genius of Socrates' *elenchos*.

One other point should be made in regard to the discursive character of Plato's dialogues. Gadamer shows that a good discussion does not have its origin in human agents making "speech acts." Instead it has the structure of *Spiel*, not as a *game* where we follow the rules but as *play* in which we join (cf. *WM* 107). Hence, although Wittgenstein, Austin, and Searle are of considerable help in grasping what Gadamer has in mind insofar as they too move beyond a narrow conception of logic and language, we must keep in mind that when Gadamer, like them, separates spoken language from scientific, methodical designation, there is nevertheless an obvious difference between his understanding of spoken language and theirs. For Gadamer language is not a tool we use but something which precedes us and whose play we submit to. That fact is made clear by the role of the word *oikeion* in the *Lysis*. If we listen to it, yield to it as uncontentious "players" yield to the play of language in a good discussion, *to oikeion*, i.e., that in which one feels at home and which pertains to one begins to reveal for us the meaning of friendship and love just as it does for the participants in the dialogue.

The two studies on the *Republic* which follow, "Plato and the Poets" (Plato und die Dichter, 1934; reprinted in Gadamer, *Platos dialektische Ethik* [Hamburg, 1968], pp. 181–204) and "Plato's Educational State" (Platos Staat der Erziehung, 1942; ibid., pp. 207–20) come from an earlier period in which the perversion of tradition by sophistic demagoguery would obviously be a vital concern. It is here in Gadamer's writing that the "critical" Plato comes to the fore, a Plato who recognizes that traditional education and traditional poetry can no longer function in a situation where the common ethos, which alone provides the foundation for the pedagogical and moral significance of poetry, has been destroyed. In such a situation where the popular consensus is that "no one does what is just voluntarily," Homer and the great tragedians are no longer secure against rhetorical misappropriation of their poetry by those who would use it in the pursuit of political power. Indeed, once in the hands of sophists, their poetry itself contributes to the further dissipation of the souls of the citizens of the state. In imitative recitation, even if only shared vicariously by the spectator, the soul forgets itself. Hence not poetry but philosophy alone, i.e., that which would restore the soul to focused self-knowledge, could heal the souls of the citizens and cure the "well nigh incurable" state. We see, then, that Plato's extreme, puritanical critique of the poets is to be taken as an ironical response to the opposite extremity of sophist unscrupulousness.

Although the critical intent of these earlier studies stands somewhat in contrast to Gadamer's later thinking, it should be noted that at the end of the second of these essays Gadamer refers to the "law of the One and the Many, of number and Being." As the subsequent essays make clear, this reference is an indication of Gadamer's growing awareness of Plato's sensitivity to human finitude and the limits of rational critique. In whatever it may be in which human beings establish oneness and harmony, be it in the soul or in the state, a principle of unboundedness intrudes, the indeterminate Two, the *apeiron*. Indeterminacy and human finitude become the themes of the essays which follow.

In "Dialectic and Sophism in Plato's *Seventh Letter*" (Dialektik und Sophistik im siebenten platonischen Brief, ibid., pp. 224–47) Gadamer treats Plato's excursus on the means of knowing: name or word, explanation or conceptual determination, example or image, and the insight itself. In accordance with his hermeneutical principles, Gadamer again insists that we pay attention to the context of the excursus and to its mode of discourse. The excursus is a recapitulation of propaedeutic oral teachings. Hence, although doctrines for the more advanced student might be implied here, e.g., *synagōgē* and *dihairēsis* in the determination of the concept and ultimately the doctrine of the One and the indeterminate Two, we cannot expect an explication of these doctrines here. What we do find is a remarkable statement of human finitude. All the means of knowing something of which human beings may avail themselves, including the insight itself which they might attain, have a tendency to get in the way and to assert themselves instead of remaining transparent to the thing meant. Thus it turns out that even if we should take mathematical knowledge with its cogent demonstrations as an ideal to juxtapose to the sophists' rhetorical misuse of the power of words to persuade (*dynamis tōn onomatōn*), and even if we should attain a momentary view of the quintessential and invariant idea behind the ordinary word with its inevitable ambiguities, in philosophical matters of the good and just we shall never come to any insight so definitive and irrefragable that someone else who does not want to see it could be made to see it. A sophist like Thrasymachus or Callicles will never see the truth and may well succeed in making it appear that he who actually does see it, does not.

In "Plato's Unwritten Dialectic" (Platons ungeschriebene Dialektik, *Kleine Schriften III*, pp. 27–49) Gadamer deals specifically with the doctrine of ideal numbers, the One and the indeterminate Two. What he finds is not at all a pair of principles from which a *system* of eidetic relationships might be deduced but, on the contrary, a statement of the limits of human insight and, therefore, of precisely the impossibility of any systematization. As opposed to Neoplatonist interpreters for whom the One is of primary significance, Gadamer stresses the equifundamentality of the indeterminate Two with the One. Against the background of that equifundamentality the One emerges as the principle of the whole of the *logoi*, the whole of language, which is not reducible to its atomic parts. The "sum" of the ideas in their interwovenness exceeds its individual components, the manifold of *atoma eidē*, or elementary ideas. Like Wittgenstein, who in criticizing logical atomism draws upon the *Theaetetus'* argument against the reduction of reality to elements, Gadamer draws upon the *Theaetetus* in presenting Plato's doctrine of the One as a critique of the Eleatic atomism of the ideas. The aspects of the One, i.e., Being, the Good, and the Beautiful, Gadamer points out, are not like highest genera which may be equated with all the species that they contain but transcendental ideas which, though present everywhere like the light of day, exceed all of that which participates in them. For Gadamer this means that as human beings we can never come to an overview of the whole which would allow us to systematize it but instead find ourselves under way within an entirety of speaking and thinking which always exceeds the horizons of our perspective. Correspondingly, if one departs from the principle of the indeterminate Two, one sees that any logos which one-ifies, defines, brings boundaries to a certain area of our experience, does so against the background and within the setting of that which remains unbounded, within the apeiron of which the *Philebus* speaks or the *ahoristos dyas*. At this point another application of the metaphor of the sum number results, namely, that the series of numbers extends infinitely beyond any specific sum which might be marked off. Thus the One and the indeterminate Two emerge for Gadamer as models that express the necessary inconclusiveness and infinality (*Unabschliessbarkeit*) in any human speaking and inquiry. Precisely here Gadamer finds confirmation in Plato of his own thesis of the priority of the question over the definitive answer (cf. *WM* 344–51).

In "Idea and Reality in Plato's *Timaeus*" (Idee und Wirklichkeit in Platos Timaios [Heidelberg, 1974]) Gadamer applies the hermeneutic principle of paying careful attention to the text's mode of discourse with remarkable results. He is able to show that within what has been generally assumed to be a continuing *mythos* which accounts for reality in terms of a mythical demiurgos, there is in fact an intrinsic phenomenological logic and that, at least in the explication of the structure of the regular solids in accordance with *anankē*, this logic is mathematically rigorous. Gadamer argues that the mythical god plays no role in this section, which has a quality markedly different from the rest of the dialogue, and that in fact here, in contrast to the *Lysis* and the *Phaedo*, Plato is indeed presenting a demonstration for those who have the mathematical knowledge (stereometry) to comprehend it. This insight leads to a further one: that anankē, insofar as it can be "persuaded" to provide the god with rationally preordered elements, is not only the negative impediment to rational order which most interpreters (Cornford) have taken it to be but also an "ontological opportunity" since what it accomplishes in furnishing the god with preordered elements is indeed beautiful even if not by design.

The final study, "Amicus Plato Magis Amica Veritas" (*Platos dialektische Ethik*, pp. 251–68) again brings Plato's number doctrine to the fore, this time by setting it off against Aristotle's understanding of the *logos ousias*. Gadamer returns here to the starting point for Plato: Socrates' unerring insight into what is good and just in a time when all others vacillate inconsistently from one opinion of these to another. Obviously Socrates sees what is just in the way that a mathematician sees the relationships among mathematical realities, i.e., with complete clarity. Consequently the mathematical, and specifically the number per se (cf. *WM* 390), become paradigmatic for Plato. In contrast, in thinking through the nature of the logos Aristotle departs from the model of the living thing. Aristotle and Plato are alike insofar as both turn philosophy to the *logoi*, to how we speak of things (πῶς λέγεται), but because Aristotle departs from the living thing, Plato's approach to the logoi appears to him to be a Pythagorean (mathematical) abstraction. For Aristotle the logos ousias is not a sum, a combination of abstract eidetic determinations; rather it states the simple (ἀσύνθετον, ἁπλοῦν) invariant character (τὶ ἦν εἶναι) of something as that character was dis-

played *in that thing*. The consequences of Aristotle's position become most evident in the matter of *pseudos*, or falsity. For Plato
falsity is an improper combination of "inharmonious" ideas, but
for Aristotle falsity is a function of the self-display of the living
thing itself. Insofar as the living thing is always a blend of *sterēsis*
and *eidos*, of privation and form, and insofar as it is in motion
from *not* being what it is toward fulfilling itself, any self-display
and, correlatively, any speaking of it remains between what the
thing "is not" and what it "is." Therefore Aristotle proves to be
an "earlier" thinker in Heidegger's sense. He maintains the
equifundamentability of being and not-being. Still, as Gadamer
points out at the conclusion, both Aristotle and Plato speak of a
higher "pure" seeing. In Aristotle that is the *theoria* of divine
nous, and in Plato the vision of the ideas.

I would add that in numerous meetings Professor Gadamer
and I worked out many changes in what would otherwise have
been a direct translation from the German. It was our hope that
the meaning would be made clearer thereby and the English text
more readable. I am very much indebted to the National Endowment for the Humanities for making these meetings possible and
for their generous support of the translation project.

1

Logos and *Ergon* in Plato's Lysis

Plato's *Lysis* has always occupied a particularly prominent position among those dialogues which are quite properly considered to belong to the early period since they stay close to the historical figure of Socrates and to his style of leading a discussion. To be sure, Socrates is depicted here as well in the familiar pose of the dialectician who educates his interlocutors by confounding them, but there are preliminary indications in this dialogue of a ground in being and idea which looms up behind all dialectical[1] disputation. This fact, together with proximity of this dialogue to the great dialogues on love written in the period of Plato's maturity, give the *Lysis* a special character. For that reason an analysis of this dialogue—which presents its own particular difficulties —could be of great value in shedding light on Plato's thought. To be specific, this discussion makes the point of Socrates' dialectical *elenchos* astonishingly clear and displays the reciprocal relationship between the line of his argument on the one hand and the level of insight of his partners in the discussion on the other.

Ironic though it might be, it is not merely a capricious jest when Socrates speaks of the Doric harmony of *logos* and *ergon*, word and deed, in the *Laches*. That harmony—a harmony which

---

1. Throughout the essays, *dialectic* will have several senses which Gadamer intentionally allows to merge with one another (cf. especially chap. 5 below). On one level it simply means the back-and-forth of discussion. In its more technical senses it can either mean the sophistic rhetorical skill of reducing a position or an assertion to an absurdity or the philosophical skill of collecting and differentiating according to essence (*synagōgē* and *dihairēsis*). There is also a Hegelian element in Plato's dialectic in the sense that the dialectical refutation of a position is not always merely negative but often points to a higher truth. However, Hegel's understanding of dialectic is essentially very different from Plato's, as Gadamer makes clear in "Hegel and the Dialectic of the Ancient Philosophers" (*Hegel's Dialectic* [New Haven, 1976], pp. 3–34). (Translator)

1

no one could be said to have achieved more fully than the Platonic Socrates himself—is posited here as something for which we must continually strive. Socrates says to Laches, who is courageous in *deed*, that their discussion could be found wanting in this harmony because Laches does not know and cannot *say* what courage is (*Laches* 193 de). To be sure, his inability to say what it is, is a common incapacity of which one becomes conscious only when Socrates demands that one account for what one is saying (λόγον διδόναι). For that is a demand which cannot easily be shunted aside. Must one not know what courage actually is when everyone is constantly speaking of it as the quintessence of virtue (*aretē*)?

It was, however, not some dispute stemming from a deficiency in knowledge but an opposite deficiency in actual deed which occasioned the Athenian's appeal to the taciturn and indefatigable Spartans and their Doric harmony. Thus in a joking and ironic manner, Socrates invents the saying which Laches, quite in accordance with the Spartan ideal, had just cited. Laches means his Spartan principle sincerely (188 c–e). The latest mode of speech-making and arguing which had captivated the spirited and oratorically gifted youth of Athens at the beginning of the fifth century B.C. seemed wanting in precisely that Doric harmony of logos and ergon. When the students of the new art enter into conversation with Socrates and submit to his examination, they are at first full of tidy new answers to the question of what courage, justice, temperance (*sōphrosynē*), and piety (*eusebeia*) are. And when their claim to know is confounded, the advocates of the new knowledge are refuted not only in a battle of words, but in deed, in their existence proper. Their presumed but ultimately useless knowledge lacks the weight of the ergon.[2] Thus it comes to pass that in Plato's ingenious fictional dialogues a good and truly Socratic answer which someone gives in response to Socrates is nevertheless overturned by the latter with the most questionable means of sophistic dialectic, for instance in the *Charmides*, where Critias himself advances Socratic

2. There is a sort of Wittgensteinian insight here. Sophistic talk in which words separate from deeds or actions, is in a certain sense, at least, "language on a holiday." (Cf. chap. 5, n. 32, below.) (Translator)

self-knowledge as an answer to the question posed. Of course Critias was known to every reader in Attica at that time as one of the Thirty Tyrants, who formed a government at the end of the war and whose arbitrary rule made earlier times seem idyllic to Plato in comparison. That this very same Critias advocates sōphrosynē and self-knowledge starkly illuminates how sharp the conflict was between logos and ergon in Plato's Athens. But as a matter of fact this conflict is not only characteristic of the Athens of that time. It is present in all philosophical knowing. It is not just at a particular hour in the history of Athens that the shadow of sophism accompanies philosophy, but always.

In this fact, it seems to me, lies the most important reason that the Platonic dialogue, as opposed to every other philosophical text in our tradition, possesses and will always possess a relevance to the present. We should remember how Plato was led to the art of these written discussions. In his *Seventh Letter* Plato himself relates how fateful the encounter with Socrates became for him and what it meant to him that this man, whom he so deeply revered and sought to emulate, was condemned to death for corrupting the youth with the then fashionable arts of sophistry. Plato's magnificent writings are dedicated in their entirety to showing that the Socrates who had to drink the cup of poison was no sophist. But Plato also seeks to make clear why nevertheless Socrates, because of his singular art of dialectic, i.e., of guiding a person in thoughtful discussion, would of necessity look like a sophist to the Attic court, provoked as it was by these latest fashionable practices. It is his own experience with this man and the latter's fate which inspired Plato's life work and his writing. In Socrates he encountered in living reality how a person could steadfastly hold to what he viewed as right—unerringly, unconditionally, and in self-reliant independence from all external influences.

Plato's *Crito* provides perhaps the most impressive monument to this fact: on the eve of his execution Socrates refuses the escape which had been readied for him, an escape which might well have been greeted with relief by the broad circle of the Attic public. And he refuses it solely because it seemed right to him, after having acknowledged the laws of the *polis* for so long and having enjoyed the protection of his rights which they afforded him, to submit to even an unjust verdict. Plato must have asked himself how a Socrates was possible in a polis whose political sense was as corrupted as the political sense of the Athens of that time. What power could have enabled someone, quite in contrast to the usual way of doing things, to hold to what is just, as though it were something real beyond all question and all dispute?

Must not the "just" have been as tangibly evident and inescapably real for him as the tangible facts of our existence are for the rest of us? Plato's answer to this question was the doctrine of ideas. What is just is not something valid by a convention whose bindingness could be disputed; rather it is something so overwhelmingly real that its existence transcends all behavior established by the social convention and all of a society's beliefs (*doxai*). We know that the doctrine of ideas formulates the conditions of all genuine knowledge in elaborating on precisely that fact.

Even the grand discussion of the state which occupies the central position in Plato's dialogues, the *Republic*, must be read as an answer to this same question. Here the answer to the question of how Socrates was possible is presented starting from the other end, so to speak. Ultimately the state which Plato has Socrates construct, the state in which philosophy would govern, is meant to answer the question of how a state would have to look in which Socrates would *not* be the exception who succumbs to a tragic fate but the accepted rule. It would be a state in which justice, i.e., the complete unity of the individual and the universal, would be the reality everywhere and whose politics would depend on men all of whom were like Socrates. In this state *idiopragein*, doing one's own work, would have to be the principle of all citizens, and in all circumstances and in all classes a knowledge and sense of the common good would prevail. When it is said that in this state the class of guardians is to watch over the common concerns of all and to assign appropriate tasks to each of the other classes, it is only to be understood as a mythical exposition of the components of the human being, the animal who forms states.

But all the smaller dialogues as well are aimed at keeping alive the question of what knowledge gives human action and behavior the unerring certainty which Socrates displayed in his life. In conforming to this aim Plato confronts Socrates with the famous chieftains of sophism so that his difference from them might emerge clearly. Without doubt, "sophist" was a word of derision in the eyes of the conservative citizenry and it took the audacity and self-confidence of a Protagoras to accept such a characterization nevertheless. But it also took all of Plato's genius and philosophical intuition to expose and refute the claim of such a hybrid artistry in 'knowledge.' Now the difference between Socrates and the sophists is in no way an obvious one; rather it is a difference evident only to someone who has not only the logos in view but also the ergon.

Socrates often avails himself of the sophistic arts of argument, but whatever the reason might be, that he does cannot in any way be attributed to some deficiency in the logic of that time. To be sure, Aristotle was the first to clarify the essential theoretical foundations of drawing correct conclusions, and in so doing he also explained the deceptive appearance of false arguments. But no one could seriously contend that the ability to think correctly is acquired only by a detour through logical theory. If we find in Plato's dialogues and in Socrates' arguments all manner of violations of logic—false inferences, the omission of necessary steps, equivocations, the interchanging of one concept with another—the reasonable hermeneutic assumption on which to proceed is that we are dealing with a *discussion*. And we ourselves do not conduct our discussions *more geometrico*. Instead we move within the live play of risking assertions, of taking back what we have said, of assuming and rejecting, all the while proceeding on our way to reaching an understanding. Thus it does not seem at all reasonable to me to study Plato primarily with an eye toward logical consistency, although that approach can of course be of auxiliary importance in pointing out where conclusions have been drawn too quickly. The real task can only be to activate for ourselves wholes of meaning, contexts within which a discussion moves—even where its logic offends us. Aristotle himself, the creator of the first valid logic, was well aware of how things stand here. In a famous passage in the *Meta-physics* (1004 b, 22 b) he declares that the difference between dia-lectic and sophism consists only in the προαίρησις τοῦ βίου (the choice or commitment in life), i.e., only in that the dialectician takes seriously those things which the sophist uses solely as the material for his game of winning arguments and proving himself right.

Let us, then, follow the evolving discussion of the *Lysis* and let us seek to uncover the correspondence between logos and er-gon in the line of its argument. And let us forgo reconstructing the logic of that line of argument in a critical, meta-discursive logical analysis. The usual approach to the line of thought in So-cratic argument in the *Lysis* has the most trouble precisely in re-gard to the discussion here, *for it fails to take the principle of the Doric harmony between logos and ergon as its guide*. As a consequence it discovers only a muddled zigzagging from one point to an-other and can find no logic at all in the discussion which Socrates conducts. But what occurs here is in fact quite clear. The youths who dare to answer Socrates' questions on the basis of their understanding of life find that Socrates has no ear for the apparent reasonableness of their answers. Mercilessly Socrates hammers their answers to pieces with the tools of soph-ism. Each time the discussion seems to be drawing near the crux of the matter, a new dialectical hurdle is put in the way and the interlocutors are diverted from the goal. Thus the young people are left behind, perplexed and disconcerted, and at the end they no longer know what friendship is. That seems to be the whole of it. But if one follows the evolution of the discussion in regard to the reciprocal relationship between logos and ergon, things take on a meaningful, sequential order. One suddenly recognizes that any discussion which Socrates conducts about friendship with two young boys *must* end in an *aporia*, for children do not yet know what friendship is and how complex a relationship an enduring friendship creates between the friends. The confusion in which these half-children are left is not to be viewed as nega-tive per se; rather it is an indication of the incipient maturation in their own existence as human beings.

The theater for this discussion is the Palaestra, one of those meeting places where boys and youths of the best social circles in Athens used to come together for sports and instruction of all sorts. Here Socrates draws a pair of friends, two boys, Lysis and Menexenos, into a conversation. Although the discussion appears harmless enough, it provides a hint of things to come. Socrates asks the two which of them is older. They answer that they are arguing about that. Then he asks which is more beautiful, whereupon both laugh, somewhat embarrassed. And then, which is richest. At that point, however, Socrates himself interrupts the conversation and suggests that one cannot ask such questions, for friends are equal in everything and have everything in common. And with that we have the catchword for the remainder of the dialogue. What do friends have in common? Socrates acknowledges that he was about to ask which of the two was more just (*dikaios*) and which more temperate (*sōphrōn*). Both words are difficult to translate. *Dikaios* implies not only what we call "just"; it also has overtones of honesty, propriety, fairness, and so on. And as the *Charmides* shows, for example, the original sense of *sōphrōn* was "having good manners" and the word corresponded to what we call "well-behaved." But its semantic vibrations pass from this range of meaning to the sphere of a higher morality of mind and spirit. In the *Lysis* the question of what these are receives no answer. One of the two boys is called away and the discussion is broken off.

Let us ask ourselves what Plato wishes to indicate with this prelude. Surely one may already surmise that the discussion will be about friendship. But one can surmise a lot more than that, and one has a presentiment of what a long way it will be from this childish form of so-called friendship to insight into what friendship really is. What does friendship mean to these boys? Obviously Socrates is addressing the two on the level of children, which they in fact are. Friendship for them is that naive comradeship of boasting and outdoing one another in which children warm up to each other. Still, this kind of friendship which develops in competitive comparisons that each makes of himself with the other, contains a first, unquestioned common ground, which provides an indication of the ultimate truth of the matter even here. To be specific, one hears, if one listens closely enough, that with the question of justice and temperance Socrates' inquiry is moving into a realm where one can no longer make these naive comparisons meaningfully since now what is truly shared and binding for each alike comes into view, i.e., that which perhaps makes real friendship possible in the first place. That an external event (the one boy's being called away) breaks the thread of the discussion is undoubtedly a sort of intimation of what is to come. In his way Plato is clear enough.

One suspects that ultimately friendship belongs to the realm of "virtues," to the sociopolitical world, and one knows, of course, that not only in the Greece of that time was having friends a prerequisite for being effective politically. For the time being the discussion is with the boys who, given their background and education, will undoubtedly engage in politics eventually but who are not yet mature enough to do so now. That they are not is specifically indicated at the end, when the dialogue terminates in confusion and Socrates says that he wants to look about for *older*[3] interlocutors with whom to continue the discussion—only to have the gathering break up. This ending too is one of those interruptions which requires one to think beyond what has been said expressly. What friendship is can indeed be asked only of those who are older. And we have the echo of Plato's *Lysis* in his doctrine of love (*Symposium*, *Phaedrus*) and his theory of the state (*Republic*) and, beyond that, in the three marvelous books of Aristotle's *Ethics* which treat friendship, taking it to be a central element of ethics in antiquity. It is self-evident that the ethics of antiquity was political ethics insofar as it always viewed the individual, his actions and his existence, within the framework of the political community.[4]

We must not forget then that ultimately the question of friendship is aimed at uncovering what the just community is. At this point, however, we are a long way from that goal. One need only think of the beginning of the above discussion, where Socrates instructs one of the young men, Hippothales, who, as

3. One should keep in mind that Aristotle expressly demands a mature audience for his ethics.

4. Attempts to weaken the bond between Aristotle's ethics and his politics (Gauthier) are not convincing.

was the custom then, is wooing the boy he loves. Socrates demonstrates to him how one is to proceed in such matters successfully. In a typically Socratic fashion, Socrates makes the boy admit that only he will be esteemed who knows how to do something and that he will be esteemed only to the the extent that he knows how to do it. In this way Lysis is humbled—Lysis, an ambitious boy spoiled by his lover and to whom Plato applies the expression, μέγα φρονεῖν, which means to be haughty but also to "think big." The vectors of meaning waver here as always, for the Platonic dialogue is played out in the field of such wavering. Lysis' haughtiness is turned to humility by the insight that he is still too young and still knows how to do so little. But although made insecure, he is at the same time made certain of the desire to learn that is awakened within him and he thereby acquires a new and more genuinely substantiated self-image. Now Greek pedagogy being what it was, it was natural that the concluding of a bond of love between a youth and a boy would simultaneously lead the boy into a higher community and put him on the way of what is called "friendship."

In the meantime Menexenos returns and Socrates begins the discussion with him. In jest Plato portrays Menexenos as particularly contentious. This portrayal is not meant as an allusion to the sophistic style of arguing; rather it is intended to make clear that the boy enjoys contradicting and disputing. But although it is not meant seriously when Socrates is cautioned that Menexenos argues so sharply, we are nevertheless given an indication of the character of the ensuing discussion, i.e., that it will have an element in it of that eristic dialectic which only confounds and does not instruct. Socrates begins in a characteristic way. He suggests that these two boys have already found what he has been seeking all his life, namely, real friendship. The reader who knows Plato's irony knows what that really means: "You two still have no idea at all what real friendship is." And as we have seen, the friendship of these two boys is in fact friendship only at the stage of innocent, childlike, ingenuous accord.

In order to understand the development of the discussion here it is necessary above all to keep the objection in mind which was made against Socrates' demand that a definition always be

given of the subject under discussion. It was argued against
Socrates that the true reality of a thing was not contained in
knowledge of what it is by definition. Even Aristotle himself says
that the important thing is not to know *what* a virtue is, but *what
brings it about*. Still, no other Socratic theme is perhaps as well
suited as that of friendship to illustrate why knowledge of what
something is is crucial after all. When we have been disappointed
by another and must say of him that "he has no idea what
friendship is," we are speaking of no mere logical deficiency in
his ability to define something, to be sure, but of a deficiency in
knowledge nonetheless. He who does not *know* what friendship is
obviously lacks both a constant supportive relationship to himself
as well as the capacity to be constant and supportive in his relationship to others. This imperturbable, reliable supportiveness,
which can be neither jeopardized nor confused, is not without a
kind of knowledge, i.e., a conscious perseverance against whatever might jeopardize or confuse it. In extolling the friendship
of these boys, who quite unproblematically display the greatest
accord, the comparison which Socrates brings to mind is obviously with the possibility of a higher, more conscious and dutiful
unanimity. Still these boys are indeed of "one heart and one
soul," albeit in an all too simple way. Plato shows that so nicely by
having Lysis, who has been humbled by what has just transpired,
request that Socrates nevertheless repeat it all for the friend who
was not present at the time. Thus the discussion with Menexenos
reflects something real although no success is had in thinking
that reality through and comprehending it conceptually.

The questions which Socrates raises are "picky" indeed.
Who in fact becomes the friend of another, the lover of a beloved, or the beloved of a lover? When Plato catches Menexenos
in an aporia here, he certainly wants us to sense that in actual
friendship it is impossible to distinguish the lover from the beloved in this way and to say who is the lover and who the beloved. Friendship obviously exists where the question of which
is which no longer arises, just as love is obviously no longer
there when one asks the other if he still loves him. Plainly the attempt to get at friendship from outside the relationship itself, i.e.,
starting from the particular existence of the individual friends,

must fail. Nevertheless here too, as the success of the Socratic discussion at this point demonstrates, it is meaningful to ask what the self-understanding of each friend is, for self-understanding is precisely what is required in real human, moral life. Knowledge is the important thing. But he who knows cannot be confused in his knowledge by another. And with that we have arrived at the claim which Plato makes for his dialectic. As opposed to sophism, his dialectic cultivates the ability to hold unerringly to that which one sees before one's eyes as true. Socrates sets the example here to the extent that he knows how to lead the way through confusion to unshakable knowledge, to use the former as a means to attain the latter. Here the confusion stems from the two meanings of *philos*, i.e., both "loving" and "dear."[5] (Language is wise enough to ensure that the word does not refer onesidedly to the subjective condition of a single individual apart from the relationship.) Socrates' questioning, which destroys the youth's understanding of friendship, plays upon a genuine experience in life, an experience which he can obviously assume is known to all. It was the experience in Greek life often had by the lover who attempts to gain the affections of a boy who is still a child. When someone loves and thinks that he can demand friendship in return even if his love is not reciprocated, the other's rejection of him can become so vehement that the other begins to hate him. Precisely this has come to pass between Lysis and his lover, Hippothales. Thus there is a great deal more to be heard in the background of the logical disjunctions between "lover" and "beloved" with which Socrates plunges this sharp-witted boy into confusion. The point, however, is obviously that these logical disjunctions are not being tested against a *real* knowledge of friendship.

Plato makes that point manifest in a marvelous way. When Socrates notes that they have taken hold of the subject matter in the wrong way, Lysis, this reserved and well-bred boy, suddenly

5. There is neither a single word in English which would express the double sense of *philos* nor two cognate words, such as the German *liebend* and *lieb*, which Gadamer uses here. Lieb poses a problem and for want of anything better, I have chosen to render it as "dear." For with all its deficiencies, it seems preferable to "cherished" or "lovable." (Translator)

shouts out, "Yes, God knows, we have indeed!" and turns red. In having the boy express himself with such agitation, Plato shows how much Lysis is engaged in the discussion. But even more is implied than this. Not only does his own childish understanding of friendship, which is based upon the sameness of friends, resist these sophistic distinctions which Socrates has been making. It seems that as a consequence of his having been so disquieted by these sophistries, something of a premonition comes to him that real friendship might be an entirely different, tension-laden thing.

Accordingly, Socrates turns to him at once and makes a new proposal based on the boy's own understanding of life, while at the same time drawing upon the wisdom of the poets. In so doing he casts aside the misdirected question "why" someone becomes a friend. Plato turns to the poets, who express what everyone thinks, to uncover what friendship really is, i.e., what this force in life is, over which "the god" has control. "Like," we are told, seeks out "like." This view is supported by a quotation from Homer and an allusion to Empedocles. The way in which Socrates treats this testimony of the ancient wisemen is characterized by an irony typical of Plato, an irony similar to that which is found, for example, in the famous passage in the *Sophist* on the first philosophers to have considered what Being is. The deep, yet simple truth which these poetic sources express, i.e., that friendship seeks what is "like," has, to be sure, something immediately illuminating about it, which Socrates states specifically. Only those who are "good" are capable of friendship, and only those who are one with themselves, which is to say, are "like" themselves, can be "like" someone else and be a friend. But this deep and ultimate insight of Plato's presupposes an understanding of *like* and *friend* very different from that which Lysis has. Thus it is quite easy for Socrates to obscure the beautiful Platonic truth that friendship is possible only between those who are good. What "like" means to Lysis, and that on which he and his friend agree, corresponds to a conception of "good" which has nothing to do with Plato's deeper insight. And for that reason Lysis cannot hold his ground against the bewildering questions which Socrates puts to him. Two who are like each other can obviously expect nothing useful or advantageous from each other, can they? And anyone who is good is self-sufficient and has no need of someone like himself.

Indeed, this argument makes the opposite possibility seem much more plausible. Again Socrates calls upon the poets, this time Hesiod. Envy, jealousy, and hate occur precisely between those who are in the same situation. On the other hand, often-times those who are in dissimilar circumstances are dear to each other, viz., the rich to the poor, the strong to the weak, the doctor to the infirm, the wise to the ignorant. Thus it seems far truer that opposites attract one another—a fact which a mere glance at the early Ionian science of nature confirms. But now it is demonstrated that this 'truth,' illuminating though it certainly is, is based upon just as meager an understanding of what friendship is as was the thesis on likeness. And in a curiously so-phistic way it too is refuted. The greatest opposition which can be thought of is the one between friend and enemy, and there-fore they would of necessity attract each other and be friends. He who accepts such an argument obviously has no real knowl-edge of what friendship is, for the argument takes the opposi-tion between friend and enemy to be like the opposition in na-ture between hot and cold. Here the mere force of attraction is taken to be friendship.

So Socrates proposes the third and remaining logical possi-bility, which brings us very near Platonic or, better said, human secrets. The reason for something's being dear to a person is that that person himself is neither like nor unlike, neither dear nor despised, neither good nor bad. Taken logically, what we have here is a familiar conceptual distinction in Plato which is known to us especially from Speusippus and which constitutes one of the first pieces of logical knowledge to be acquired in Plato's school. Besides the two alternatives in a conceptual opposition there always remains the third possibility of "neither/nor." This third possibility really does seem to be the case with friendship; he who feels friendship for someone sees in the other something which he himself is not, but the thing which he sees, which he is not, is more like something which has not yet been achieved in himself, something more like a potential in himself, which leads

him to look for a model in another. All beginning friendships
which have left the level of boyhood friendship behind are in a
way such a choosing of a model, and all subsequent enduring
friendships preserve something of this element in them although
in a reciprocal relationship which establishes the friendship on a
new basis.

Socrates deduces an important consequence from this possibility. If someone is neither good nor bad, it means that something must be "present" in him, present as a lack, as something
which he needs. Here Socrates calls that which is missing in a
person, this lacking of something, the *parousia* of something bad.
Parousia is the mode of being of the bad here. We know this expression, parousia, to be one of the most important, basic ontological concepts in Plato. Here it obviously has a quite simple,
harmless meaning, but even so, the concept implies a subtle distinction which begins to charge this harmless word with tension.
Socrates chooses a truly grotesque example to illustrate the driving force implied here in friendship or love. When a young man
disguises himself and colors his hair gray, the color of his hair is
gray, to be sure, but the gray is not there in the way it is when I
am gray. On the contrary, we have here the mere presence of
something bad, the appearance of a deficiency, as it were, which
does not mean that something therefore *is* bad. Obviously in the
case of the feeling of deficiency which provides the basis for
friendship, we are dealing with just such a presence. In a certain
sense, it is a "false" presence, which is to say that it points back to
something concealed behind it which underlies it and is the truth
of the matter. This makes good sense generally from a human
point of view even if we give it a specifically Platonic interpretation. If one who is neither good nor bad is capable of loving the
good, it means in the first place that despite the presence of a
deficiency, the presence, that is, of something bad, he himself is
not bad. But taken positively, it means further that he transcends
himself insofar as he *longs* for something not there. Longing has
the structure of such self-transcendence. On the basis of this argument some of the most fundamental conclusions in Plato are
now drawn, e.g., that the *sophos* or wise man, like the god, does
not philosophize, nor does he who is simply ignorant, but only

he who knows that he does not know. One can see why the answer which Socrates has arrived at (218 c) is greeted triumphantly. Friendship has its basis in a "neither/nor" which longs for the positive, longs for the good.

This passage is striking. One understands what is happening in the exchange only if one does not seize solely upon the inevitable thwarting of this apparently felicitous result when it is pressed by logical counterargument. One must look beyond its logical insufficiencies, which are ultimately to be taken as insufficiencies in the conception of friendship which has prevailed up to this point. For if it is experienced positively, what we now have is the germination of a deeper insight into what friendship means. If one clings to the sense of *like* and *dear* within which the understanding of things has moved up to now, it will seem right away as though the friend were nothing more than a means, as though he were there only to rid me of my deficiencies. There is no denying that there is a profound human truth here. An infinite number of human involvements do have their origin precisely in the fact that a person can stand himself no longer and throws himself into the arms of one nearby. Even so we would be reluctant to say that the essence of true friendship consists in one person's being the means of remedying the deficiencies of another. We know, as a matter of fact, that he who understands friendship in this way and who would thus reduce his significance to that of being there solely for the other, destroys the communal basis of the relationship. However if friendship, being what it is and constituted as it is, never permits one person to be the means for another's needs, then we can say that what is really "dear" no longer serves any purpose at all. Generally speaking it may be the case that I would hold something dear because I have a specific need, for example, of a drink of wine when I feel weak.[6] But true friendship cannot be like this. In friendship one cannot be dear merely according to the sense of the word (*rhēmati*), i.e., insofar as he is useful.

---

6. To say that wine is "dear" admittedly taxes English usage more than it will bear. The problem results from the fact that *dear* does not always coincide with the German lieb. (Translator).

Rather he must be dear in reality (*tōi onti*) (cf. above on the *Laches*). Only then is he truly dear. Thus the way of friendship in the *Lysis* leads to a first result and serves as a prelude to the famous way of love upon which Diotima leads Socrates in the *Symposium*. The interpreters are mistaken when they find this train of thought unfounded or arbitrary and hasty in its *logic*. On the contrary it is quite logically thought out. Real friendship can exist only where what or who is dear to me does not depend upon any conditions which make it dear. For conditions, as we know, can always change. Friendship and love are fundamentally defined by the fact that something or someone is never dear to me because of this or that pleasure or advantage which the other thing or person provides for me. On the contrary, where friendship and love exist, there is something primary and fundamental: an unconditional being dear of something which is dear in itself and which lies outside the whole chain of things which are held dear as means to an end.

Prima facie Socrates' argument juxtaposing what is really dear with what is only conditionally and mediately dear does indeed seem logically unsatisfactory. It appears that he conflates two distinct things, means and purpose. A thing is dear because of its usefulness as a means, but it is dear in this sense only because of the purpose it serves. Socrates gives an example which is irreproachably lucid. One loves the doctor and medical treatment *because* one is sick and *for the sake* of health. The goal is health, the doctor or the medicine, the means. The reason that one needs the latter is the presence of something bad which has befallen one. Here the cause as the "because of" (*dia ti*) and the purpose as the "for the sake of" (*heneka tou*) are clearly distinguished. But Socrates can nevertheless still interchange dia ti and heneka tou just as in German one interchanges *wegen* and *umwillen*. Thus we can say, for instance, that the wine is dear on account of one's feeling weak in the sense of the German *um . . . willen*, meaning on account of (German: wegen) the strength which it gives us. The actual "for the sake of" (*Worumwillen*) is the state of health and not the sickness. But language is never unknowing, and thus it is quite convincing here when it speaks in this way. Means do present themselves as purposes; they are encountered in a context of getting to a goal. Thus we are not dealing here with a logical mistake, i.e., the confusion of a causal determination with a final determination, but with the intertwining of both determinations in human experience.

This intertwining is obvious in friendship. What appears to be the highest purpose to Plato, to be "primary" love, is strictu sensu not uppermost and highest in a hierarchy ascending to the ever higher. Calling it primary is Plato's way of expressing what will later be more precisely elaborated in the unified context of the doctrine of ideas. What is meant is *a different mode of reality or being* and not an elevation in the same reality. At the basis of friendship is something which is dear in a very different sense from that of "being useful" to me. What emerges when one ascends to higher and higher means is not greater and greater utility but another mode of being altogether: that which is "good" *eo ipso*. Our own experience of friendship and love illustrates this convincingly. What is dear in itself is not dear in the same sense as that which is conditionally dear, dear for the sake of something else. In explaining to oneself the fundamental difference between these two senses of *dear* and in experiencing their difference, one transcends everything conditional and rises to what is truly real, *to ontōs on*. Concepts like "good" and "right" and "dear" do not take on their full and satisfactory meaning when one thinks of them as a *pharmakon* or remedy, as a means to something else. If all longing were really possible only because of the lack of something, if I could long for something only because I lack it, then the being dear to me of anything would presuppose this lack. Thus, someone is dear to me only so long as he helps me in remedying my deficiencies or is of some use or other, and I in fact would understand *dear* to mean only that which is useful and advantageous. That cannot be what makes love what it is. Since what is useful to me always varies, I would never be capable of what really constitutes love or friendship.

But is all longing really of such a nature that it depends upon a deficiency, upon what I lack? If such were the case that which is longed for would cease to be good once my need were fulfilled. And is there not something dear which remains when the bad thing, the privation, is gone (221 c)? Is all longing a need which has passed when it is satisfied in the way that thirst is quenched when one has drunk something? Is it really sufficient to say that one values something to drink only when one is thirsty? Or is it not much more the case that one enjoys something in the drink which is good in itself, e.g., in the good wine which is not to be washed down with water and the goodness of which does not depend on my being thirsty and having nothing else around to drink. This trivial example can easily be carried over into the realm of friendship. Does the proper attraction which brings and holds friends together consist in a person's being for another what the other lacks? And does it last only as long as he lacks this thing? Or is there a mode of attraction which is not governed by the law of self-termination but which of itself nourishes and augments itself, as it were, so that we can say of friends that they are always becoming more for each other? This does not mean at all that one absorbs the other or that they must eventually get on each other's nerves. On the contrary, does not friendship between human beings consist in the fact that a person finds his self-awareness, his self-confidence through the other, and not that he merely wishes to forget himself and his needs in the other?

As a matter of fact Socrates finds a word to express the character of this tension-laden relationship in which need and fulfillment coexist. It is the Greek word *oikeion*, i.e., that which pertains to the household, to the *oikos*. It is an ordinary expression for relatives and house friends, i.e., for all who belong to the household. Oikos, household, thus has the broad sense of an economic unit such as the Greek household characteristically was. But oikeion is just as much an expression for that place where one feels at home, where one belongs and where everything is familiar. We too have usages similar to the usage of the Greek oikeion which display this double aspect in the conceptual field of household. In German, *hoi oikeioi* is rendered as *die Angehörigen* and in abstraction from this normal usage we have come to speak of *das Angehörige*, meaning everything which pertains to the household and not only those people who belong to it.

In das Angehörige, however, there are always overtones of

das Zugehörige too, i.e., of that which is proper to the household, that which belongs to it: das Zugehörige is that which answers to me and that to which I answer[7] because it pertains to me. Socrates uses oikeion and its semantic field to say that there is a need in me of das Zugehörige, a need of that which pertains to me. And that is a need which does not cease when it is met, and that in which the need finds fulfillment does not cease to be dear to me. That which pertains to me and to which I belong, is as reliable and constant for me as everything in my household. Socrates concludes that when someone loves another as a friend, his longing is directed to the other person in such a way that the former fulfills himself in his longing. Ultimately what he seeks is that quality in the other which pertains to him and which gives his longing legitimacy.

At this point the discussion, which Socrates has thus guided to the edge of Plato's doctrine of the true being of the idea, suddenly becomes a live dramatic scene. The human, real-life implications of what has been said become obvious when the lover, who has been unlucky in his love until now, concurs passionately in this legitimization of his passionate longing, while Lysis, on the other hand, who has no eye at all for the lover who pursues him so persistently (and who in fact does not see him at all because Hippothales has carefully hidden himself behind the others), falls silent and only unwillingly admits that the boy for his part should love the true lover too. Obviously the result is not to his liking. Like Socrates' irony and like his complicity in aiding Hippothales woo his beloved, Lysis' shyness and his unwillingness to accept the result are intended by Plato to show indirectly how the discussion now touches upon its actual subject matter, the word, upon the deed. And in fact the boy backs away from the possibility of "friendship" just as he backs away from the

7. *auf das man hört oder das auf einen hört.* Gadamer follows Heidegger here in stressing the element of *hören* (hearing) in the German *Zugehören* (belonging) and he applies Heidegger's insight to *das Angehörige* (that which pertains). Heidegger's point, upon which Gadamer tacitly relies, is that, as opposed to seeing, in any form of *hören* I am never a theoretician viewing something from above, which I have put before me (*vorgestellt*), but instead always under way within an occurrence which transcends the horizons of my awareness. My relationship to *das Angehörige*, for instance, has this structure of being under way within. (Translator)

lover who is pursuing him. The logos here has not yet revealed something in deed (*ergoi*) to this boy, whose experience still lags behind what Socrates has been saying.

Socrates plays a singularly reserved role here. Indeed it is more accurate to say that he makes every effort to obscure the truth to which the discussion leads. *The reader* might notice that the answer, "to oikeion," contains the deeper meaning of what was meant by "the same" at an earlier stage in the discussion, and very likely it will not be lost on him that what is called "oikeion" and "the same" can also be called "good." But Socrates confuses his young friend by falsely making it seem that a distinction must be maintained among "oikeion," "the same," and "good." This distinction leads again into the cul de sac into which the discussion had gotten earlier. The conclusion now becomes inevitable that neither the lovers nor those loved, neither being the same nor being different, neither being good nor "pertaining" to each other can be said to constitute friendship. One must know oneself what friendship is if one is to grasp once and for all that in it sameness and difference, longing and fulfillment, growing intimacy with others and with oneself, are all one and the same thing. And precisely this the boys do not yet know.

The discussion which Socrates has conducted with the boys and which he would have liked to continue with someone "older" ultimately points beyond itself to a growth of actual friendship and to a knowledge of what being a friend is. The way is paved for the Doric harmony of logos and ergon which Plato's philosophical utopia will subsequently construct—although again only in words.

2

The Proofs of Immortality in Plato's *Phaedo*

In many respects Plato's *Phaedo* dialogue must be considered one of the most marvelous and significant writings in all Greek philosophy. Certainly not the least reason for this is that it is the *Phaedo* where Plato has his teacher, Socrates, speak of the expectations one may have concerning death and the beyond—this on the last day of his life in a final discussion with his friends. No doubt, too, it is this theme of the afterlife and the way in which it is treated which have given credence to the idea that the *Phaedo* is to be understood as a kind of counterpart to the Christian's overcoming of death. Precisely Socrates' proofs of immortality, so it seems, might be taken as the pagan prefiguration of the overcoming of death in Christianity. This of course, is a misconception, as will soon be made plain here, but nonetheless it has been a productive misconception for the eighteenth century in particular. The comparison of Socrates to Jesus is inappropriate. In arguing against it, I would like to show that Plato's dialogue raises the very different question of what may be saved of the ancient religious tradition in an age in which scientific explanation and understanding of nature are in the ascendant and have supplanted the mythological picture of the world, and in an age, as well, in which logic begins to come into its own and assert itself. Plato raises the question of what account one can give of death in this situation where conscious, rational accounting of things is the order of the day.

To be sure, we must not overlook the mimetic character of Plato's dialogues. We are dealing here with a poetic presentation, which should never be measured against a one-sided criterion of logical consistency. Rather, the presentation recounts a human discussion which must be understood as discussion. The proofs of the immortality of the soul which follow one another in this discussion all have something deeply dissatisfying about them. That, it seems to me, must be presupposed in any examination and analysis of this dialogue. The arguments themselves are unconvincing, however much the human presence of Socrates *is* convincing—the presence of this Socrates, that is, who on the last day of his life quite cheerfully leads and dominates this conversation with his friends, driven on as he is by an unconditional dedication to the subject matter itself, and who at the end of the day drinks the cup of poison with complete composure and peace of mind and takes leave of his friends without yielding to the slightest fear of death. As Nietzsche has so aptly put it, this figure of the dying Socrates became the new ideal to which the noblest of the Greek youth now dedicated themselves instead of to that older heroic ideal, Achilles. Thus the *Phaedo*'s poetic power to convince is stronger than its arguments' logical power to prove. But Plato cannot be faulted for that since in saying this we are merely following Plato himself. He has Socrates and the latter's friends ponder the mysteriousness of death and brings them to admit that despite all proofs of immortality, however convincing, the child in us does not cease to be afraid of death. Thus it seems appropriate to me to first examine Plato's mode of demonstration to see if it indicates whether Plato was fully aware of the insufficiency of these proofs and, if we find that he was, to ask then what the actual intent of his demonstration is. It seems clear that despite the inadequacy of all these proofs they have a sort of logical order to them and display increasing cogency, but it is just as clear that ultimately these arguments must be thought of only as expositions of an assumption and not as conclusive demonstrations.

As a point of departrue for our questioning let us first consider the fictional setting itself which Plato selects as the scene for the discussion in the *Phaedo*. The discussion proper takes place between Socrates and two "Pythagorean" friends.[1] I find this significant, for these two "Pythagorean" friends, Simmias

---

1. Of course just about anyone is called a Pythagorean in the tradition, but that is exactly the point. Not only those contemporary with Plato are the so-called Pythagoreans (Archytas et al.). And as precisely the *Phaedo* teaches us, it was one-sided of Frank to think that they were.

and Cebes, in no way represent a religious group of the sort established by the forefather of the Pythagorean sects. Instead they stand for that particular sort of mathematical investigation, theory of music, and cosmological knowledge which has, as not the least of its sources, Pythagorean teachings. And beyond this, as we shall see, they are quite at home in the natural science, biology, and medicine of their day. Now one should keep in mind that in the *Apology* Plato represents Socrates, not as an expert in modern science at all but, on the contrary, as one who himself repeatedly asserts his own ignorance of science and who restricts himself to the moral problems of mankind and to self-knowledge. When Plato has Socrates, in the hour of death, enter into conversation with "Pythagorean" representatives of contemporary science, that is obviously meant to show that Plato saw it as his own task to unite the moral introspection for which Socrates stood with the scientific knowledge represented by the Pythagoreans; and perhaps it will prove to be the case indeed that "Pythagorean" science is not without importance for the great human questions which Socrates would have us pause to consider.

If we depart from this hypothesis in undertaking our analysis, we see right away that the actual exchange is ignited by a specific religious problem. Plato knows how to make important things clear by emphasis. After an extended introductory discussion, the conversation turns to suicide, i.e., that form of self-annihilation expressly forbidden in Pythagoreanism. It is at the moment when this question is posed that Socrates raises himself and begins to lead the whole discussion from his sitting position. It is striking here that he asks the Pythagoreans what they know of their teacher's, Philolaos', prohibition of suicide, and they admit that they know nothing definite about it and that Philolaos hardly ever spoke of it. Their ignorance gives us a clear indication that they are no longer interested in the religious content of the Pythagorean teachings and that they therefore genuinely represent the modern scientific enlightenment. It is Socrates who must remind them of the religious background of this Pythagorean doctrine.[2] One small thing in particular makes espe-

2. The other teachings of Philolaos which parallel the *Philebus* so remarkably play

cially evident how far removed these Pythagoreans are from the religious tradition of Pythagoreanism. When Socrates questions how such an inflexible prohibition could be established when in many cases it would obviously be better to die than to live on in an unendurable fashion, Cebes states his agreement in a remarkable way. He falls back into his Boeotian dialect! (62 a). Plainly Plato wants to show where the heart of the man is and how totally the ideal of rationality and reasonableness dominates these ' Pythagorean friends. Their attitude is confirmed directly thereafter in the argument which Cebes advances. Although the ancient Pythagorean prohibition of suicide was clearly intended to reinforce the religious ties of the human being and the doctrine of transmigration, to stress the *salvation* of the soul, Cebes converts the argument against suicide into a criticism of Socrates' readiness to die. He shows that this readiness is incompatible with Socrates' own admission that he presently lives under the auspices of benevolent gods. The truth of the religious tradition has paled to such an extent for Cebes that the fate of the soul in the beyond is no longer of any concern to him. And in quite the same manner, Simmias simply laughs when Socrates declares "dying" to be the crux of all philosophy (64 a).

All this stands very much in contrast to the emphasis with which Socrates' activity was characterized at the beginning of the discussion as some sort of divine work and Socrates himself as a successor to Apollo, a device which is facetiously carried to the extreme of portraying Socrates as a composer of verses. Although Socrates most certainly does justify his readiness to die in availing himself of the idea of the purification of the soul at death, it is clear nonetheless that in Socrates the older Pythagorean conception of purity has given way to a new one. Purity for him is no longer to be identified with prescribed cultic rites of purification, to which the members of an order cling as their *symbola* without the least bit of self-understanding. On the contrary, for Socrates *purity* means the new awareness of oneself

---

no role here. Thus the authenticity of what is said here hangs precariously in the balance. But one would certainly be well advised not to set Philolaos, who seems to come in the third generation after Pythagoras, too far apart from those pursuing mathematical cosmology. The theme of suicide was evidently no longer central even for him.

found in the life of the philosopher who concentrates upon thinking. Again it is significant that this recasting of the ancient tradition (66 d) is readily and heartily accepted by the Pythagoreans. For "pure thinking" is indeed what characterizes "science," i.e., the mathematics, which was central for the Pythagoreans of this generation. (To be sure, an adequate understanding of what mathematical purity is, is first made possible by Plato's doctrine of ideas, which, as the course of the discussion will show, these Pythagoreans cannot yet really comprehend.)

Thus it is quite in keeping with the "this worldly" attitude of these men that they trumpet a crude materialism which, in opposition to the accepted Homeric religion, thinks of death as the total dissolution of the human soul (70 a). These modern doubts about the beyond and immortality give the discussion its actual theme: It must provide proofs of the immortality of the soul in opposition to such skepticism. The discussion is neatly divided into two parts. It starts with a series of three proofs, to the last of which Socrates appends an impressive moral exhortation which is described as profoundly affecting his listeners. Then, as is clearly marked by a fresh set of objections, the discussion enters a new and deeper dimension. Thus in a certain way the first three proofs are closely tied to one another.

The first proof, which is based upon the universal cycles of nature and the balance prevailing in it, obviously relies upon the same ancient Ionic doctrine of opposites which had served as a schema in Pythagorean philosophy of nature. What is striking about the proof is that it is obviously unsuited to prove the point which it is supposed to prove. The fear of any thinking person that, like the last breath, the soul might escape with the final exhalation from the body and dissipate, is a widespread and natural uncertainty, one which the Pythagoreans here do not invent but only articulate. And the inappropriateness of any recourse to the universal cycles of nature to deal with this uncertainty is palpable. It almost seems, in fact, as if Plato specifically wanted to confront the reader with this obvious inappropriateness. In any case all the manuscripts which we have (without exception!) would have it that from this proof one can deduce not only that the souls of the dead exist but also that existence after death makes things better for good souls and worse for bad ones. This conclusion makes so little sense that, in accord with Stallbaum's proposal, it has been deleted in the modern editions (72 e) on the grounds that the similar but not identical turn of speech at 63 c 6 might indicate that that is its proper locus. Logically Stallbaum is right. The argument does not follow here at all. But is it not the case, perhaps, that the reader is supposed to notice that it does not follow? Is it not ultimately the very deficiency of this proof which prompts Cebes to introduce what is properly speaking not his idea but Socrates', i.e., *anamnēsis*? And to do so with a direct reference to the argument known to us from the *Meno*?

But neither can this anamnēsis proof, the intent of which is ultimately to display the acquaintanceship in a previous life with true essences (ideas), an acquaintanceship which precedes all experience on earth and is independent of it, suffice to counter uncertainty about life *after* we die—even though it is a masterful example of Plato's ability to simultaneously analyze and elucidate. Its insufficiency becomes quite obvious at the conclusion of the argument, when this proof is treated by the Pythagoreans as only half a proof, which leaves the question of the afterlife of the soul open (77 a,c). Their response speaks volumes, and Socrates' proposal to combine the first two proofs only underscores the position of the Pythagoreans. As if these two proofs could actually complement each other! For certainly it cannot be overlooked that "soul" in the one means something quite different from "soul" in the other. The Pythagoreans do not think at all in terms of the Socratic "soul" which knows itself. Although they have often heard of Socrates' doctrine of anamnēsis, they have trouble remembering it and they stay within their perspective, which is defined not by the self-understanding of the *psyche* but by their investigation of nature and living things in nature.

The limitations of their point of view are exposed indirectly when Socrates intimates that the two of them might still have the fear which every child has, namely, that the soul might simply blow away at death (77 d). But even so he appeals to these Pythagoreans as especially qualified to follow his argument. When the complaint is voiced by both of them that after Socrates dies no one will be able any longer to use thought to allay the fears of the child in us, Socrates not only points to the fact that there already are others in Greece who are able to allay such fears in the way he does, he appeals in particular *to these two themselves*: "It might well be that you yourselves are the easiest to find and the best suited of those who are able to do that" (78 a). This seems to me to be an indication that mathematicians and those knowledgeable in mathematical science have a requisite capability of which they need only be made aware with sufficient clarity, namely, that of "pure" thinking which applies to an order of reality different from that given in sense experience. In his anamnēsis proof Socrates had clearly emphasized the appropriateness of mathematical knowing for grasping the concepts of true Being and the soul, and in first departing from that basis he had proceeded to draw "moral" conclusions: οὐ γὰρ περὶ τοῦ ἴσου νῦν ὁ λόγος ἡμῖν μαλλόν τι ἢ καὶ περὶ αὐτου τοῦ καλοῦ καὶ αὐτοῦ τοῦ ἀγαθοῦ καί δικαὶου (For our argument was concerned with the Equal but just as much with the Beautiful in itself, the Good in itself, and the Just) (75 c). Furthermore, this repeated allusion to mathematics had earned him Simmias' enthusiastic agreement on the anamnēsis proof (77 a). The third proof, which Socrates is now ready to present, very specifically brings into the foreground an ontological distinction known to mathematicians: the distinction between invisible and visible reality.

Socrates is plain enough. After the proof based upon his elaboration of anamnēsis has been termed half a proof he does not spare his partners. For one thing, he proffers the synthesis of the first two proofs as a completion of the demonstration in a way which patently falls short of what is logically required. But worse than that, he returns his two partners in the discussion to the level of the dogma of the common man, which holds death to be the escaping of one's life breath and hence something to be feared as the dissolution of oneself. This devolution of the discussion indicates nothing less than that the two friends with whom he is speaking have not yet really grasped the meaning of *psychē* as that concept is worked out in the doctrine of recollection. The third proof which follows the other two after the important intermezzo therefore attempts to break down the ontological foundation upon which the popular misconception of the soul is based. After several runs at it, Socrates finally makes it plausible that the soul has a different mode of being from the body. The soul belongs to the realm of true Being. Of primary importance here is the conceptual correlation of "being dissolved" and "being composed of parts." *Neither* of these can be said of the soul and its knowledge of true being. And when one starts with this fundamental distinction between visible and invisible reality it can be deduced that in death the soul of the philosopher, who seeks to detach himself from the senses and thereby to free himself for knowledge of the true reality, attains just that knowledge, which is to say, happiness. Thus the specific purpose of this proof within the whole of the discussion is to found the immortality of the soul in concepts of genuine invisibility and permanence as opposed to, and beyond, the relative permanence given in the sense world, e.g., that of mummies.

Now this purpose accords with pre-Socratic thought certainly, but it by no means assures that the proper concept of the psychē which Socrates desires to inculcate has been grasped and that the appropriate understanding of oneself, which alone would provide a moral foundation for *philosophia*, has been achieved. Indeed the *inadequacies* of this third proof in fact generate the ensuing discussion. Still it should be noted how readily the Pythagoreans acknowledge the superiority of the soul which strives for wisdom and that they are quick to accept this reinterpretation of the ancient and traditional doctrine of the transmigration of souls—a reinterpretation which borders on the comic. To be sure, the humor and irony of the exposition here (81 c–82 d) are camouflaged and the moral exhortation to pursue asceticism outweighs them. Nevertheless we are meant to see that this is a joke which rational thought is playing with traditional religious dogmas, for that is Plato's way of indirectly emphasizing the continuing inadequacy of the demonstration up to this point.

This might also be the place to remark that it is precisely this third proof which was expanded upon in Moses Mendelssohn's eighteenth century reworking of the *Phaedo*.[3] Mendelssohn, of

---

3. *Phaidon oder die Unsterblichkeit der Seele* (Berlin, 1776).

course, stresses the concept of alteration rather than the simple concepts of being dissolved and being composed of parts, for he wishes to show the impossibility of something suddenly ceasing to be. The continuity of natural processes guarantees for him the impossibility of a sudden cessation and annihilation. Thus his is a very different proof, one built upon the *lex continui*. In general it can be said that Mendelssohn reproduces more the poetic motif of Plato's dialogue than the logical content of its arguments. But the third proof of *Phaedo* and Mendelssohn's proof do have one thing in common: both would prove the immortality of the soul on the basis of a particular understanding of nature. In Plato the concept of the noncomposite, invisible, and permanent provides the foundation of the argument, while Mendelssohn, in going beyond that foundation, extrapolates from the concepts of alteration and continuity in time, to the being of the soul.

But Plato's dialogical mode of presentation, of course, has nothing in it of the deductive logic which Mendelssohn claims for his demonstration, the "dogmatic" character of which was exposed in Kant's famous critique. On the contrary, it should never be forgotten that in the case of Plato's 'demonstration' of immortality we are dealing with a mere stage in a dialogical exposition, whose deeper concern is not immortality at all but rather that which constitutes the actual being of the soul—not in regard to its possible mortality or immortality but to its ever vigilant understanding of itself and of reality. Thus after the point of dramatic equilibrium of the whole, marked by the stunned silence of all and the hushed whispering of the two Pythagoreans, the discussion resumes with the objections of these two friends, objections introduced with the qualification that in regard to matters as uncertain as the question here, one may at best seek the answer least likely to be refuted (85 c). In short, Socrates does not promise an adequate proof but only a defense against objections which result from a deficient understanding of what he means by soul. To this extent the objections may be said to follow consistently. If one thinks of the soul as a harmony, this harmony is certainly invisible but dependent upon the existence of the body nevertheless. And if one thinks of the soul as the perpetually self-renewing power of life which animates the body and holds it together, the soul is indeed more enduring than the parts of the body which come and go, but by no means can it be concluded that its power is *never* exhausted and that it itself is not eventually destroyed. Both of these are serious arguments and we should be aware of their scientific basis. They are metaphorical formulations of genuine scientific questions. Simmias' argument obviously uses a Pythagorean theme drawn from a mathematics which takes itself to be a science of nature, and Cebes' argument appears to be taken from a biology which conceptualizes the lifegiving power of the soul, its capacity to integrate organically, in terms derived from contemporary physics and medicine.

The response of the assembled friends to the introduction of these new elements into the discussion makes the background completely clear which determines the whole discussion, namely, the scientific enlightenment and the resultant collapse of the heretofore unquestioned validity of the religious tradition. Plato underscores this in a special way. The doubts which surface here, doubts which fill these Pythagoreans and which cut so sharply to the roots of the religious beliefs and mythical accounts of the soul, are so grave that their undermining effect spreads from the situation of the earlier discussion of these matters to the situation of those recounting that discussion, Phaedo and Echecrates. At this point Plato disrupts the framework adhered to up to now in the dialogue. If we are properly informed, Echecrates, who was himself a Pythagorean, considered the harmonic structure of the soul to be an established fact, and he is dismayed here by Simmias' skeptical treatment of this doctrine. It is self-evident that the latter's materialistic interpretation of the soul is not actually Pythagorean but a materialistic conclusion constructed in opposition to Plato's idealism. And it is certainly in keeping with the way things stand at this point that Socrates finds this the occasion to say something about the danger of skepticism and, specifically, of the misology which tends to develop when the struggle for clear insight repeatedly miscarries. That is a danger which Plato obviously sees in the sophist's art of confounding and confusing—and not without historical justification.[4] As we shall see momentarily, it is precisely this danger

4. Consider the role played by Protagoras and Gorgias, both of whom Plato places

which gives the doctrine of hypothesizing the *eidos* its real significance.

If we examine the counterarguments on which Socrates now falls back, we notice first that the two Pythagoreans wholeheartedly endorse the concept of anamnēsis and evidently not so much because of its role in the Pythagorean doctrine of salvation as because of its importance in founding science (cf. the *Meno*). But Socrates has an easy time making them aware of the incompatibility of that doctrine with the Pythagorean teaching on harmony (92 a ff.). The indestructible and unalterably precise numerical determinacy of harmony which underlies the Pythagorean number theory also provides the basis for the Pythagorean beliefs on the soul and its transmigration. Simmias, in contrast, is obviously arguing on the basis of a theory of the balance of opposites, a theory which derives from contemporary medicine. And Cebes' objection makes definitively clear that this way of thinking is not really Pythagorean at all. In his version the religious doctrine of the transmigration of souls is expressly and emphatically reinterpreted in physiological terms. The many bodies in which the soul is incarnated do not imply different "lives" but rather a single life, the vital power of which repeatedly changes its material "stuff." At 87 d it is said that any one soul would use up many bodies, especially if it should live for many *years* (not "lives"), and the body would fade away "while the human being goes on living."[5] Here the transmigration of the soul with its repeated incarnations is, as it were, only the result of the surplus power (ἰσχυρόν τι) which the soul has already displayed in this life (88 a 7; cf. 91 d 7). The argument that Socrates uses to refute Simmias' skepticism goes to the core of Pythagorean mathematics. It turns on the distinction between *being* harmony and *having* harmony. The soul which *is* a harmony, i.e., the soul conceived of in terms of number theory and which is said to participate in the indestructible harmony of the

---

in the framework of tradition-bound *paideia*, as sponsors of this newly developing skepticism.

   5.   One would be rid of the whole problem which results from the destructibility of harmony and the incompatibility of that destructibility with Pythagorean beliefs about the soul, if one would pay proper attention to the analogousness of the argument here with the harmony objection.

world, is vulnerable to the 'scientific' objection that it is dependent upon a material substrate. Consequently, number theory cannot succeed in justifying the religious dimension of the soul. On the contrary, soul must be thought of as Socrates thinks of it: by departing from our human self-understanding. From that perspective it can be seen that the soul can *have* a harmony and lose it, for it is characteristic of the human soul that it must endeavor to maintain its own order. Thus at this point human moral understanding and the Pythagorean concept of harmony converge. When they do, a distinction becomes necessary which is of quite a different sort from the Pythagorean distinction between visible, perceptible being and the numerical, harmonic ground of the latter, which in Pythagoreanism emerges as the true being of things behind the fluctuating facade of appearance. Although mathematical science necessarily distinguishes between mathematical being and perceptible being, it is evident that prior to Plato a clear ontological conception of this difference in being was lacking. As is well known, traces of the Pythagoreans' insufficient understanding of what they themselves were doing were to be found even in the mathematics of Plato's time (cf. my study of Plato's *Seventh Letter* below, on the squaring of the circle). It is Plato's interpretation of Socrates' concern for the soul which first provides the Pythagoreans with an appropriate understanding of their own mathematics. The world does not consist of numbers even though it is true that the recurrent rhythms in the processes of nature obey numerical determinations (if only in the mere approximations of which perceptible being is capable). The being of the soul, however, which understands itself and its own being,[6] is not the numerical being of nature or a *being* harmonious. To consider it as such is a "naturalistic" fallacy.

Indubitably the high point of the whole dialogue is the refutation of Cebes' objection. And that it is, is underscored once again with characteristic dramatic means. Socrates remains silent for some time, completely withdrawn into himself, and only then

6. *die sich selbst in ihrem Sein versteht*. The phrase should be understood against the background of Heidegger's analysis of *Dasein's* understanding (*Verstehen*) of itself as it projects itself toward its future possibilities (cf. *Sein und Zeit* [Tübingen, 1960]).

does he enter upon the famous account of his way to philosophic thought. He describes his dissatisfaction with natural philosophy, his hopes and disappointment in regard to Anaxagoras, and finally he expatiates on that second best way, the way through the *logoi*, i.e., the procedure of hypothesizing the eidos. Though he is still under way, this hypothetical procedure promises to return him from the perplexity, into which science had plunged him, to a clear understanding of himself and his pursuit. This is not the place to explicate the procedure of hypothesizing and to establish its far-reaching consequences for Plato's dialectic. But since for neo-Kantians this first exposition of Plato's doctrine of ideas was taken to be the most important evidence in support of their linking of Platonic and Kantian idealism, it is necessary that we correct some current misconceptions and point out that the function of this doctrine within the whole of the discussion of this dialogue is quite different from that implied in the modern methodological concept of hypothesis, with its scientific overtones. As a matter of fact Socrates says quite clearly how this procedure of hypothesizing the eidos would free him from a perplexity into which he had been led not so much by the science of his time as by the sophistic application and distortion of that science. Far from being a modification of scientific procedure, the hypothesis is introduced here as a dialectical tool with a purpose relative to the task at hand: combating sophism. The new element in the procedure does not consist in the invalidation of a previous hypothesis and replacement of it with another when it is found to contradict the facts—that is taken for granted. The new requirement which Socrates establishes is in fact the converse. In contrast to the modern procedure of verifying a hypothesis, the hypothesis of the eidos is not to be tested against an "experience" which would validate or invalidate it. Such a procedure would be totally absurd in respect to a postulated eidos: that which constitutes being a horse could never be proved or disproved by a particular horse. Instead, the test which is to be applied in respect to the eidos is a test of the immanent, internal coherence of all that is intrinsic to it. One should go no further until one is first clear about what the assumption of the eidos means and what it does not mean. It should be noted that consequently the hypothesis is not to be tested against presumed empirical consequences, but conversely the empirical consequences are to be tested against the hypothesis, i.e., that from the start everything empirical or accidental which the eidos does not mean and imply is to be excluded from consideration. This means above all that the particular which participates in an eidos is of importance in an argument *only* in regard to that in which it may be said to participate, i.e., only in regard to its eidetic content. All logical confusion is a consequence of failing to distinguish and separate the eidos from what merely participates in it. Where one fails to make the distinction, one is easily caught in apparent [sophistic] contradictions, such as saying that the number 2 can be "generated" by addition on the one hand but also by division on the other (cf. *Phaedo* 101 b ff.). A proper testing of the eidos hypothesized here would exclude as extrinsic and sophistic everything which the concept "generates" introduces.

Thus only once the hypothesis, which is to say the communicative agreement implied by it, has been secured, is one in a position to test its validity and to proceed to further hypothesis. We see, accordingly, that hypothesis is designed to fend off the dialectical tricks with which the new sophistic *paideia* had armed itself and in reaction to which Plato's Socrates risks that second best journey: the journey, namely, into the logoi themselves, into this new and perplexing element in which he seeks and finds firm ground. It strikes me as highly significant that Cebes, who has shown himself so well informed about the science of his time and who certainly must be well acquainted with the mathematical concept of hypothesis spoken of in the *Meno*, has especial difficulty in understanding the first exposition of the hypothetical procedure here (100 a 8)—significant, it seems to me, for all those who do not recognize the difference in principle between the function of the hypothesis in science and the function described by Socrates which it has in dialectic, but significant and definitive too for the mathematician, who wants no part of the sophist's ψιλοὶ λόγοι (derisive comments) (*Theaetetus* 165 a). Certainly both the Pythagoreans and Socrates need to fend off such talk and Plato reinforces this common ground between them in the strongest possible way with the dramatic means which the dialogue form makes available to him. The hypothesis of the eidos is the defense against the newly developed art of blind eristic argument. In that, both friends emphatically concur. They speak with one tongue, so to speak, "ἅμα." And to heighten the emphasis Plato again interrupts the recounting of the discussion. For Echecrates and Phaedo too fully agree that this latest fashion of sophistic double talk must be exorcized.

But it is obvious that even here the Pythagoreans still do not see the real implications of the doctrine of ideas. As the discussion unfolds, Plato indicates that fact to the reader, who should be thinking these matters through on his own. Once again his way of indicating their ignorance is most ingenious. Socrates bases the rest of his demonstration upon the established fact that opposites exclude each other and that consequently Death *and* Soul and Death *and* Life may not be combined. At this point an unknown person joins in (103 a). Now why does the narrator no longer remember who it was? Could it be because no one present (except Socrates) could possibly raise his objection? In any event the unknown person, in calling attention to the beginning of the discussion, demurs: "Have we not already admitted the contrary, namely, that opposite always comes from opposite, larger from smaller, smaller from larger, and indeed, that all becoming is from opposite to opposite? And now it would appear that that cannot be." The passage here is clearly accented. Someone *unnamed* speaks up (this alone underscores the point) and then comes Socrates' answer, which plainly blames Cebes for the confusion expressed in this argument (107 c). Even though Cebes does not want to admit it, one must allow that he himself does not clearly see the decisive difference between "idea" and what "becomes," between opposites themselves and that which has opposite qualities. *And precisely therein lies the limitation of the Pythagorean explanation of number and world: Pythagoreans take numbers and numerical relationships for existence itself and are unable to think of the noetic order of existence by itself.* Obviously the crucial point in refuting Cebes' objection is that the discussion of the "cause" of all coming-into-being and passing-away (95 e) led to the ontological distinction between the idea and what becomes, between *ousia* and *genesis*. It is the world of ideas from which science is derived and which alone makes science possible. But there could hardly have ever been an interpreter of Plato who could not see that this proof of the ontological relationship of idea, life, and soul, as marvelous as it might be, is incapable of demonstrating anything more than the character of the universal *eidē*, Life and Soul, and that it most certainly cannot allay the fears which the specific individual soul has of being destroyed, fears which pervade its self-understanding.

The thesis which I am seeking to establish here is that actually Plato himself did not expect this fact would escape anyone, and that he by no means overestimated the power of this proof. In essence that can be seen in the way in which the result is formulated (107 a). Cebes says that he is convinced, but Simmias, from whom a response is also expected, is much more cautious; to be sure, he can find no reason to be incredulous, at least not on the basis of what has been said. But given the importance of the matter and given our human frailty, he finds it necessary to remain skeptical nevertheless about what was stated (107 b). And Socrates emphatically agrees with that! As convincing as the discussion might have been, the conclusion is drawn that the proofs are not sufficient and that one must continue to test their premises insofar as is humanly possible. Evidently in questions of this sort one cannot expect greater certainty.

Thus all that remains of these demonstrations is their application in the moral realm. *If* the soul is immortal, it is right and necessary to show proper concern about it now in this life. For that will be of critical importance for its entire being. The same moral application is repeated after the colorful portrayal of that other world below and the same conclusion expressly drawn at 114 d. One must, as it were, keep "singing" these future prospects to oneself (ἐπᾴδειν ἑαυτῷ). This brings us back to the splendid metaphor of the child in us, whose fears of death are never quite to be allayed by rational arguments, however convincing. It seems to me that in this metaphor and in the return to it here the question regarding the point of the whole demonstration is answered. The fear of death which is never quite to be put to rest is in fact correlative to our having to think beyond the surrounding world given to us in sense experience and beyond

our own finite existence. Plato certainly does not want to say
that he has proved the same immortality of the soul which is basic to the religious tradition. But what he does want to say is that
the spreading skepticism resulting from the scientific enlightenment does not at all affect the sphere of our human life and our
understanding of it. The growing scientific insight into the
causes of coming-into-being and passing-away, into the course of
natural processes, does not obviate the need for thinking beyond
the reality of this world, and it has no authority to contest religious convictions. Thus the point of the demonstrations, it seems
to me, is that they refute doubts and not that they justify belief.
And how indeed should the phenomenon of death in all its im-
mensity ever become comprehensible for human reason and insight, and yet how much even so does it continue to demand
from human beings a response to its imponderability. Evidence
of this fact is provided above all by that silent yet eloquent ances-
tor worship and tomb art which projects human feeling and
imagination beyond the inner certainty of one's own being alive
to those departed in death and which preserves the dead one as
a member of the family. It seems that Plato has in mind especially this answer of the religious tradition when he says that the
task of giving ourselves courage, "singing to ourselves," and al-
laying our fear of death is never completed. In particular the solemnity with which he says that after his death there will be men
enough who can indeed reassure us points to the gamut of questions concerning man's existence and thoughts about death:
"Great is Greece and many excellent men there are in her. Numerous too are the foreign peoples among all of whom one must
seek those who can reassure us. No expense and effort are to be
spared, for there is nothing toward which one could better apply
one's life and possessions" (78 a). When it is said that the search
for the right reassurance should go beyond the community of
those who speak the same language, is that not an indication that
the question being asked transcends the community of any language and what can be conceived of in it? We see today that it
was the role of the Greeks in world history to have made science
with its special capacity for clear insight the foundation of human culture. But even science cannot let this question drop, and

it cannot evade the task of finding an answer to it, the task which our human existence and our urge to think beyond the perceptible and proximate world assign to us. This fact is expressed in the linking of *psychē* and eidos in Plato's thought.

To be sure, Kant displayed the fallacy of the 'rational' demonstration which Mendelssohn developed in his rethinking of the *Phaedo*. But Kant's own philosophical insight comes very close to that of Plato's dialogue. Kant's critique 'proved' human freedom just as little as Plato proved immortality. But it did prove that the a priori validity of causality underlying all natural science could not disprove our human sense of being free. For Kant freedom was the only rational fact. Plato called that same fact something else: *idea*.

3

Plato and the Poets

> Difficult though it might be to detect it, a certain polemical thread runs through any philosophical writing. He who philosophizes is not at one with the previous and contemporary world's ways of thinking of things. Thus Plato's discussions are often not only directed *to* something but also directed *against* it.
>
> Goethe

In his *Republic*, a work which develops an ideal order for the state and for its program of education, Plato condemned Homer and the great Attic dramatists to permanent exile from the state.[1] Probably nowhere else has a philosopher denied the value of art so completely and so sharply contested its claim—which seems so self-evident to us—to reveal the deepest and most inaccessible truths. Perhaps the most difficult task to confront the German mind in its efforts to assimilate the mind of the ancient world (and perhaps the most unpalatable too given the self-image of the former) has been that of justifying Plato's critique of the poets and grasping its meaning. For it is precisely the art and poetry of the ancients which the aesthetic humanism of the German classical and romantic periods took to be the epitome of classical antiquity and which they made an obligatory paradigm

---

1. The following analysis was presented on January 24, 1934, at the meeting of the Society of Friends of the Humanistic Gymnasium in Marburg. The published version here is thus also directed to the wider circle of those interested in its subject matter. For that reason prefatory remarks and citations of supporting texts are omitted for the most part. Moreover the excerption of Plato's critique of the poets from the *Republic* as a whole makes it impossible to consider here some of the most central elements in its overall argument, e.g., the dialectical explication of the traditional concept of justice in book 1, the Socratic transformation of the ancient doctrine of the virtues in book 4, and above all the doctrine of the ideas in books 5–7, which in proceeding beyond the doctrine of virtues, completes the definition of man and state. (Cf. chap. 4 below.)

39

for themselves. And Plato himself, the hostile critic of this art of classical antiquity, was felt by the romantics to be one of the most splendid embodiments of the poetic genius of the Greeks and was admired and loved from their time on just as much as Homer, the tragic poets, Pindar, and Aristophanes. Moreover the scholarly research which resulted from this revitalization of the classical ideal in Germany justified this response to Plato in its own way. It inquired into the particular law of form governing Plato's dialogical compositions and discovered in Plato's work the wonderfully artful synthesis of all the elements of form which had defined the development of literature from Homer through Attic tragedy and comedy. Indeed Plato himself proved to be the only one who meets the requirement which is established in the *Symposium* in the night-long discussion of Socrates with the tragedian Agathon and the comic poet Aristophanes, namely, that the true tragedian must be the true comic poet. Furthermore this situating of Plato in the history of developing poetic forms is supported by the ancient tradition, which tells us expressly that as a youth Plato himself composed tragedies.

But this same tradition also tells us that Plato burned these youthful attempts after he became a disciple of Socrates. He who understands this account understands Plato's critique of the poets. For certainly we cannot take it to mean (as the ancient authorities would suggest) that Plato, having been awakened by Socrates, abandoned the misguided ways of his youth. We cannot interpret it, in other words, as we would ordinarily interpret such a biographical account of a creative individual, i.e., as a report of his discovery of his own true talent. If this story is actually true and not in fact some fictitious formulation of Plato's later critique of the poets, the truth of it is not that Plato recognized that he did not have the *ability* to be a great poet but that he recognized that he did not have the *desire*. For the encounter with Socrates as a very epiphany of philosophy had brought home to him that being a poet was no longer worthwhile.

Obviously there must be a measure of the value of poetry besides the one with which we are familiar and which Plato uses to oppose the classical poets so sharply. In book 10 of the *Republic* we learn the reasons for Plato's rejection of the beloved Homer.

Homer, it is said, had not founded a better state than Charondas or Solon. Nor did he have any ingenious discoveries to show for himself like those of Thales or Anarcharsis. Nor was he influential in the private sphere; unlike Pythagoras, who established a Pythagorean way of life for the few, Homer created no Homeric life as the leader of a circle of followers. Nor could he even compare to the great sophists in being an effective and successful educator, but instead he found himself living an unstable rhapsodic existence. Now when we read this and hear what the standard is by which Homer's poetry is to be evaluated and rejected, how could *we* be won over to the philosophers and turned against the poets? For we, certainly, would no longer presume to apply this standard to either poets or philosophers or, in fact, to apply it at all as a measure of intellectual significance.

We must attempt, therefore, to reach a new understanding of Plato's standard if we intend to assess his decision against poetry and his criticism of the poets. It cannot be our purpose to dispose of Plato's decision by saying that it is merely the function of some particular distant and irrelevant moment in history. On the contrary we wish to make it possible for this decision of Plato's to mean something to us too. When Plato burns his tragedies, he does not settle an eternal dispute about the priority of philosophy over art or vice versa, by establishing which provides the deeper interpretation of life. Rather he recognizes that in the hour of his decision Socratic philosophy is not to be circumvented. And the poets fail just as much as anyone else to face up to this necessity.

I would call to mind here Socrates' remarks in the *Apology*, in which he relates how he had tested the saying of the oracle that no one is wiser than he. He examined statesmen, poets, and craftsmen and found them all to be ignorant. The interrogation of the poets, however, elicits something which distinguishes them from all the others. Although the poets themselves can give no answer to Socrates' question about what true virtue is, their *works* might contain a valid answer. The poets confirm the Delphic utterance only to the extent that they take themselves to be great knowers although they, like seers and interpreters of the oracles, say what they do only from divine inspiration. Though their poetry might always be prophetic, Socrates' examination reveals that they themselves are less qualified to interpret it than any of their listeners.

> The poet, when he sits on the tripod of the muses, is no longer in his right mind. Like a fountain, he willingly lets whatever enters him stream forth. And since his art is only imitation, he is forced to create characters which oppose each other and thus always to speak against himself (to contradict himself), and he does not know if the one thing or the other of that which he has said is true (*Laws* 719 c).

> The poets say what they say, not from their own wisdom, but in being filled by the god and possessed. . . . They create their poems like Bacchants creating honey and milk out of rivers (*Ion* 534 a).

And they tell us,

> that they harvest the honey of their songs from streaming well springs in the gardens and meadows of the muses and bring it to us like bees, they themselves being in flight. And they are right: the poet is something buoyant, winged and holy, and he cannot create until he is filled by the god and without consciousness and until there is no more reason in him (*Ion* 534 b ff.).

This acknowledgment of the poet's *enthousiasmos*[2] is fraught with the most dangerous ambiguity. Despite the glowing description of the poet, a basic tone of irony and criticism predominates. Although poetry might be divine madness and possession, it is in any case not *knowing*. It is no skill (*technē*) which could account for and justify itself and its truth. The pictures of life which the poet most powerfully evokes remain equivocal enigmas like life itself, and Socrates cannot learn the true art of living which he seeks from them. Thus it sounds like undisguised irony when Socrates advances the poets as "fathers of wisdom

---

2. Here to be taken literally as *en-thous-iasmos* or "being filled with the gods," *Götterfülltheit*. (Translator)

and leaders," and in fact he most sharply contests that Homer "educated all of Greece."

Nevertheless this is not all that lies in Plato's treatment of poetic enthousiasmos. Socrates really has no intention of settling whether the "divine men" say the truth or not, and whether in times which were nearer to the gods the truth of their poetry might in fact have been understood although it is no longer understood today. He knows only his own lack of knowledge and the lack of knowledge of those whom he can question. Thus the "yes and no" of the irony here in respect to the poets demands that we inquire philosophically into what might justify his critique of Homer.

Exactly why does Plato reprove Homer? First, for his picture of the gods, i.e., the human appearance, so well known to us, which he gives the gods—gods who in the heights of their Olympian existence quarrel and transgress, plot and scheme in much the same way that men are forever doing. And second, he resists Homer's image of Hades, which must necessarily arouse the fear of death. He objects to the excessive bewailing of the dead, the excessive scorn and ridicule, and the wanton passions and desires in Homer's gods and heroes.

All this seems to be more a critique of myth such as it exists in Homer than a critique of poetry per se. And Plato is not alone in his criticism of myth. His predecessors here include philosophers such as Xenophanes, Heraclitus, Pythagoras, and Anaxagoras, all of whom had similar criticisms of Homer's theology. But above all it is the later poets, Pindar and the tragedians, who are in agreement with Plato. It is they who purified and exalted the imagery of the gods and heroes by building upon the old myths while expressly rejecting the traditional form of the legend. And they built upon the old myths and extracted new truths from them, new moral and political significances, not in opportunistically conforming to the fancies and expectations of their audiences but in following an intrinsic necessity in their poetic production, to which all their skills had to be subordinated. Poetry is finding the right myth, and as Aristotle says, myth is the soul of tragedy. Is Plato, then, the last in this line of philosophical critics and poets who recast the old myths? Is he the most radical of those who purify the great tradition of myth and translate the ancient myths into a new ethos?

One might think so in view of his criticism of the Homeric gods and heroes. That criticism seems to be in the same vein as Xenophanes' attack on the crude anthropomorphic picture of the gods in Homer and as Heraclitus' assertion that Homer deserved to be banned from the competitions and flayed with sticks. But Plato also seems to be basically of one mind with the *poets* of the post-Homeric period insofar as they reject the traditional accounts of the misdeeds and vices of the gods as minstrels' lies, and thus it seems that Plato went beyond the poets only in the rigor of his adherence to a requirement which they themselves acknowledged. In fact even his motive for purifying the traditional myths seems to have been the same as theirs. Both Plato and the poets reject what is false, not just because it is false, but for *pedagogical* reasons. The poets themselves know that their greatest effect is on the youth. As Aristophanes puts it, anyone who tells little children some story can be their teacher. But the teachers of young men are the poets. Thus they may say to them only what is right.

But Plato's criticism goes infinitely further. Drama too falls before his critique, for he is as unrestrained in applying his immoderate critical standard to the form of poetry as he is in applying it to the form of myth. Poetry presents its content in narration, in direct imitation, or in a mixture of both forms as dithyramb, as drama, as epic. And now we are told that all imitative presentation, insofar as anything but an exemplary ethos is displayed in it, is to be discarded. Consequently next to nothing remains of Homer's poetry. In regard to Homer, in fact, Plato deliberately heightens the provocative element in his attack by changing the direct speech, at its first appearance in the classical beginning of the *Iliad*, to indirect speech:

Homer: A 33 ff.:

> He having said this, Chrysēs was afraid and
>   did what he was told.
> In silence he passed along the shore of the
>   murmuring sea;

And as he wandered on, now alone, the old
    man
Implored Apollo, the son of long-locked
    Letho, fervently.
Hear me, oh God, who with silver bow dost
    bestride Chrysa
And holy Cilla, thou who art the mighty lord
    of Tenedos.
Smintheus! If ever I have built a lovely
    temple for you
If ever I have burnt for thee choice
    shanks
Of bulls or of goats, then grant me this,
    my desire:
May the Achaeans pay for my tears under
    thy shafts.

Plato: *Republic 394 a:*

And the old man on hearing this was frightened and departed in silence, and having gone apart from the camp
he prayed at length to Apollo, invoking the appellations
of the god, and reminding him of, and asking requital
for, any of his gifts that had found favor whether in the
building of temples or the sacrifice of victims. In return
for these things he prayed that the Achaeans should suf-
fer for his tears by the god's shafts.

Of course this conversion is only meant to illustrate the difference between narration and imitation, but it is an intentionally malevolent example. For if the norm it establishes is strictly
adhered to, the opening of the *Iliad* would have to be purified
of all direct speech. Neither the imitation of Agamemnon's out-
break of rage nor the imitation of the priest's prayer for revenge
could be allowed. Thus it is no longer in any way remarkable
that Plato proceeds to reject Attic drama as a whole and that he
just as ruthlessly censors the specifically musical elements of
Greek music, melody (harmony) and rhythm, so that in the end
nothing remains save dithyrambic songs in praise of the gods,
heroes, and virtues, i.e., representation of the right ethos in a

simple, strict musical form.

And as if this censure of the poets were not enough, at the end of the *Republic* (the beginning of book 10) Plato specifically returns to the theme of driving the poets out of the state and repeats in an even sharper form his demand that they be exiled. To be sure, the grounds which he gives seem serious and compelling, but nonetheless they serve only to heighten, not diminish, the provocativeness of his argument. With great hesitancy (which Plato underscores) Socrates begins again to settle his accounts with Homer, inhibited as he is by a love for Homer which has been with him since childhood and by the awe and respect which he feels toward the poet, and enchanted as he still is by him. But this hesitancy only makes all the more clear the enormity and violence of this settling of accounts. The poet is classed among the handworkers. He is said to be a sophist and magician who produces only deceptive appearances of things. And what is worse, he ruins the soul by stirring up in it the whole range of its passions. Hence it proves necessary to exile all the "sweet muses" from the state, however poetic they might be.

That *in nuce* is Plato's position. It is clear that the reason for this shocking attack on Homer and the poets is more than the sense of pedagogical responsibility which had prompted previous philosophers and poets to purify the traditional myths. Plato's criticism is no longer poetic criticism of myth, for unlike the poets he does not preserve ancient poetry in a form purified by criticism. He destroys it. To that extent his criticism becomes an attack on the foundations of Greek culture and on the inheritance bequeathed to us by Greek history. We might perhaps expect something of this sort from an unmusical rationalist but not from a man whose work itself is nourished from poetic sources and who cast a poetic spell which has enthralled mankind for thousands of years. Although Plato assures us to the contrary, is not his inability to do justice to the poets and to the art of poetry nevertheless an expression of the age-old rivalry between poets and philosophers?

It is mistaken to try to minimize the provocative and paradoxical nature of Plato's critique in any way. Of course Plato himself alludes here to this age-old conflict between philosophers and poets, and precisely in order to assure us that this longstanding enmity is *not* reflected in his criticism. And it is true too that his critique of Homer's myth is not without its equally radical predecessors. Furthermore there can be no doubt that Plato's arguments against the art of poetry are much more likely to sound strange to the reader of today, who is no longer familiar with the role of the poets in Greek education. It was the practice then to justify the whole of one's knowledge—in any area—by recourse to Homer (just as Christian writers justified their knowledge by recourse to the Bible). In addition, listening to poetry had often completely given way to fantastic allegorization and hairsplitting exegesis, and, given the dominance of the spoken word in the Greek world, a poetic formulation taken out of context as creed or maxim went from the ear to the soul without the poet's overall intention defining and limiting its application. But all these considerations in no way diminish the extraordinary strangeness of Plato's criticism. Also mistaken is the defense of Plato which would argue that his critique is not of poetry as such but only of a degenerate contemporary form of it which contented itself with mere imitations of scenes from real life. For it is precisely Homer and the great tragedians who enthrall Socrates and his friends but who are criticized nonetheless. It is also of no help in understanding the matter if one presupposes Plato as the metaphysician of the doctrine of ideas and then demonstrates that his critique of the poets follows logically from his basic ontological assumptions. On the contrary, Plato's attitude toward the poets is not a consequence of a system of thought which prevented him from more fairly evaluating poetic truth. Rather, his position is the quite conscious expression of a decision—a decision made as a result of having been taken with Socrates and philosophy, made in opposition to the entire political and intellectual culture of his time, and made in the conviction that philosophy alone has the capacity to save the state. There is good reason that Plato places his critique of the poets in two prominent places in his *Republic* and explicitly elaborates it there. For the pedagogical significance of Plato's new and different philosophy becomes evident precisely insofar as that philosophy breaks with the poetic foundations of Attic education and asserts itself against the whole of the tradition.

Any interpretation of Plato's thinking here depends upon the context in which the expulsion of the poets from the sacred temple of Greek life occurs. Consequently any interpretation is wrong from the start which neglects this context and seeks to pass judgment on isolated statements which Plato makes. To do so would be to assume that Plato's position on art is explicitly articulated in these statements and that he means his argument as some sort of apology which would ultimately permit us to love the poets just as much as their adversaries. But the actual truth of the matter is that the meaning and intent of this critique of the poets can be established only by departing from the place where it occurs. It is found in Plato's work on the state within a program of education for the guardians of that state, a state which is erected before our eyes in words alone from the building blocks which alone suffice for it. The critique of the poets can be understood only within the setting of this total refounding of a new state in words of philosophy, only understood as a radical turning away from the existing state. Only then does the quite simple purpose of it become plain.

Plato himself relates in his *Seventh Letter* (the famous autobiographical manifesto addressed to his political friends in Sicily) how he came to abstain from practical, political action and how, after a long wait for the right moment to act, he realized that a rebirth of the state could be brought about only by philosophy. For not only his father city but all existent states were poorly constituted and well nigh incurable. Plato's *Republic* is the expression of this insight. It stipulates that philosophers must become the rulers of the state since the affairs of the state are to be put in order only by philosophy.

Everything said in the *Republic* about the order of the state is subordinated to this requirement and serves as a justification for it. One misses the full seriousness and importance of that requirement, however, if one takes the projected educational program and the ordering of the state literally. This state is a state in thought, not any state on earth. That is to say, its purpose is to bring something to light and not to provide an actual design for an improved order in real political life. Plato's state is a "paradigm in heaven" for someone who wants to order *himself* and his own inner constitution. Its sole raison d'être is to make it possible for a person to recognize himself in the paradigm. Of course the point is precisely that he who recognizes himself therein does not recognize himself as an isolated individual without a state. He recognizes in himself the basis upon which the reality of the state is built, and he is able to recognize that basis in himself however deformed and degenerate the actual state in which he lives may be. The proposed curriculum of education, which completely overturns the existing order of education, is actually only meant to remove the question of man's political nature, the question of the true essence of justice from any particular, relative form which the ordering of one's life might take and to transfer it to that ground in the soul of the individual which is the basis of the state insofar as it still exists and the basis of whatever state could come into being in the future.

Thus Plato's purification of traditional poetry can be understood only in relationship to the purpose of the whole of this paradigmatic constitution in the *Republic*. And the proposed purification of poetry, like the constitution, is not to be taken literally, i.e., as a set of instructions for reconstructing traditional education, a purification of the curriculum according to new standards. The very requirement with which it starts is seen to be totally unrealistic and immoderate when measured against the claims which one normally makes for the pedagogical importance of poetry. Any instruction in the ancient poetry was taken then and is to be taken now like any real instruction, i.e., as something auxiliary. In this case the heritage of the poetic tradition is applied in educating youth. What is of primary importance in education, however, occurs by itself. The most significant pedagogical results are never to be attributed to the specific means of instruction but to the "laws of the state" and above all to its unwritten laws, the ethos prevailing in the society which, though concealed, secretly molds human beings. Thus the secret pedagogical efficacy of poetry is due to the fact that in it something is expressed which reflects the ethical spirit prevailing in the community. Homer's effect on Greek youth was the same as that which he has in the youth of any individual today.

He provides magnificent paragons of heroic virture—courage, honor, willingness to die, magnanimity, endurance, intelligence —and he does this without allowing the dissension among the gods, their deceit, base scheming, or cowardly weakness to influence us as negative models of behavior.

Given this fact, Plato's censorship of poetry seems to betray the moralistic bias of an intellectual purist. For here poetry is given a burden which it cannot carry and does not need to carry. Its content is to be purified so that it might attain an educational effect on its own. Through play, it is supposed to inculcate the genuine ethos in young souls and to do this by itself with no existing ethos in the communal life of young and old to guide and define the effect of the poetic word. That task amounts to an overburdening of the pedagogical function of poetry, an overburdening which is to be accounted for only by the critical motive behind what Plato says. Plato's Socratic insight was that a binding political ethos, which would assure the proper application and interpretation of poetry, no longer existed once sophism had come to define the spirit of education. To be sure, justice and the virtue of the political man were precisely what the sophists' education sought to inculcate too. But Socrates had uncovered the real content and dogma of their new ethos. For the sophists, justice is only the conventions of the weak which protect the interests of the latter. For the sophists, ethical principles are no longer valid in themselves but only as a form of our mutual "keeping an eye" on one another. The "just" is that by means of which one person can assert himself against another with help from everyone else and, as such, it is adhered to only out of mutual distrust and fear. It is not the justice intrinsic and internal to me myself. All the many variations of the sophists' theory of justice are alike in providing a 'foundation' for justice. And whether the sophists conceive of themselves as conservative or revolutionary, indeed even when the sophists think that they are giving a foundation to the authority of civil law, in principle they have already perverted the sense of justice. As judges of justice they fail to acknowledge it even if they "acquit" it. Thus Callicles' and Thrasymachus' declaration that might makes right only serves to disclose the mentality which prevails in all sophism: *No one does what is right voluntarily.*

When such a truth has suffused the spirit of a state, the positive pedagogical effect of poetry converts into its opposite. To the person with Thrasymachus' and the other sophists' teachings ringing in his ears, the world of poetry, which for generations had provided the models of higher humanity for youth, now is made to attest to the perverted spirit itself. Thus in the speech of Adeimantos at the beginning of book 2 the poets themselves are held accountable for the weakening of the proper sense of justice; they urge justice upon children not for its own sake but for the advantages and rewards which it brings. And all traditional poetry is guilty of this same thing. Beginning with the heroes and continuing to the present, injustice is never faulted on its own account and justice never praised for its own sake. But Adeimantos hints that this is not his own view on the truth of ancient poetry when he ends by saying that Thrasymachus or anyone else is able to state such a theory of justice and injustice only once he has brashly converted the real meaning of these concepts into its opposite.

Therefore it falls to Socrates to sing the true praises of the just and right. He must accomplish what no one else, especially the poets, can. Plato's "state" must now propound the true praise of a justice which will remain victorious evermore over the sophists' perversion of its meaning. What is just and right is not the right that someone *has* in opposition to another. Rather it is *being* just: Each *is* just by himself and all *are* just together. Justice does not exist when each person watches the other and guards against him but when each watches himself and guards the right and just being of his inner constitution.

Thus in the ideal state which Socrates now develops, the poetic tradition is purified to the point of totally eliminating the ancient heritage, for there must be no more witnesses in support of the sophists' perversions of the truth. The very excessiveness of this purification, which exceeds a thousandfold the boldest dreams of power ever entertained by any moralist-pedagogue, should teach us the point of a reordering of education such as Plato has in mind. *It is not intended to display how poetry would have to look in an actual state. Rather it is intended to disclose and awaken the powers themselves which form the state* and from which the state as a whole derives. For that reason Socrates erects a state in words, the possibility of which is given only in *philosophy*. This state appears to be one which rests entirely upon the power of its educational system, i.e., to be a new beginning ex nihilo with no history which results solely from a rehabituation of man. But actually it is a picture, justice "writ large," in which the soul can recognize what justice is. However, the soul on its way to knowledge must not be guided by traditional poetry and the traditional world of ethical custom. *Indeed, even this state of new habituation must be left behind* as the soul, in proceeding through mathematics, learns to distinguish between appearance and truth. The road back to real political action is open only to him who in philosophizing has transcended the shadow world of "reality." And only the philosopher is called upon to travel it.

Thus the exposition of this ideal state in the *Republic* serves in educating the political human being, but the *Republic* is not meant as a manual on educational methods and materials, and it does not point out the goal of the educational process to the educator. In the background of this work on the state is a real educational state, the community of Plato's academy. The *Republic* exemplifies the purpose of that academy. This community of students applying themselves rigorously to mathematics and dialectic is no apolitical society of scholars. Instead, the work done here is intended to lead to the result which remained unattainable for the current sophistic paideia, with its encyclopedic instruction and arbitrary moralistic reformulations of the educational content of ancient poetry. It is intended to lead to a new discovery of justice in one's own soul and thus to *the shaping of the political human being. This* education, however, the actual education to participation in the state, is anything but a total manipulation of the soul, a rigorous leading of it to a predetermined goal. Instead, precisely in extending its questioning behind the supposedly valid traditional moral ideas, it is in itself the new experience of justice. Thus this education is not authoritative instruction based on an ideal organization at all; rather it lives from questioning alone.[3]

---

3. In *Wahrheit und Methode* Gadamer elaborates on the priorities of the *question* over the *answer* in Plato in particular, and in authentic discourse in general, a priority which

Plato's critique of the poets is thus to be interpreted in terms of the two faces which the *Republic* presents: on the one hand, the strict utopian constitution of the state and, on the other, a satirical criticism of existing states. The very immoderation of this critique of the poets gives us tangible evidence of the purpose which Plato has in mind. It is his aim to bring about the possible, i.e., the actual, education of the political human being by providing a picture of the impossible, i.e., an organized paideia whose unlimited capability derives entirely from itself and in no way from a given ethos. This paideia must be understood as the antithesis of what the Greeks of that time had taken paideia to be and of what we today, as heirs of Greek humanism, conceive of under the headings of education and culture, namely, the "cultivation of what is specifically and purely human in all spheres of life," "the development of the harmonious human being."[4] To be sure, when Plato, at the beginning of his critique of the poets, reviews the forms of paideia, he declares that one could not find better forms than those which the past has made available: music for the soul, gymnastics for the body. But this pious adherence to the long tradition of Greek education actually carries concealed within itself that impious and inflexible censorship of the grand Greek tradition of poetry which has been the object of our investigation up to this point. And now, when we ask what could justify this inflexibility, we come to see clearly what an unbridgeable chasm separates Plato's paideia from all other existing education—be it through the mores and customs of the forefathers, the wisdom of the poets, or the instruction of the sophists. Paideia for Plato is not the traditional cultivation of musical facility and physical agility in the child. Nor is it the heightening of

---

distinguishes Plato's philosophy from that which follows him and which keeps his thinking closer to the natural movement of discursive inquiry. The opposite position is that occupied by Hegel, whose extraordinary insight into the dialogical, dialectical movement of thinking is blunted, Gadamer argues, by the goal which Hegel sets for himself of closing the system. Hegel's idea of a completed system must necessarily suppress the open-endedness of thinking, in which alone the question can maintain its priority over the answer. (Cf. *WM* 344 ff. on the hermeneutic priority of the question and chap. 5, n.11, below.) (Translator)

4. This formulation is Werner Jaeger's. Cf. *Platos Stellung im Aufbau der griechischen Bildung* (Berlin, 1928), p. 17.

Justice ① shaping of an inner harmony of the Soul
② harmony of self (sharp & the mild)
willful + philosophical
③ tuning of an inner dissonance inherent in people

54 | *Plato and the Poets*

enthusiasm and spirit in the young by the use of hero-models
from myth and poetry, nor the cultivation of political and practical wisdom by the use of such a reflection of human life as myth
and poetry provide. Rather it is the shaping of an inner harmony in the soul of a person, a harmony of the sharp and the
mild in him, of the willful and the philosophical.

Such a description seems reminiscent of the humanist ideal
of the "harmonious personality" which is to be formed by developing the whole range of one's human potential—an aesthetic
ideal to be achieved by a proposed "aesthetic education of the
human race." But for Plato harmony means the tuning of a *dissonance* which is inherent in man (*Republic* 375 c).[5] Education is the
unification of the irreconcilable: the schism of the bestial and
the peaceful in the human being. The guardians of the state,
whose education alone is the concern, are not by nature just, so
that one need only develop their "potential." Paideia is essential
in order to fit together in a unified ethos what, according to
their potential, has necessarily split in two. And as a matter of
fact, the class of the guardians is, properly speaking, the class of
all human beings.[6]

The "city of pigs," that idyll of a healthy vegetative state
which Plato describes with an inimitable mixture of nostalgia and
satire, and in which peace and pacifism are automatically present because each in doing what is right and necessary for all does

5. The point is even clearer in the *Republic* at 410 c ff. and is most sharply accentuated in the *Statesman* at 306 ff.

6. Of course the guardians are only the class of the leaders in a state which is made
up for the most part of people with "professions." But it is significant that paideia as
such, i.e., the paideia which leads to knowledge of justice, becomes thematic only when
the class of guardians comes under consideration. This should suffice to make clear that
justice in the professions, *idiopragein*, is only a shadow-image of true justice. Of course the
"truth" of justice is not found only in the guardians. But only in starting with the guardians, and only in reference to them, can the "professional" man be seen to take part in
true justice. For the latter, idiopragein, doing one's own job, means not intruding in the
business of the other *classes*, i.e., of the warriors and guardians, more than it means not
intruding in the work of other *professions* (434 ab). Hence it means letting oneself be
guided. And ultimately this whole picture of the state is to be applied in interpreting "the
inner state," the constitution of the soul of each individual, whose justice as inner action
provides the norm for whatever he does, be this in the acquisition of wealth, in his providing for bodily needs, or in his political or private transactions (443 de).

what is just—this state, tightly organized as it is for the provision of needs, could never exist in human history and is thus no genuine ideal for mankind. For since it is without history, it is without human truth.[7] Unlike socially organized animals, ants, for instance, whose social drives could be satisfied with purposive order providing only the necessities of life, man is not merely a natural creature. Man is a profligate being who desires to progress beyond his present circumstances. Thus quite by itself his state transcends itself as his needs increase. And as the ultimate consequence of this wild growth, the class of warriors emerges and within it the new, specifically human phenomenon: political existence.

For the warrior's work is the only work not aimed at the production of something which one needs and which does not consist in merely performing a skill. On the contrary, it is demanded of the warrior that he be free and detached from his

---

7. The "city of pigs" (*Republic* 369 b–374 e) is only an ironic counterimage to the reality of human political life. For there is no human state in historic or even prehistoric times which did not go beyond providing for the necessities of life and which, in precisely so doing, did not enter the realm of history, where there are flourishing and decay, corruption and recovery. However for Plato this fact means that in all states everything depends on the right paideia. The healthy mode of living enjoyed by the inhabitants of the city of pigs is in essence completely ahistorical in the transmission of this healthy life from one generation to the next (372 d). Thus no real answer to the question of what justice is, is to be found in this image of the state; the question of right has no actuality here. For the interaction of its people with one another is limited to the reciprocal need they have of one another in the production of what is needed by all of them, and thus their relationship to one another fulfills itself in the consumption of their products. The shift in style to irony at 372 a is specifically intended to indicate that in Plato's view the matter cannot rest with this hypothetical construction. The just state is not to be found in this condition of "good health." *The question of justice arises only once injustice has also become possible*, i.e., once society has progressed beyond merely regulating and organizing the production of necessities. It arises in a state where there are lords and servants, where there is the beautiful and noble (*to kalon*), and where there is the desire to invade the sphere of another (*pleonektein*), where there is war. The just state is the state which has been *brought back* to moderation (399 e: *diakathairontes*) from a historical excess.

In his instructive treatment of the city of pigs (*Platon* [Berlin, 1919], 2: 214 ff.) Wilamowitz correctly identifies Plato's dissatisfaction with this "ideal" condition as the reason for the irony and caricature. But he did not see that in this first division of human professions it is not the *external* threat which is omitted and, as a consequence, the class of warriors but rather the *internal source of that threat*, namely, human discontent. For this reason Wilamowitz failed to see the necessity of a detour through healthy and rampant states in coming to an insight into what justice is.

work. He must be able to distinguish between friend and foe. In essence then, his skill is knowledge, i.e., knowledge of when and where and against whom he should or should not apply his craft. His being, therefore, is that of a guard: the warrior is also a guardian. Now guarding is both guarding *for* someone and guarding *against* someone. Guarding for someone, however, means having power over him and using this power and one's strength for him and not against him. Thus being a guardian is something different from practicing handwork. Guarding requires reliability and self-restraint in addition to carrying out the work of the warrior. But this constancy implies still more: namely, loving the friend just because he is a friend (and not because, or to the extent that, he does good things for you but even when he does something bad) and conversely, hating the enemy even when he does something good, just because he is the enemy. Plato characterizes the new element which now emerges alongside the force of the warrior's will as man's philosophical nature and he depicts the unity of these opposite natures in the metaphor of the loyal watchdog. In that the dog is friendly to the houseguest simply because the guest is known to the household, the dog is a friend of what is "known," which is to say, of knowledge. He is quite literally a philosopher. Thus the guardian, which is to say man, must cultivate the philosophical nature in himself while at the same time reconciling this nature with the violent drives in himself of self-preservation and the will to power.

It is the goal of paideia to bring about this unification which keeps the human being from becoming either a tame herd animal (a slave) or a rapacious wolf (a tyrant). For the potential of the human being to be a human being among other human beings, in short, to be a political being, depends upon this unification of the philosophical and martial natures in him. But this potential for political existence is not given to man by nature, for even if both these elements in him are natural and necessary, man becomes a political being only *insofar as he resists the temptations of power which arise from flattery* (cf. Alcibiades, *Republic* 492 ff.). This means, however, that he must learn to distinguish the true friend from the false one and what is truly just from

flattering appearances. It is philosophy which makes such distinguishing possible, for philosophy is loving the true and resisting
the false. Thus philosophy is what makes man as a political being
possible. Paideia, consequently, is not the cultivation of some
skill; rather it produces this unity of power and the love of
knowledge. It only calms the inner strife which, though dangerous, is nonetheless essential to man. For although that strife will
always prevent his pacification, it provides the energy proper to
each man individually and common to all. Only a life with this
dynamic tension is a human life.

Thus Plato's idea of paideia incorporates within itself the insights of the sophist enlightenment into the dangerousness of
man, insights into his tyrannical will to independence. But Plato
demonstrates as well that the philosophical potential of man is
just as fundamental.[8] Thus in Plato justice of the state is not
founded negatively on the weakness of individuals whose prudence leads them into a contract. Instead the human being is political in a positive sense because he is capable of rising above his
insistence on himself, capable of being for others. Indeed, the
yardstick against which the guardians are measured proves to be
whether they hold to and guard this principle: that not their own
well-being is to be preserved but the well-being of the state. The
guardian is the guardian of justice only when he guards himself.

Thus in Plato the conflicting elements in man are to be reconciled and unified without robbing him of his power and the
poets evaluated, and their "lies"—for they only tell lies—ad-
judged beautiful or not, on the basis of whether they bring
this reconciliation about or hinder it. Hence they should no
longer be allowed to sing Homer's and Hesiod's tales of how the
gods quarrel and deceive both one another and man. And they
should not sing either of anything discouraging or immoderate
in heroes or in men, lest someone, taking these tales as his exam-

8. *gleichursprünglich*. The word is one which Heidegger often uses to indicate the essential and inevitable concomitance of Being and Not-being, e.g., in being authentic and
being inauthentic, being in truth and being in error (guilt). Gadamer finds acknowledgment of this same insurmountable duality in Plato's anthropology. For Plato man is "always already" (*je schon*) both philosophical and tyrannical. Thus the task of paideia cannot be to eradicate the "tyrannical" but to harmonize it with the "philosophical."
(Translator)

Part's dictum → promote ethos of harmony + justice of the Soul

ples, might become tolerant of his own unjust actions. The true poetic singing of human life must always proclaim the truth that the just man alone is happy. All imitation of an unjust ethos must, therefore, be excluded. For to the degree that imitation is anything other than play which preforms one's own character, it always loosens the precarious tuning of the harmonious soul and dissipates the soul in the all-absorbent medium of appearance, in which it is lost to itself. And when communal property, communal living, communal women and children are made the rule for the guardians and for all education, musical and gymnastic, and when finally even the begetting of proper new generations is to be determined by a number calculated in some profound and mystic way (and when the decay of the state is said to begin with a mistake in the calculation of the calendar of wedlocks)—all this *is supposed* to make one aware that this educational state is not meant as a proposal for some actual new ordering of man or the state. Instead it teaches us about human existence itself and the basic impulses in the latter which make it possible to establish a state: The state is possible only when the difficult and delicate tuning, the aforementioned harmonization of the schism in man, succeeds.

Thesis repeated.

Plato's paideia is thus meant as a counterweight to the centrifugal pull of those forces of the sophist enlightenment being exerted upon the state. His critique of poetry develops this counterweight in the form of an explicit critique of existing paideia and of its trust in and reliance upon human nature and faith in the power of purely rational instruction. In opposition to this sophist paideia, Plato advances an arbitrarily and radically purified poetry, which is no longer a reflection of human life but the language of an intentionally beautified lie. This new poetry is meant to express the ethos which prevails in the purified state in a way which is pedagogically efficacious.

*   *   *

In book 10 Plato repeats his critique of poetry and justifies banning all imitative poetry from the state. The critique of poetry here is simultaneously an ultimate justification for Plato's writings. Prima facie it seems that this last critique is directed at

the very idea of poetry, and it uses arguments which are even
more foreign to modern consciousness than the moralism of the
preceding strict pedagogical purification of poetry. For modern
consciousness holds that in the symbolic presentation of art one
finds the deepest revelation of a truth which no concept can
grasp. Thus however compelling the train of thought of **Plato's**
critique might be, its presupposition is bound to put one off. He
sees art as essentially nothing but imitation. The distinguishing
feature of this critique is that Socrates develops his argument
throughout in departing from the painter, and he even places
the poet together with painter under the rubric of "handworker." In the representative arts a relationship does indeed
exist between the picture and a "reality" which is pictured
—although the essence of these arts is by no means exhaustively
defined by this relationship. Numbered among such "realities"
are the things which the handworker "really" produces, and insofar as the handworker for his part looks to the "idea" of the
implement which he produces, the reality of the picture may be
said to occupy the third and lowest level of a hierarchy leading
up to the idea, viz., picture, implement produced, idea. For the
individual implement which the handworker produces is itself
only a darkened rendering of the idea, a mere "something of the
sort like" the true being of the thing, and one among many exemplars. Thus the painter who copies such an exemplar and
copies it not even as it is, but only as it appears in one specific
respect among many possible others, is most certainly an imitator
of mere appearance and not of the truth. The better his rendering is, the more "deceptive" it is. Such art has an unlimited capacity of rendering the shape of anything in the medium of appearance since it aims at nothing more than mere deception.
The artist is like a man who can do anything, like a magician or
sophist.

But Plato's argument is not intended as a theory of the plastic arts, and whether they might be essentially different from a
copying of the appearance of reality is thus not the issue here.
Even so—and whatever the answer to this question might
be—Plato's criticism of *the poets* requires precisely *this* illuminating analogy with the plastic, formative arts. The claim

which poetry makes for itself is a most exalted one. Poetry is not
a plastic art, which is to say that it does not form its picture of
things in shapes and colors in a foreign material. The poet turns
himself into the tool of his art. He forms by speaking. But instead
of things, what the poet forms is more often than not the human
being himself as the latter expresses himself in his existence, as
he experiences himself in action and suffering. And the pedagogical claim of the poet is based upon this fact. But once such a
pedagogical claim is made it must be questioned. Does the poet,
who is a good talker himself and who knows how to make any
man who understands some particular thing sound good, com-
pose his poems with knowledge of all the human sciences and,
above all, with knowledge of man's self-knowledge (paideia,
aretē), or not? The analogy with the mimetic copying of the
painter which aims solely at rendering the mere appearance of
one aspect of the thing provides us with a prefiguration of the
answer to this question.

For the poet who really understood education and human
aretē would dedicate himself fully to them instead of contenting
himself with ineffectual laudations. Thus only the poet who was
really an educator and who really shaped human life could play
the game of poetry in real knowledge of what it was about: Only
those poets can be taken seriously who do not take their poetry
writing to be ultimate. For this reason Homer fails the test which
Solon, for instance, passes: the test of having been effective in
shaping human life. Homer's poetic play turns out to be the
mere pretense of knowledge which dazzles us with the colorful
splendor of its poetic language. But when the decorative poetic
speech is stripped away by a Socrates, who asks the poets what
they really mean, it is shown that poets actually understand nothing of what they present so forcefully. Then their wisdom looks
like those faces which appeared to be beautiful when young but
which prove to be not really beautiful once the charm of youth
has departed. Here Socrates' imagery points to the real object of
Plato's polemical, dialectical critique of poetry: Socrates' argument causes not only poetry to lose its charms; those forms of
morality which the poets' colorful decorative art made appear so
beautiful now display their decrepitude.

Here indeed we have the "second half" of the argument to be advanced against the pedagogical claim of the poets. It is not only the case that they have no real knowledge of men and of the Beautiful. In that regard they are no different from handworkers who must first learn the guidelines of their craft and what is correct and proper from someone who knows how to use the tools of the trade. But in contrast to the handworkers, the poets do not even know how to do what they do correctly in the areas where they claim to be knowledgeable. They do not present something, e.g., human existence, as the beautiful or bad thing which it *is* but only as it appears beautiful to the *polloi*, who themselves know nothing. Thus just as the painter takes the guidelines for his copying not from the real measurements of things but from the appearance which the things display to the crowd from a distance, so too the poet's portrayal of human existence is shifted away from the real dimensions of human nature to the false forms of morality which appear beautiful to the crowd to which he presents them.

Although Plato does not specifically say so, this critique of the art of poetry implies a break with the entire tradition of education which had always presented the moral truths of any given time using models taken from the heroes of Homer's world. The break is made manifest by the critical conclusion which Plato draws and in his subsequent exposition of the effect which poetry has. The real object of Plato's criticism is not the degenerate forms of contemporary *art* and the perception of the older, classical poetry which the contemporary taste in art had defined. Rather it is the contemporary *morality and moral education* which had established itself upon the basis of the poetic formulations of the older morality and which, in adhering to aging moral forms, found itself defenseless against arbitrary perversions of those forms brought on by the spirit of sophism.[9] Accordingly Socrates

9. In his *Platon* (Berlin, 1954), 2: 138 ff., Friedländer (whose earnest discussion of the motives for Plato's *mimēsis* critique is to be recommended on the whole) seems to me to have gone against his own insights. It is of course true that here, and in what follows, the way in which Plato speaks of painting and the illusions which it creates leads one to think of the art which predominated in his time, just as what he says of poetry reminds one of Euripides and popular drama. But that only explains why Plato *could* argue in the

rejects the current interpretations of poetry and questions
whether we still understand the wisdom of the ancient poets at
all. It may be that in a world defined by binding actions and
definitely prescribed morals the words of these "divine men"
were the most noble and powerful statement of the moral world
which fathers could speak to their children for their moral
edification. But in a time of decline a message which could stop
the advancing corruption of the political spirit was not to be
found in even the loftiest poetry of the past.

Therefore when Plato asserts that poetry falsifies and de-
ceives, he means it primarily as a critique of the aesthetic reality
of artworks, which would measure these against the concept of
true reality. Above all, this apparently ontological critique of the
art of poetry is aimed at the content of poetry, the ethos which it
represents, wherein, fatefully, virtue and happiness are placed in
opposition to each other. Such a juxtaposition can result only
from a false conception of virtue and happiness which makes
them seem incompatible.

Socrates thus buttresses and completes his critique of poetry
with a critique of its *effect,* a critique which repeats and deepens
the motifs of the preceding critique of the poets. Socrates points
out that it is the very power which poetry has to enchant and impress us which makes poetry inimical to the true purpose of education and destructive of the right ethos.

For corruption of the soul is the inevitable consequence of
deceit. The illusion which the painter creates bedazzles one's vi-

---

way he does, not why he did argue this way against art. The decisive point is that this critique is valid for the classic ancient art as well; for ultimately it does not bear upon the
conception of art which Plato's contemporaries had but upon the *moral content* of art. The
research of Werner Jaeger collated in his *Paideia* (Berlin, 1959) makes clear just how
fitting it is that Homer becomes the object of Plato's critique of the poet's vision of *aretē*.
All aretē without *phronēsis* is of Homeric origin, and throughout all the changes in Greek
political life Homeric aretē preserved its role as a paradigm. This fact makes all the more
evident, it seems to me, that the Socratic–Platonic critique of this aretē-ideal is a plea for a
δικαιοσύνη μετὰ φρονήσεως (justice by means of phronēsis) (*Republic* 621 c) precisely in
opposition to this powerful Homeric tradition. He who in an earlier life shared in virtue
through "custom without philosophy" (ἔθει ἄνευ φιλοσοφίας) chooses the life of a tyrant in
the new allotment of lives! (619 b ff.). This mythical motif restates symbolically what had
been worked out in the long dialectical movement of the *Republic* and completed with the
critique of the poets (cf. *Phaedo* 82 bc!).

sion and makes the thing appear now one way and now another—until a man of mathematical science, for instance, arrives on the scene and establishes the true dimensions of the thing by measuring, counting, and weighing. Like the painter the poet is ignorant of the true measures of the thing which he portrays, ignorant of the measures of good and bad. And just as the painter raises doubts about what is real and what is not, the poet creates disconcertion and an enervating lassitude in the soul of the spectator when he conjures up outbursts of the volatile human passions. Here Socrates is painting the effect of all imitative poetry in the colors of the Athenian theatrocracy. The poet, who wants to impress the crowd, is led by both the taste of his audience as well as his own nature to whatever is opulent and vivid and can be portrayed as such, that is, to the shifting storms of human feelings. Conversely he is put off by the constant disposition of those who, whatever their fate, preserve that quiet energy which grows from resolve. That which lends itself to poetic representation, gestures and expressions of the passions, is, if measured against the true ethos, superficial and untrue. Thus art repeats what in reality is already the "hypocrisy of life" (Hegel).

Art repeats it, however, in an ingratiating way, i.e., in an apparently innocuous "mere" imitation. Hence the decisive thing wrong with imitation is found in the ill effect of its charms on the human soul. All imitation is imitation of something else and, in particular cases, of some*one* else. The intention of the imitation can, of course, not really involve the person imitated and be reflected back upon the imitator himself, for imitation of another person can have the formal structure of appropriation of something for myself. In that case the imitation is not aimed at the other at all. Rather the interest in the other is actually an interest in how one does a certain thing. What a person learns from someone's "showing him how" and in the imitation thereof is not so much something which belongs to the other as something which I can appropriate for myself. The purpose of such imitation is thus not to imitate but to learn how to do something myself.

In contrast, he who really imitates and only imitates, in

[handwritten top margin: between a double negative > imitator is not-Hamlet (i.e. himself) but more than himself, he is not not-Hamlet (i.e. an actor)]

[handwritten left margin: Imitation / as a turning away from oneself]

mime, is no longer himself. He gives himself an alien character. But even so he only (imitates) the other, which is to say that while he is not himself, he is not the other either. This (imitation) thus implies a split in the self. That a person is himself but still imitates another means that he imitates the other from outside and seeks to become what the other is externally by shaping his own exterior to match the exterior of the other. But orienting oneself toward the [exterior of someone else,] copying his superficial accidental gestures (if it is done earnestly and not consciously as a game for the sake of demonstrating something) implies turning oneself away from oneself, away from that which one is inwardly. Such imitation is thus carried out in forgetfulness of oneself. Insofar as the intent of the imitation, making oneself like someone else, is fulfilled in looking exactly like that individual (as occurs, for instance, when an actor has fully immersed himself in his role), we no longer have simply the imitation of an alien exterior in which the imitator, even if oblivious to himself, could be said to preserve himself. Here imitation has become self-exteriorization, self-estrangement. Thus the actor does not merely act out someone else's gestures. On the contrary, all his expressions are the display of an inner nature which is nevertheless not his own human nature. All forgetfullness of self in imitation fulfills itself, therefore, in self-alienation. And even he who merely watches such imitation without acting himself yields to the thing imitated in sympathy, which is to say that he forgets himself in vicariously experiencing through the other whom he sees before him. Thus even looking on, to the extent that it is the self-forgetful yielding of oneself to the vibrations of an alien emotion, always implies at least some self-alienation.

[handwritten left margin: Isn't this only possible as a play-Chorus?]

It is clear that this effect of mimetic representation remains fundamentally the same even in other modes of poetic portrayal less suggestive than acting. And it is in this light that Plato's *Republic* presents the effect of imitation. The charm of imitation and the joy taken in it are a form of self-forgetfulness which is most pronounced where what is represented is itself self-forgetfulness, i.e., (passion.

[handwritten left margin: Passion / is self-forgetfulness]

Thus this critique of mimetic poetry cuts much deeper than it had at first appeared. It not only criticizes the false and dan-

[handwritten bottom margin: cf Bertold Brecht's [Short Organum] — principle of "estrangement"/ "alienation" to ensure audience maintains a critical, judgment rendering consciousness ←]

Critique of moral consequences of ["aesthetic consciousness"] (ie aesthetic forgetfulness of self) → the antidote is philosophical questioning

gerous contents of mimetic art or the choice of an unseemly mode of representation. *It is at the same time a critique of the moral consequences of "aesthetic consciousness."*[10] The very experience which is had in delusory imitation is in itself already the ruination of the soul. For the deeper analysis of the inner constitution of the soul has made evident that aesthetic self-forgetfulness opens the way for the sophists' game with the passions to infiltrate the human heart.

The question arises, accordingly, whether there is any poetic representation at all which is immune to this danger. And when Plato, in holding to the idea of education through poetry, affirms that there is, the further question arises in what sense this new poetry can be said to be imitation. The key to this last question—one which we shall see is decisive for all of Plato's work—is to be found in Plato's observation that the only poetry which withstands his criticism is hymns to the gods and songs in praise of good individuals. To be sure, something "unreal" is poetically represented in these; gods and men themselves appear as speakers here in an imitation in the strictest sense. Nevertheless such poetry differs from the powerfully suggestive representation of the rest of poetry. It is representation in praise of someone. But in [the song of praise] and in the form thereof which transcends the human realm, i.e., the hymn to the gods, there is no danger of that self-estrangement induced by the potent magical play of poetry. In praising, neither the one who praises nor the one before whom the praise is made is forgotten. On the contrary, at every moment both are present and expressed as

the potent magical play of poetry

10. *ästhetisches Bewusstsein*. A central theme of Gadamer's *magnum opus*, Wahrheit und Methode, is announced here, i.e., Gadamer's own critique of "aesthetic consciousness" and the subjectification of the art work which is its correlate (cf. *WM* 77 ff.). Gadamer is arguing that in effect Plato foresaw the moral consequences of the subjectification of art which Kant and post-Kantian philosophy were later to complete. For aesthetic consciousness our encounter with the work of art becomes an inner experience, or *Erlebnis*, which for its duration falsely dissociates us from the practical world (cf. Gadamer's analysis of Schiller's *Über die ästhetische Erziehung des Menschen* [*WM* 77–78]). Plato sees the deleterious effect of such an aesthetic Erlebnis on the soul of the individual who cultivates it in mimēsis. Hence for Plato the aesthetic education (*Erziehung*, paideia) which Schiller advocates would be ruinous. For it is the very antithesis of true paideia, which far from deepening the soul's obliviousness to itself, raises it to the clarity of Socratic self-knowledge. (Translator)

Erlebnis (an inner experience) — falsely dissociates one from the practical world → antithesis of true Paideia (ie education) meant to deepen soul's self knowledge; not its obliviousness to itself!

they are in themselves. For praising is not a representation of what is laudable. Of course the song of praise will always contain an element of representation of the laudable, but in essence it is something distinct from this representation. He who praises addresses both himself and the one before whom he praises (and in a certain sense even the one who is being praised), for he speaks of that which binds them all to one another and gives them all a common obligation. He who praises avows his commitment to something, for in praising, the standard by which we evaluate and comprehend our existence is made manifest. Now representation of an example in which the standard which we all share becomes evident is certainly more than drama and more even than the representation of something exemplary. It is a way of giving the model new efficacy, i.e., in and by representing it.

In essence, then, the song of praise in the form of poetic play is shared language, the language of our common concern. It is the poetic language of the citizens of Plato's state. To be sure, even this mimetic representation would be subject to the previous ontological argument, for like all poetry, it is mimesis of something which has been produced. It itself does not produce the true ethos; it only represents it poetically. But in the true state, the state of justice, such a representation would be an avowal of commitment to the spirit shared by all, an avowal which in lighthearted play would celebrate that which is taken truly seriously.

But what poetic form should praise of true justice take when the communal bond formed in the practices, customs, and patterns of life in the state is no longer felt and when allegiance to it thus can no longer be pledged in a song of praise? What form should the song of praise take in states which in fact are "almost incurable"? What form must it take so that even as representation it might be genuine praise, a language of what is of concern to everyone? As a matter of fact, in raising this question we have done nothing less than uncover the locus of Plato's dialogues in his intellectual enterprise. For when justice remains only as an inner certitude in the soul and is no longer to be clearly identified with any given reality, and when knowledge of it must be defended against the arguments of a new "enlightened" consciousness, a *philosophical discussion* about the true state becomes the only true praise of justice. And the only valid way to represent that discussion becomes Plato's dialogue, that song of praise which affirms what is of concern to everyone and which throughout the "play" which represents the educational state does not lose sight of the serious issue: the cultivation of the political human being and of justice in him. Plato's critique of poetry, a critique which culminates in his rejection of aesthetic consciousness, is intended to support the claim which he makes for his own dialogues. Plato does not simply put a new incantation into the field against the aesthetic forgetfulness of self and the old magic of poetry; rather he advances the antidote of philosophical questioning. One must do what one who has fallen in love does when he recognizes that his love is bad for him and forces himself to break away from it. The critique of the poets which Plato assigns to Socrates in his discussion of the state is intended as just such an antidotal spell which—out of concern for the condition of one's own soul, the inner state, the state in oneself—one casts upon oneself to rid oneself of the old love.

Thus the poetry of Plato's dialogues is certainly not the model for that poetry which would be allowed in the ideal state. But it is the real poetry which is able to say what is educational in actual political life. And just as poetry in the ideal state must fend off aesthetic misinterpretations of its mimesis, Plato's dialogical poetry must resist any aesthetic misinterpretation. Thus there is complete conformity between the norms which Plato establishes for poetry and his own dialogical compositions, a conformity which is hinted at, in fact, at the end of the *Republic*.

This conformity can even be found in the Platonic form of composition closest to the traditional concept of poetry: Plato's myths. It is self-evident that the content of his myths, the images of the gods, of the beyond, of the afterlife of the soul, all adhere strictly to the theology set up in the *Republic*. But the power which Plato draws upon and the means which he applies in charging the mythical subjects of the previous age with new mythical luminosity (those very mythical subjects which his critique had purified of their magic) are significant. The content of his myths is not made to fade away into the glorious twilight

of some primordial past, nor does it close into a world unto itself
whose inscrutable meaning, like an alien truth, overwhelms the
soul. Instead it grows up out of the center of the Socratic truth
itself in a play in which the soul recognizes itself and the truth of
which the soul is most certain. That its happiness lies in justice
alone clearly echoes back to the soul from all distant horizons toward which it resounds. All the mythical content which Plato appropriates, belief in the beyond, in the transmigration of souls,
in the superterrestrial governance of eros, in the cosmic interrelationship between the soul and the stars and between the
world of the state and the world of the stars—all these mythical
powers are not conjured up so that they might cast their own
spell. Rather they derive their existence from the inner certainty
of the soul insofar as they are linked to the truth which the soul
discovers in philosophizing. Thus essentially the soul receives no
new truth from outside itself here. Plato's myths are therefore
not *mythos* and not poetry, if *mythos* means the undeciphered
truths of ancient belief, and poetry the soul's representation of
itself in the mirror of an exalted reality. There can be no interpretation of Plato's world of myth since the world made of
mythos here is not a world at all but the projection into the cosmic of the lineament of the soul's interpretation of itself in the
logos. Plato's myth is not to be experienced as an ecstasy which
transports one to another world. Instead by being tied back into
man's experience of himself, the old legendary material of these
myths acquires new meaning as magnifications, inversions, views
from afar, and ironic counterimages of the real world. Thus
these myths are in no way representation and theater whose
mere charm delight us and the mere viewing of which could
satisfy us.

The very form of narrative is also determined by the fact
that the soul cannot and must not forget itself in illusory flights
of fancy. Plato tells his tale "poorly," showing no concern for the
requirements of any narrative which is intended to absorb the
narrator and listener alike in the spell cast by the shapes which it
conjures up. Indeed, it is astonishing how much indirect discourse there is in these myths. The myth at the end of the *Republic*, for instance, is related almost entirely in indirect discourse.

This practice allows us to see in retrospect the deeper meaning of Plato's critique of the poets, which in regard to Homer appeared at first to be little more than malevolent nonsense. Everything is so designed that the mythic fable cannot remain in the distance which a lovely fairy tale preserves for itself. In the middle of a surge of poetic ecstasy we are suddenly made to recognize (sometimes only by a genuinely Socratic phrase) that we are enveloped in Socratic air here and that the age-old legend supposedly being rescued from oblivion is not a resurrected ancient myth at all but a Socratic truth which rises up in front of us in three dimensional presence while the illusory fable completely recedes before it. Plato's myth is an elegant demonstration of Socrates' argument that appearance is false and a confirmation of Socrates' paradoxically inverted measuring of the real world against another, "true" world. But even so it is suffused with irony, which should warn us never to forget that it is not by fortunate coincidence alone that we shall attain to the noble truth and escape the serious consequences of Socrates' criticisms.

Nevertheless, one cannot say that the sole function of such myth is to make Socratic truth understandable by expressing it allegorically. Of course one should never be in doubt here about who is speaking and about the knowledge which underlies what the speaker says. But the fact that this Socratic knowledge of one's own self is expressed in the form of a play of mythical images tells us something about the kind of certainty which this knowledge has. Socrates encounters in his soul something inexplicable which resists illumination by the enlightenment that had succeeded in clearing up and destroying mythology. We should not interpret the limits which Socrates sets to such explanation as a vestige of a faith to which the soul clings despite the success of the enlightenment in explaining mythical apparitions and events as natural processes, and in thereby eliminating the magical element in them. When the enlightenment tries to explain the soul itself and to eliminate the mystery which surrounds the powers of justice and love by reducing them to clever (or weak) contrivances or infirmities, Socrates emerges opposite its so readily understandable accounts as the visionary who sees his own soul. And in images of the judgment of the dead and the hierarchy of worlds and with the open eye of the seer and the wry smile of the man of irony he proclaims an inexplicable certainty which the soul has—a certainty which establishes the limits of human philosophizing as well as its dimensions and horizons. To be sure, in these poetic myths the soul does not transform itself into a variety of figures which assert themselves against us while keeping us in ignorance of their truth. But the soul does return from its journey through the surreal realms of myth in which Socratic truth rules as the real law of things chastised and set right in its beliefs. These worlds make all too obvious the importance of its philosophizing, a task from which no revelation there sets it free.

In the dialogues themselves the difference from mimetic poetry is even clearer than in the mythical tales, embellished as the latter are with a curious, elusive poetic charm. The dialogues are, of course, "representations" of real people, Socrates and his partners. But the important feature of these figures is not the powerfully graphic representation of them and not the invention of speeches which are in accord with the character of each and which give each his due. Ultimately these dialogues are more than philosophical dramas and Socrates is not the hero of these poetic compositions. Even the representation of Socrates is meant as an inducement to philosophize. The intent and purpose of these discussions are neither to portray human beings nor to recount statements and responses. It is not coincidental that Plato is fond of representing these discussions in a recapitulation and he does not even hesitate to have Socrates repeat the ten-book-long discussion of the *Republic* on the following day. Plato is not concerned with vivid and forceful accounts but with what makes any such repetition worthwhile: the maieutic power of these discussions (*Theaetetus* 149 c ff.), with the movement of philosophizing which redevelops in every repetition. Precisely because of the seriousness of his purpose, Plato gives his mimesis the levity of a jocular play. Insofar as his dialogues are to portray philosophizing in order to compel us to philosophize, they shroud all of what they say in the ambiguous twilight of irony. And in this way Plato is able to escape the trap of the ever so vulnerable written work, which cannot come to its own defense, and to create a truly philosophical poetry which points beyond itself

to what is of real consequence. His dialogues are nothing more than playful allusions which say something only to him who finds meanings beyond what is expressly stated in them and allows these meanings to take effect within him.

However, the theme voiced continually in Plato's critique of the poets is that they take seriously what is not worth being taken seriously. Here and there Plato gives us indications that his own creations, because they are in jest and are only meant to be in jest, are the true poetry. In the *Laws* the Athenian, in whom more than anyone Plato has most obviously hidden himself, says that he is in no need of a model for the right poetry for educating the young:

> For if I should look back over the speeches which we have been making from this morning on—and not, it seems to me, without a touch of the divine spirit—these would seem to me to be spoken as a kind of poetry. . . . For in comparison with most of the speeches which I have read or heard, in poetry or prose, these seemed to me to be the most appropriate and best for the young to hear. Thus I know of no better example to recommend to the guardian of the laws and education, and he should stipulate that the teachers teach these to the children. And he should apply them as a standard to evaluate whatever other poetry might be suitable. And above all he must compel the teacher to learn them and to value them (811 c ff.).

> And if tragic poets should come into the city and wish to perform their plays, we would say to them: oh best of the foreigners, we are poets ourselves, who have composed the best tragedy which there can be. For our state is nothing but an imitation of the most beautiful and best life and that indeed is the truest of all tragedy. You are poets and we are poets too, your rivals and competitors in composing the most beautiful drama. And only the true law—that is our hope—can succeed in composing the most beautiful drama (817 b ff.).

How Plato conceives of his own literary work and how he envisions the subject matter which is his real concern are mirrored in the mimetic sphere in such passages—passages from a discussion which is to provide the foundation for a new state. Plato is guided by the one important task of creating the inner constitution of mankind on the basis of which alone the order of human life in the state could be renewed. And for Plato the literary dialogues, including the representation of the just state and the just legislation, are only a *prooimion* to the true laws: "a prelude and preface, most artfully prepared, to that which must be completed subsequently." No one yet, he says, has created such preludes to the laws of the state which, like the introduction to an anthem, move the soul to open itself willingly to the laws. Plato's work is just such a true prelude to the true law of human existence. His clash with the poets is an expression of this, the exalted claim which his work makes for itself.

4

Plato's Educational State

Plato research in Germany after World War I indeed uncovered a fruitful point of departure by using Plato's political life as a basis to reach an understanding of his works and his philosophy.[1] As a consequence of this approach the *Republic* came to occupy a more central position than it had ever held before. But although one can find many specifics situated in the huge edifice of the *Republic* which bear on Plato's later political theories, doctrines regarding an actual structure of the state or its institutions are in fact not basic to this earlier work. Indeed the concern here is not even with the right laws for the state but solely with the right education for it, education in citizenship. Ultimately, however, the latter is education in philosophy. This dialogue is a philosophical discussion in which an ideal state is constructed, a utopia which lies far removed from any reality. For here Plato demands a state in which philosophers rule and rulers are taught by philosophy how to rule.

We know from Plato's biography and above all from the unique testimony which he himself gives us in the *Seventh Letter* that Plato by no means used abstract theory to deduce this requirement that philosophers rule. On the contrary, it arose as the natural consequence of the political experiences of his youth. Also, we know that his entire life's work is rooted in the conclusion to which he came, that there is an indissoluble tie between political and philosophical activity. Thus like any other of Plato's writings, the *Republic* belongs not only to his philosophical but also to his political life, and its special character must be defined starting with that fact.

1. Cf. among others Wilamowitz, op. cit., and K. Hildebrant, *Platon* (Berlin, 1933).

Plato himself tells us (*Letter VII* 324 c ff.) that he came from one of Athens' foremost families, that he had decided upon a political career, and that the political circumstances in his homeland seemed particularly favorable for him. For a revolution following the Peloponnesian War had produced (in reaction to it) an oligigarchic regime in sympathy with Sparta. And among its so-called Thirty Tyrants were some of Plato's closest relatives, who at once called upon him to serve. But the idealistic hopes which he had harbored in his youth that everything would now be better and more orderly were not fulfilled. The democracy which he had previously spurned soon seemed idyllic in comparison to this regime, and this truth was brought home to Plato most acutely by its attempt to involve Socrates, whom he so respected, in its despicable deeds. So it came about that Plato greeted the reinstatement of the democracy with renewed expectations—until these hopes too were dashed by the trial and condemnation of Socrates:

> When I saw that, and above all what sort of people concerned themselves with politics and laws and morals, and as I became more mature and began to see through it all, the more difficult it seemed to me to carry on the matters of state properly. For in the first place I recognized that nothing could be accomplished without friends and reliable allies. Nor was it easy to find such people, for our state had long since ceased to live according to the principles and customs of our forefathers. Nor was it possible to win new allies in the usual way. In the second place the laws being promulgated and the public morality had both deteriorated to an incredible extent. Thus when I, who at first so ardently desired to be politically active, now looked upon all of this and saw the chaos and confusion, my head began to swim. To be sure, I did not give up thinking about how this particular situation and the political organization in general could eventually be improved. But I found myself waiting longer and longer for the opportunity to act until I finally realized that all the states of today are constitutionally unsound. For their means of lawgiving suffer, as it were, from an incurable disease—incurable, that is, unless a reform of quite extraor-

dinary proportions could succeed. And I found myself forced to assert that fact by praising the right philosophy and proclaiming that it alone makes it possible to know what is just in private and civic life. For that reason the evils of mankind will not cease until men of a genuinely and truly philosophical sort have come into political power or, by some divine dispensation, those in power begin to philosophize genuinely (325 b ff.).

Although this passage is quite well known, it was necessary to cite it in its entirety, for its value in interpreting Plato's literary dialogues is disputed. My view is that this autobiographical statement reveals something about the purpose of all of Plato's writings. Note that it does *not* say that Plato gradually came to the realization that his political aspirations were in vain after he was already an influential writer. On the contrary, it relates how Plato abandons any political career and only then begins to try to influence the course of events through his writing, to try to summon people to philosophy and to urge that the leaders responsible for the state be educated in philosophy. This is precisely the point of what he has Socrates say in the dialogues from the very beginning. And later when we see him follow the advice of his princely friend and student, Dion, in the Sicilian adventure and when he takes the young ruler of the Syracusion kingdom to be a God-given opportunity to put his philosophical ideas into political practice (327 e ff.), this injection of himself into Sicilian affairs, as unfortunately as it might have ended, is anything but a deviation from the principle which is stated in the *Seventh Letter*. Plato tries no other route to power than philosophical education, and the failure of the Sicilian project is the failure of the *education* of the young tyrant. Even when Plato is called upon to give political counsel, he does not give advice based on his experience, advice how a particular political situation might best be exploited; rather he gives the same advice in all situations (331 d), the same advice which underlies the philosophical education which he advocates. Only justice can bring about a solid and enduring state and only he who is a friend to himself is able to win the solid friendship of others. These two statements contain the whole of Plato's political philosophy. They establish the essential correlation between state and soul, on the one hand, and politics and philosophy, on the other. And we shall see that ultimately the epigrammatical formula used by Aristotle to characterize what is special in Plato—that he unifies aretē and *eudaimonia*, virtue and happiness—in fact expresses the same basic truth. Precisely in unifying these two Plato proves to be the authentic heir of Socrates, the fate of whom determined Plato's own development. In Socrates' name and *persona*, as "a young Socrates become beautiful," Plato practices his apolitical education—in both writing and live discussion. Nevertheless, this education proves to be of fundamental value in constituting the state. Plato is no more a statesman than Socrates but no less either.

It is in his capacity as the true political educator that Plato writes his *Republic*, and most certainly this can also be taken to mean that the pedagogical state which he develops there refers as well to the actual, living community where such education was being practiced in the academy. But we should not lose sight of the central truth of the matter. We should not be diverted by the fact that the form of a utopia, the projection of a state whose relationship to reality was quite thoroughly camouflaged, did indeed exist as a literary genre before Plato. Nor should we be diverted by the fact that a writer with immediate political intentions would obviously choose such a form of light ironic allusion to advertise his political program because of the chance it affords to mix criticisms and promises so ingratiatingly. No, precisely because it disregards the intrinsic link between politics and lawmaking and because it concentrates exclusively upon proper education of the leaders, Plato's ideal state has only a roundabout, but all the more real, political significance. He justifies his requirement that philosophers must be the rulers and the critique of existent circumstances to which his experience had led him, by considering the essence of the state and human faculty which makes it possible: *dikaiosynē*. Or put another way, his philosophical inquiry is prompted by the question of how someone like Socrates, the just man in the unjust state, could possibly exist.

Dikaiosynē is the true political virtue. It means more than

the justice which distributes justly, a justice which prima facie seems to imply the German *Gerechtigkeit*. It has the ancient and traditional sense of the quintessential civic virtue underlying any community and any authentic government, a virtue the inculcation of which must be the goal of any education. Dikaiosynē is what justice, integrity, rule by law, and a civic sense are, all in one. And Plato's bold and consciously paradoxical argument is that philosophy is necessary not only to know what it is but to acquire and maintain it. (For previously philosophy had been merely a final and highly valued step in the education of the young prior to their entry into the political arena.) To verify Plato's argument we must follow the course of the discussion in the *Republic*. We must see the sequential logic and the overall unity of its development. For that reason, the construction of the *Republic* is not only a problem for literary critics concerned with questions of form and style. On the contrary, exactly at those places where contrived coincidences and arbitrariness determine the construction or even where tangible, unerased traces of its development can be identified, a unified philosophical movement is nevertheless actually unfolding. We shall make it our task here to bring this inner unity to light and to illuminate thereby the sense of the discussion as Plato intends us to understand it. We shall do this by departing from the critical junctures encountered in our ascent to the center of the whole, but we shall not allow ourselves to become involved in the particular philological problems raised here. To be specific, the question raised by Socrates at the beginning concerning dikaiosynē seems to have been answered twice, and each time, accordingly, the discussion seems to have come to a conclusion: at the end of book 1, which indeed appears to have originally been an independent dialogue concerning justice, and at the end of book 4. There can be no doubt that on both occasions a new level of insight is our reward for persisting through a dark moment in the discussion.

Let us begin with the upbeat, book 1, the polemic against the definition of justice fashionable at the time, i e , the definition taught by the sophists. Plato's thought never grows old but remains relevant to the present largely because of the

fact that he always keeps the counterimage of philosophy, sophism, in view. At this point in the dialogue an essential definition
of justice, the virtue underlying all civic order, is extracted from
a sophistic kind of thinking which lies closer to the modern
theory of the state than Plato's own. If viewed historically this
kind of thinking, as it has come down to us via Plato himself and
Thucydides, can be seen to have been of decisive importance in
shaping modern theories of the state insofar as the latter are
founded on the concept of power. The doctrines of the sophists
are more than a logical, dialectical sport. They are an expression
of that decay of Greek public morality which Plato tells us
defined the political experience of his youth. All this is made evident at the start by the striking contrast of the old man who, as a
kind of venerable, natural mirror image of philosophical life,
praises freedom from sensuous desire and extols the joys of dis-
cussing things, and who in conforming to cult and custom, builds
his existence upon a practicable rectitude: "telling the truth and
paying one's debts" (*Republic* 331 d). His son and heir, however,
no longer has the privilege of being so uncritically at home in
what is clearly dictated by cult and custom. In him there dwells
something quite in contrast to the contented self-assuredness of
the old father, something in contrast to the self-confident attitude of one who is certain of being in accord with himself and
with his traditional upbringing. Thus the son is forced to account for what he claims to know and to justify it, and as is always the case, what appears at first as a breakdown in the logic
of his attempt to do so is in fact the disclosure of a deeper discrepancy in his existence. Justice, he says, is paying back one's
debts. In the days of Simonides this might have been as tidy and
unequivalent as any maxim (331 d e ff.). But the concept of
"debtor" becomes problematic for Socrates' partner in the
discussion when the sophistic case is introduced of the insane
man who wants his dagger returned to him.[2] And with the concept of debtor the concept of justice also becomes a problem, for

2. Cf. Xen. Kyr. 1. 6, 31: Dialexeis, Diels, *Die Fragmente der Vorsokratiker* (Berlin,
1934), 90, 3. (Chapter 5 below, on Plato's *Seventh Letter*, deals specifically with the sophistic techniques of "confounding any insight" and the problem which these techniques pose
for philosophy.) (Translator)

it is no longer evident what action justice would dictate here. Obviously paying a debt is "just" only in an external sense. What is just and right is not always determined by what claim another has to anything in my possession. Within a higher relationship to another person, a community more genuine than that established by merely lending him something, it can be more just to reject his "just" claim—in this case, for example, where he has lost his senses. The just thing here is "to do his thinking for him." What is just in this instance is defined by the higher duty resulting from ties between individuals, ties in the political realm which require distinguishing between friend and foe, between who is to be helped and who is to be hurt (332 ab). Even with that refinement, however, such justice seems to be limited to circumstances of war, for only then does one have friends and enemies. But is true and essential justice to be restricted to war? In peacetime (which for this merchant's son is nothing more than the occasion to make money [333 b]) the whole matter becomes ambiguous again. Under certain conditions, protecting someone's money for him can require keeping it from him. So justice can convert into thievery insofar as I deal for the other individual and conceal the transaction from him (334 ab). Obviously this sort of difficulty will ensnare anyone who seeks to define justice in terms of some action which I perform for another. For justice is not some sort of ability in social dealings (332 d).

But even when the distinction between friend and foe *is* clearly discerned, as it is in war, the matter is not entirely straightforward. Here too the question arises whether being a friend means anything other than being united against an enemy, and whether justice is sufficiently defined as the applied art of helping the friend and hurting the enemy. To be sure, "Hurt the enemy!" is an unequivocal maxim, but it can be asked whether justice consists in this, whether justice is to be found at all in the feeling of self-superiority derived from some art—however obvious it may be how to apply the latter. Does not the idea of justice imply a shared orientation toward the Good, toward the order and rule of the Good, which, where it obtains, also includes the enemy as one whom I do not actually harm but set right with force? This certainly holds for factions within a single state and perhaps even for any possible supernational order among states. Thus there is more than superficial meaning in the fact that the reformulation of Simonides' saying here is claimed not to be his at all but that of some tyrant such as Periander and Xerxes, men whose self-image is based on mere power, i.e., the ability to do whatever they want (336 a), and whose talk of justice therefore always implies their opinion of themselves as superior to others. Tyrants have no friends.

This interpretation of Simonides' saying is of course a deliberate and ironic twisting of it, which shows how little understanding people still have of him by Plato's time. There can be no doubt that the dialectical confusion into which Socrates has plunged his interlocutor discloses a latent element of the tyrannical in the latter's definition of justice, an element to which he himself remains oblivious. But this disclosure allows *us* to perceive the genuine meaning of justice, which Socrates' partner in the discussion would have to be taught to "recollect." The discussion is on the verge of educating someone by "recollection."

At this point, however, comes the well-known scene: Thrasymachus, the sophist rhetor present, blurts out the undisguised thesis that justice is the advantage of the stronger, i.e., of those who rule (338 c). However, if this means that the ruler seeks his advantage by using that which he sets up as just as a means, the possibility indeed remains that he can be mistaken about what is truly to his advantage. In that instance justice would become something which harms the one who rules (339 b–e). Hence if he really understands how to rule, he does not at all understand his *own* advantage but only what is advantageous for ruling (342 c–e). The deeper meaning of this definition, accordingly, proves to be that the virtue of justice for those who *are ruled* is to the advantage of those *who do the ruling.* Thus for those who are ruled it is an alien advantage,[3] the advantage of someone else who himself does not hold to what is just. Justice is what is to the advantage of the unjust. So the definition of justice as the advantage of the stronger provides no answer at all to the question of

---

3. ἀλλότριον ἀγαθόν, which is taken here, in opposition to its traditional rendering, in its literal sense.

what justice is in essence and what justice means to the one who tries to live according to it. This definition says only that it is to the advantage of the tyrant, i.e., the one who violates what is just with impunity, that everybody else continue to adhere to the code of justice. This means, however, that justice amounts to naivité (341 c). The hollowness of this position is now clear. What is said to be just, the advantage of the stronger, is only just when it is not taken to be what it really is, i.e., not taken to be the advantage of the stronger but taken to be "just." A justice which is postulated and advocated using mere power as its rationalization cannot suffice to explain why what is based on power is valid as *just* and not merely as what is coerced. One may add that the founding of justice in power would be conceivable only if what was so founded was just for the one who rules as well as for those ruled, and if his power was thus not his but the rightful power of the state to enforce what is just for all.

The ideal of the life of a tyrant which Thrasymachus develops thus contains no real answer to the question of what the essence of justice is. Rather it is only a declaration of his rejection of justice. However, the argument that justice is true prudence and virtue, genuine strength and real happiness (349–54) also evades the question of what justice is in essence. And its failure to address this question (insofar as it glorifies the merits of justice but does not define its essence) gives this first conclusion of the discussion a negative and tentative character (354 a ff.). Hence Socrates compares himself here to a glutton who has allowed himself to be taken in by the unending variety of treats offered in the feast which his opponent has prepared for him (354 a). This comment makes clear that in a polemical discussion, where one ethos is pitted against another, the opponent determines the horizons of the whole. Hence the very failure of the discussion to define justice shows us how accurate Plato was in his characterization of the existing state as decadent. What began as mere ignorance of the just order in society and ignorance of justice as the power in the soul which sustains that social order, has now developed into a total perversion of justice.

At the beginning of book 2 Plato's two brothers enter into the dialogue, and the discussion here is thereby set off from what has preceded it. The questioning does in fact move to another level. Even someone who does not consider justice good in itself but, given his fear of suffering injustice, holds it to be the lesser of two evils, can see that in practice justice is preferable to injustice. Thus out of prudence and the knowledge of how weak he is by himself, each individual may enter into an agreement or contract with others which will establish what is right and assure that justice is valued (358 e).

Here we have a theory of justice which seems to be both politically and pedagogically realistic. But the positive evaluation of justice need be only conditional, for it obviously depends on correctly assessing how the conflict between powers will be resolved. Hence it is not valid in itself but only relative to what might emerge in that conflict. Quite in contrast to this approach to justice stands the undertaking to which Plato now turns, an undertaking reminiscent of Kant's rigorous analysis of the concept of duty. It must be demonstrated that injustice is always bad and justice always good, i.e., good independently of its practical application and even in the most extreme cases where one was mistaken regarding the just course of action. However, in contrast to Kant, Plato does not have in mind a deduction of the inner moral world of the unconditionally good will, a moral world apart from the realm of political action. Plato seeks precisely that power of the human soul which constitutes and sustains the state, its political "fertility," as it were (γόνιμα, 367 d), from which arise the state and what is right and just. The authentically existing human being does not concern himself with his own prosperity and advancement while living in opposition to the state. In that case right and justice would consist only in each human being's worried alertness vis-à-vis the others (367 a). Instead human existence is so constituted that precisely that basis of the existence of the state itself which makes the state possible and which is present in it at least to a small extent in even its most corrupt forms, is to be found in the souls of its citizens. It is to be found in the idea of justice.

Now to interpret something is to reach an understanding of it by returning from the conclusion to what has led up to it. Hence the problem posed here cannot be interpreted at all without knowing the solution to it in advance. That solution lies in distinguishing between the prevailing common opinion and the *idea* which underlies it. It will become evident in what follows that only this distinction, as it is made in Plato's philosophy, makes a real statecraft possible, i.e., a statecraft which shapes the political reality and does not merely wend its way among given forms of the latter. He who in making this distinction sees through current opinions to the *idea* is already a philosopher, and only he who penetrates in this way to that which endures is capable of politics on a grand scale, that is, of forming and maintaining a stable political reality. Thus the paradoxical philosopher-king, though long kept in the background and explicitly introduced only after considerable delay, is essentially implied in the way the question is put from the beginning. Or stated another way, Plato's philosophy springs from the existence of Socrates. Insofar as it inquires about the possibility of what is just in the midst of prevailing injustice, it discovers the "just in itself."

The question of what justice is in itself, of its essence, stands quite apart from any question of power or of what is generally accepted in the state. It necessarily asks what the state is essentially, in itself. But what the state can be depends upon the virtue of its citizens. I will not repeat the demonstration that this state, constructed as it is in words alone, only assumes a political character involving actual power and sovereignty once the discussion comes to the warrior class (cf. chap. 3 above). Nor shall I restate why it is that at this point the state develops internal political tensions—and simultaneously the need of a course of education to surmount these tensions—from the conflict inherent in it between the sovereign power on one hand, and the overriding order of the whole, on the other. Suffice it to say that the disclosure of what justice is starts by displaying it in the order of a just state and then proceeds to a translation of what is seen there, into justice in the soul (427 d ff.). The ancient table of values of the πάτριος πολιτεία thus recurs in Plato's so-called cardinal virtues, virtues which are curiously interwoven and made to convert, one into the other, until they ultimately resolve into the one virtue of Socratic knowing. Wisdom, i.e., thinking for everyone, belongs to the leaders, and courage to the warriors, but not the

Fascinating proposition> given today's emphasis on racial + religious idintities. justice presupposes one transcends one's own class interest to assume the greater interest of all.

84   *Plato's Educational State*

elementary animal courage of the fighter, rather the political courage of the man who uses weapons for the sake of all and never for himself (429–30 d). Sōphrosynē belongs to all the classes, to the rulers as well as the ruled, i.e., sōphrosynē as unanimity about the "thinking for everyone" and the "fighting for everyone" carried on by the governing classes (430 d–432 a). The justice of the state, however, consists in something which all these classes, with their specific virtues, presuppose: in everyone's doing what befits him, or idiopragein (433 b). Idiopragein is required of the class of workers as well as the governing classes and it alone gives the state its unity. Only insofar as the individual is oriented away from his own class and committed to the political order relating these classes as a whole, is the state possible. This commitment alone changes sovereignty from the mere possession of the power to coerce, to administration of the rightful power of the state.

It is not hard to detect that this principle of idiopragein, cast as it is in an order of distinct classes, contains a specific criticism of the degenerate Attic democracy (434 b). But as a matter of fact, it is primarily the state as a whole which is emphasized here, not its particular divisions. The state is an ordering of government and populace founded upon the fact that the whole is present in each individual and his action.

Now it is obviously of decisive importance for the life of the whole that the principle of "doing what befits one" does not turn political justice into a special case of division of labor. Division of labor represents only an "image" of justice, a linking of the action of the individual to the whole such as one finds in any technē (443 bc). Plato's concern, however, is with something more than the integration of the products of work into the community of consumers. To be sure, any work is there for all who will make use of it. Nevertheless, the work of a political leader or a warrior is not just a technē of that sort but eo ipso directly related to the whole of the state. The political leader knows that he acts for all, and what he does and does not do depends upon this, his knowledge of the whole (cf. *Charmides* 166 ff., *Euthydemus* 291 ff.). Every other worker too is directly related to the whole, not by virtue of his integration into the coordinated work of the

whole but as a citizen, i.e., by virtue of his harmony with the
whole of the sovereign order to which he belongs. The political
idiopragein of the classes is thus to be distinguished from the
idiopragein of technē, and it follows that the disruption of this
class order is the real political misfortune (434 c), i.e., a destruction of the structure of governing such as became visible in the
decay of the Attic democracy.

The definition of justice as idiopragein in reference to the
larger image of the state is now carried over to the soul. It seems
as though a mere analogy would be required here: The order of
the state would of necessity correspond to that of the soul (435 b
c ff.). Like the state, the soul must have the potential for being at
one with itself, but it is also susceptible to dangerous disorders
and strife. And in a quite remarkable analysis Plato shows that
there are indeed three parts to the soul, which correspond to the
three classes in the political order: love of knowledge, zeal, and
desire. Desire is attraction to something and knowledge is dis-
crimination in saying "yes" and "no." Between these, however,
lies what one could call engagement for the "yes" and "no." This
doctrine of the soul is deduced from phenomena which display
the soul's inner division and hence it is worked out in reference
to the instances of man's being divided against himself. The
proper ordering of the parts of the soul becomes the metaphor
from which the cardinal virtues are derived, and justice appears
in the soul as the same thing which it was in the state: here as the
idiopragein of the parts of the soul, as it was there the
idiopragein of the classes. It appears that we have now come to
the requisite result which the attempts of the first book had
failed to attain. In the case of the state political justice could not
be found in the economic principle of the division of labor
among the professions but only in adhering to, and showing concern for, the inner order of the state, i.e., in bringing about the
reconciliation and unification of the three classes. And it was
shown that the actions of the state can be right and just only on
the basis of that order. In precisely the same way it is demonstrated that the justice of the soul does not consist in some external act which it performs, not in integrity in money matters or in
aligning oneself with what emerges in the interplay of interests

of those competing for political power. Rather, as was the case in the state, it consists in an "inner" action, the action of the soul by which it too attains to a unity in the diversity of its strivings and drives, and to friendship with itself (443 cd ff.). An action is just which is in conformity with this inner order of the soul and which brings about and sustains that order. Thus the constitution of oneself as an internally well-ordered soul is the true measure of *Dasein's* self-understanding,[4] i.e., of *sophia* (443 e). Conversely, the destruction of the soul is *amathia* (444 a), the diminution and darkening of this inner capacity to govern oneself.

The inwardness of justice is most certainly not an inwardness of disposition, not that good will "which alone of all things in the world may be called good" (Kant). On the contrary, Plato's inwardness is the measure and origin of all valid *outward* expression in human activity. It is no sanctified realm of the heart known only to God but rather an order of governance and a constitution of the soul's being which maintains and fulfills itself in every action.[5]

The discussion might seem to have reached a genuine and successful conclusion insofar as it has established what is the one essence of justice common to both the state and the soul. Indeed,

---

4. *Sich-Verstehen des Daseins.* I have left Dasein (being-there, existence) untranslated since it is used here in the special sense which Heidegger gives it in *Sein und Zeit*. Here, as throughout his study of the *Philebus* (*Platos dialektische Ethik*, Hamburg, 1968), Gadamer is able to apply Heideggerian insights in his exegesis of Platonic texts. *Sophia* is grasped as a mode of Dasein, a relationship of the self to itself in self-understanding. In contrast, *amathia* is shown to be the absence of self-understanding, which characterizes a person turned away from himself in "curiosity." Cf. below, n. 9. (Translator)

5. Here as in many other places, traces of Gadamer's encounter with Hegel are evident, an encounter which opened up insights quite apart from anything in Heidegger's thought. The allusion here is to the dialectic of the "Law of the Heart" in Hegel's *Phänomenologie des Geistes* (5 B b). There, as in Hegel's exposition of conscience and the "beautiful soul" (6 C c), Hegel works out his critique of a merely subjective morality, a criticism which, as Gadamer shows, does not apply to Plato and ancient thinkers generally, who in that respect emerge as far superior to modern thinkers. The problem with the "Law of the Heart" (Rousseau) or the good will (Kant), is their inability to reconcile what is thought subjectively with what occurs in the external world of actions. As Hegel points out (6 A), no such discrepancy afflicts Greek moral philosophy, which lies before the dichotomization of consciousness and world. Cf. chap. 3, n. 10 above on "aesthetic consciousness." (Translator)

this definition of justice is no longer dependent upon what is generally accepted as just or whatever might be deduced from "everyone's" opinion. Instead it goes to the very idea of justice, its being as it is in itself: the health of the soul which is also the precondition of the health of the state. Justice is a being of the soul in relationship to itself and this is the very thing which Socrates means when he appeals to us to care for our souls.

With that, however, we have arrived at the second of those critical junctures in the dialogue which we have made it our task to illuminate. For at this point the development of the subject matter leads to a concluding expatiation on the philosophical education of the guardians and leaders. And as was the case before, this turn in the discussion is not the result of some editorial hindsight on Plato's part but of the logic of the subject matter itself, however circuitously that subject matter might assert itself. Our task here is to grasp this logic. Plato himself noted the preliminary nature of his extrapolation from the classes in the state to the parts of the soul (435 d) and he provides us with abundant, if muted, indications of its provisional character. The description of the philosophical education of the rulers which follows is indeed the elaboration of a point in the pedagogical program of the state which had remained ill defined (cf. 503 b, 503 e), but in essence it is much more than that. It was the purpose of this education to strengthen the philosophical element in the guardians in order that the general and universal (Hegel: *das Allgemeine*), the κοινῇ συμφέρον, might prevail. It is an inevitable characteristic of rulers that they are susceptible to the temptations of power and to the tyrannical drive in man, and this weakness can lead to a darkening of the philosophical element in them and to the destruction of the civil order. The same susceptibility can be found in the soul of any individual: it appears as the danger of the self's splitting in two when it is seduced into pandering to those with power or catering to the senses. And it is precisely here that the preliminary nature of the psychology of the three parts of the soul and of the definition of justice based upon this psychology comes to light. The doctrine of the parts of the soul cannot be dissociated from the definition of the virtues

insofar as the latter is based upon the former.[6] But Plato does
not so much propose a psychology as a doctrine concerning
the dangers of division in the self, a division which is the
counterimage of the self's unity with itself when the virtue of
justice prevails in it. Whether the soul is to be one in form or
whether it is to be many (612 a), a many-headed monstrosity so
to speak (cf. *Phaedrus* 230 a), is not a question for a merely theoretical psychological science. Rather it is the primary concern in
the right and just guiding of one's own life by knowledge. However, the possibility of such guiding and the issue of what direction it should take open up a new movement of questioning
within what has been achieved up to this point (even in the
definitions of the virtues), a movement of questioning which will
eventually lead us up to the center of Plato's philosophy as a
whole.

How matters stand here in regard to the soul can be
clarified by the image Plato uses of health (444 de). All health is
inner harmony against the background of possible disharmony.
Only in disharmony and derangement do both the soul and the
body become sensitive to their inner division. But the analogy
between bodily and psychic health has an obvious limitation. We
tend to say that nature takes care of, helps, itself. A good bodily
constitution is thus one which has the greatest capacity for re-
pairing itself naturally, and any doctor only assists in the natural
process of self-reparation, as does the individual person who
takes care of himself and protects his health.

The healthy soul, on the other hand, is not simply in the
hands of some "nature" which takes care of it; it does not possess
a natural good constitution which could be said to govern it. The
soul is always aware of the danger of disharmony because it must
knowingly aim at being in unison with itself. It must pay constant
attention to ensure that it maintains its accord with itself; or, put
another way, its self-accord is endangered at every moment. The
Greeks have a lovely expression for this intrinsic correlation between the good constitution of the soul and Dasein's knowledge

---

6. Wilamowitz (op. cit., 2: 219) declares the right interpretation to be wrong. Cf.
Republic 504 a!

of itself. They call it sophrosynē, which Aristotle glosses as σώζουσαν τὴν φρόνησιν (*Nicomachean Ethics* 1140 b). In preserving *phronēsis*, in existing as *knowing*, Dasein attains to a lasting governance of itself. Thus in the case of the soul it is not sufficient to have merely characterized its healthy state. The real concern is to preserve it from being led astray. The definition of justice arrived at was the sound, good constitution of the soul, but what has been attained in arriving at that definition is only an ideal picture of the just state and of the just soul, a picture of the true political and psychic health. It can be said of both, however, that they are not of a certain "nature" and are not good by dint of a good "nature." This holds for the soul just as much as it does for the state. The state with such genuine political health as the one which Socrates has constructed here in words alone lives from an excess of wisdom in its institutions. It is so ordered that it cannot be anything but healthy. But who constructs such a state and who such a soul? Where are there human beings so dedicated to the state and where are there souls whose passions yield so totally? The real question is not what justice, as the ideal health of state and soul, looks like but how justice has the power to bring itself about and preserve itself. To ask that, however, is to ask how this state could possibly exist. And as a matter of fact that very question introduces the grand philosophical discussion which now begins, viz., the question of how this state is possible, the question of possibly bringing it about (471 ff.).

Even if the picture of the true state and of true justice is only a model and thus, like the ideal picture of a painter (472 cd), immune to the question of whether it is possible, it is not accidental that this question of an *actual* justice sets the philosophical discussion here in motion. The paradoxical answer which Socrates gives is contained in his demand that philosophers rule. It is—in virtually the same words (473 d)—the demand which the *Seventh Letter* repeats. In the *Seventh Letter* political power and philosophy were to be unified by educating the young ruler of Syracuse. And here in the *Republic*, similarly, the possibility of philosophers ruling is obviously tied to education. For that reason primarily the sons of rulers are named (499 b), and for that reason the temptations are delineated to which a young man in

- The True Philosopher: one who yearns "to see" (true being beyond)
  vs
- One who yearns (to see): dazed, in a dream, swayed by
  diversion + novelty

the state is exposed (cf. the portrait of Alcibiades, 494 c). So now
everything turns on the more precise characterization of the true
philosopher, from which the transition is then to be made to the
description of the course of philosophical education for the
leaders of the state. However, it is fundamentally impossible to
say what the true philosopher is without first focusing philosophically on that which the philosopher *sees*. Even the description of a philosophical education is not possible without simultaneously experiencing this philosophical education as the di-
recting of one's vision to "true being."

Socrates describes the figure of the philosopher by both
comparing and opposing. He first likens the philosopher to the
eroticist (474 c. ff.). Both are dominated by passion, and insofar
as the lover is able to find something beautiful in everyone who
is young, insofar as he is forever finding new occasions for his
love and is not predisposed to any specific love in preference to
others, he shows that he aims at fundamentally one thing in all
loves. So too, the philosopher turns to all kinds of knowledge
and is not swayed by any preferences. For him too any particular
form of knowing is only a pretext which he himself sees through.
Now passion has precisely this quality. It can find in anything,
even in the most meager stimulation, that one thing at which it is
aimed.[7] Thus it can be said that the philosopher is possessed by
the passion to behold the truth.

Still the passion and yearning to see can be something quite
unphilosophical too (475 d ff.). Certainly, the one who yearns to
see thrives on seeing all beautiful things. So does the philosopher, who is made to merge with the eroticist in this regard (476
b f.), just as before (403 c) erotic love had been exalted into a
love of the muses, which is to say, into *philo-sophia*. But unlike the
philosopher, the one who merely yearns to see does not see the
one absolute Beauty in all things. On the contrary, dazed and as
if living in a dream (476 c: *onar*), he is always taken by the many
which displays itself to him. He seeks diversion in the many and
he lives by comparing one thing with another, his criterion being
novelty. Thus his passion is to be wherever something is going

7. Compare the *philotimos* (lover of honor), 475 ab.

on.[8] As opposed to this dreamer, the philosopher is awake. He is one who, whatever might happen, stays on his course, one who can tell the true from the false and who looks to true Being.

This differentiation of the philosopher from the one who yearns to see is intended to remind the reader of the beginning of the *Republic*. There (327 a ff.) the philosopher leads those who have stayed behind—in the hopes of seeing something—into a conversation instead of to a torchlight race on horseback in honor of the goddess. And therein we have precisely the philosophical event which occurs wherever Socrates is.

Being able to see true Being in itself, the idea, the paradigm, as opposed to that which only participates in it, the adulterated and turbid—is what characterizes the philosopher. And from the start, that which alone makes the healthy state possible, i.e., the proper attitude of the rulers toward the office and power by virtue of which they rule, was obviously this ability to see. The rulers must recognize that the power which they have is not theirs, not power at their disposal. They must resist public adulation and the hidden seductiveness of power which tempts the one who has it to seek his own advantage by any means of persuasion and to call such action "just." They must be unaffected by all these appearances and keep the true well-being of the whole in mind. All this was to be achieved by the education of the guardians in the ideal state. Thus the truth which had been avoided for so long is finally declaimed: The leaders in the ideal state must be philosophers (503 b).

In this way Plato's political intuition that the remedy and cure for the unhealthy condition of the states of his time is only to be expected from a rule of philosophy fuses with his projection of an ideal state (501 e). Philosophy alone, it is held, makes

---

8. Cf. 328 a, where Socrates alludes ironically to the desire to see: "Besides there is to be a night festival which will be worth seeing. For after dinner we will get up and go out and see the sights and meet a lot of the lads there and have a good talk." Again Gadamer draws upon Heidegger's *Sein und Zeit*, specifically the analysis there (§ 36) of *Neugier*, curiosity, or literally, the lust for the new, but Heidegger, as he himself points out, is drawing upon a long tradition which goes back through Kierkegaard's analysis of the eroticist in *Either/Or* to Augustine's treatment of *cupiditas* and *curiositas* and ultimately, of course, to Plato. In showing the link between Plato and Heidegger, Gadamer succeeds in closing the historical circle for us. (Translator)

that state possible in the first place and preserving the state would require leaders educated by philosophy. This can mean only one thing, however: Looking about for a cure for ailing states and constituting an ideal state in words is nothing other than education which cultivates that thing in every state which makes the state possible: the just political attitude of its citizens.

Here is not the place to discuss this philosophical education, which culminates in the science of dialectic. Such a discussion would lead us beyond the idea of justice to the idea of the Good, which transcends any specific ideas; rather it presupposes the latter. In any order in which a many becomes a unity, in the state and in the soul, in knowledge and in the structure of the world, it sees the law of the One and the Many, of number and Being.[9]

9. Cf. chap. 6 below, where Gadamer works out the line of thought concerning the doctrine of number in Plato, which he leaves undeveloped here. (Translator)

5

Dialectic and Sophism in Plato's *Seventh Letter*

Just what is dialectic in Plato? It is generally recognized today that it began with those talks which direct and guide the interlocutor—the kind of talk for which Socrates is famous and which made his life such a signal event in European history. And we see now that it was precisely the interpenetration of this initial dialectic with logical concerns which gave rise to Plato's subtly ingenious theory of concept formation, i.e., the procedure of *hypothesis* and *dihairēsis* in which, he tells us, the art of the dialectician consists. Paul Natorp and Julius Stenzel are principally responsible for this insight. And in my own *Platons dialektische Ethik* I used phenomenological methods to show that the basic determinations reached by the art of dialectic in the *Sophist, Statesman,* and *Philebus* do indeed have their root in live, philosophical dialogue.

To be sure, what we have now generally come to call dialectic can be only partially accounted for in terms of its origin in dialogue. More than anyone else the most singular monologist among philosophical dialecticians, Hegel, could claim to have founded his thought upon the art of leading a conversation which Socrates practiced in his encounters with "tractable youths." For even though it is principally Descartes' methodology which guides him, Hegel can claim for his method of systematic, universal development of all determinations of thought precisely that same directly sequential logic that we find in Plato's dialogues. Nevertheless, the reason we call Hegel's procedure dialectic is not that it can be said to originate in dialogue but that it is based in thinking in contradictions, *in utramque partem disputare*. The source here is *Eleatic* dialectic: the skill of developing the consequences of opposed assumptions even while one is still ignorant of the τι ἔστιν, the "what" of what one is talking about.[1] That is the skill which we first find displayed in Zeno and in Plato's *Parmenides* and which since Aristotle has been called dialectic. Surely one of the most difficult problems which Plato's philosophy presents is that of establishing how these two procedures which he develops from Socrates' art of conversing, i.e., the exercise of thinking in opposites, on the one hand, and the differentiation of concepts, on the other, are related to each other.[2] We know both only from literary expositions, in which an element of playfulness is always present. Indeed, the same method of differentiating concepts which Aristotle criticizes with such pedantic seriousness for lacking a convincing proof of its results is always introduced in Plato's dialogues with a touch of humor and irony. The *Parmenides*, especially, reads almost like a comedy and leaves us quite perplexed in regard to its actual meaning. Even if the Neoplatonic interpretation of the dialectic of the One does touch upon the truth of the matter, it must be said that in the *Parmenides*, at least, this truth is cloaked in irony and intentionally obscured.

More and more, Plato scholars have come to acknowledge what Werner Jaeger had stated back in 1912: namely, that in spite of everything "it will continue to remain a mere expedient when in the absense of other sources we attempt to get information concerning Plato's doctrine of ideas or number theory from his dialogues."[3] Consequently Plato scholarship has concerned itself to an ever greater extent with the didactic discussions of the academy, of which we no longer have any direct knowledge. We explore the reflections of them in Aristotle and his contemporaries, and the more we take Plato's "philosophy" seriously in this way—in Germany as well as elsewhere—the more one-sided it appears to us to treat Plato's dialogues in the manner of those

1. Aristotle, *Metaphysics* M 4 1078 b 26.
2. For further elaboration on the relationship of Hegel's dialectic to Plato's see "Hegel and the Dialectic of the Ancient Philosophers" in Gadamer, *Hegel's Dialectic*, pp. 5–34. (Translator)
3. Werner Jaeger, *Studien zur Entstehungsgeschichte der Metaphysik Aristotles* (Berlin, 1912), p. 140.

in Germany in the first half of this century who emphasized the "political Plato" (Wilamowitz, Friedländer, and, in extreme exaggeration, Hildebrandt) and the "existential Plato," for whom (in keeping with the existential philosophy of the 1920s) the dogmatic form of the doctrine of ideas virtually disappeared.[4]

However, we are not faced with an either/or here. In the first place, there must be a reason that Aristotle could count Plato among the Pythagoreans. Aristotle's perspective may well have been restricted by his own rejection of mathematics and his deliberate recapitulation of the thought of the older "physiologists." Nevertheless it may be accepted as a fact that Plato's philosophy did indeed construe the "principles" of the One and the Many arithmologically. In the second place, it does not suffice to interpret Plato's characterization of the practice of philosophy as dialectic in a merely biographical or literary sense. This characterization must have its basis in a most intrinsic, essential tenet of his philosophy, a tenet which both the division of concepts in the style of the *Phaedrus, Sophist,* and *Statesman*, as well as the thinking in opposites such as that presented in the *Parmenides*, should illustrate in some way. The particular literary form which Plato invented for his Socratic discourses is not merely a clever hiding place for his "doctrines"; it is a profoundly meaningful expression of them within the possibilities which the art of writing allows.

Perhaps a solution to our problem here can be found in the puzzling description which the *Sophist* gives of the activity of the dialectician 253 d).[5] For this much is clear: the passage provides a logical account of the procedure of concept division, but as the double antithesis of its sentence structure proves, this procedure also implies eo ipso an element of thinking in contradictions. Conversely, the "exercise" of the *Parmenides* which provides an example of the dialectic of proceeding on opposite assumptions confirms that that procedure is to be understood in relationship

---

4. Cf. H. J. Krämer and Konrad Gaiser, who with comprehensive and precise philological techniques work out the consequences of the methodological approach spelled out by Jaeger. The research of Robin, Natorp, and Stenzel, among others, has been leading us in this direction for some time now.

5. See my treatment of this passage in *Platos dialektische Ethik*, p. 74, n. 2.

to the overall vision of the dialectician, who knows how to proceed in discussion, in argument, and counterargument. In particular, when the concern is with the postulation of ideas, it is repeatedly said to be a task of infinite difficulty to prove their
validity to one who would contest them. As is so often the case in
Plato, the discrepancy between what one sees and what one can
defend against an opponent is emphasized specifically.[6] The
force of the arguments made by the opponent appears so great
that a victorious proof of the validity of the ideas would require
extraordinary means. In this regard one might recall the well-
known anecdote about Plato's defense of his doctrine of ideas
against Antisthenes: "He who has no eye for the idea could not
be made to see it even by a Lynceus."[7]

Now the discrepancy between an insight and its demonstrability is precisely the issue for the much disputed excursus of the
Seventh Letter. Here too it is assumed to be self-evident that the
truth of an insight must assert itself in discussion, i.e., in opposition to any possible counterargument.

In the form of an excursus of four precious pages in length,
Plato's *Seventh Letter* treats the question of the means by which an
insight may be reached. The authenticity of the letter has long
been contested and most recently the so-called excursus in particular has been called into question by many because it presumably does not concur with Plato's well-known doctrines.[8] It is also
true that the line of thought here is presented in a vague, circui-
tous way and that the argument is sometimes astonishingly sim-
plistic. Nevertheless, I believe that until now we have failed to
observe and evaluate a very simple fact which would suffice to
explain all that. These pages do indeed constitute an excursus,
but not in the sense, obviously, that they could be extracted from

---

6. Plato often makes clear that he sees a distinction between a correct assertion and
an irrefutable one. Cf. the *Parmenides*, 133 b and 135 b, where the cases of seeing something oneself and of teaching an insight to someone else unambiguously and irrefutably
are specifically said to be two different things.

7. Cf. Simplicius, *in Categorias* 208, 30 ff.

8. My interpretation of the excursus which I have been presenting in my lectures
for decades now, will, it is hoped, justify itself on the basis of the philosophic subject matter. Only in those places where I cannot agree with the recent interpreters on specific
philological questions have I taken a position on the issues they raise.

their context as a subsequent insertion. (Attempts to do that, however tempting they might seem, are destined to fail.) Rather, they are an excursus in the sense that they are characterized by the author of the letter as a self-citation and possess an inner completeness and unity which clearly distinguish them from the letter itself, insofar as the latter was occasioned by particular circumstances.⁹ The notions developed here are not being thought out to rebut the philosophical presumption which Dionysius II had displayed in his tract on Plato's philosophy.¹⁰ Instead the

9. 342 a. ἔτι δὲ μακρότερα (still more at length) points up this distinction, as does the πολλάκις (frequently).

10. I am not implying that the language of the excursus indicates that this argument was not intended originally for the purpose it serves here. On the contrary, no stylistic features would require us to separate the excursus from the rest of the text. In fact its vagueness, digressions, pleonasms, etc., remind one of the *Laws*. My exposition is merely meant to indicate that the argument here must be understood as purely exoteric. Only an argument which in no way claims to say what is ultimate and most profound can be sensibly inserted in a political letter like this one. H. J. Krämer has seen the essence of the matter when he writes, "The excursus has only methodological and not substantive meaning" ("Aretē bei Platon und Aristoteles. Zum Wesen und zur Geschichte der platonischen Ontologie," *Heidelberger Akademie der Wissenschaften*, 1959, p. 459). For just that reason I would caution against interpreting it in terms of substantive references to the teachings in περὶ τοῦ ἀγαθοῦ (On the Good) although it might indeed be correct that this argument was presented in response to the treatise published by Dionysius, which corresponded in its content to "On the Good."

In general I find that the literature on the *Seventh Letter* lacks the proper hermeneutic principles. A dialogue is not a statement of doctrine and an open letter is not a dialogue. The autobiographical statement at 326 b is unquestionably an interpretation of Plato's own development made after the fact and is obviously a reference to the *Republic*. But it is just as clear that it is made here in the context of Plato's attempt to influence Dion and Dionysius II, a point made over and over again in the letter. Thus one must stress the second of the alternatives ("until the actual rulers begin to seriously philosophize") in the way in which it most likely was meant. For it is unlikely that, conversely, true philosophers would ever accede to political power. That seems to me to be obvious. What indeed is one supposed to make of Plato's political utopia? It will not do, I think, to view the *Republic*, as Hildebrandt does, as a form of political action and a step in the taking of power. (Of course the whole *Republic* is full of deliberate provocations! But these are not meant politically.) Nor is it a statement of doctrine—despite Aristotle's peculiar way of always ciriticizing the dialogues pedantically with regard to their "content." Rather it is a brilliant literary utopia in which a counterfeit civic order is made to represent (indirectly and with pointed allusions) the course of instruction in the academy, the propaedeutic training for the doctrine of ideas. Cf. my own earlier attempts above at interpretation of this issue, "Plato and the Poets" and "Plato's Educational State," which still seem hermeneutically correct to me. (Regarding the question of whether what Plato sets forth in this indirect fashion was philosophy, see the conclusion of the latter essay, in which it is text of the letter itself reveals that the concern is with a train of thought which Plato had often set forth previously. Plato himself says—with no trace of irony—that what we read here had been presented in lectures many times before. To me there is no doubt that these presentations occurred in the context of Plato's oral instruction and that what is explicated in the excursus had a propaedeutic function within that instruction. It is to be viewed as a prefatory appeal to give oneself over to philosophic instruction and didactic discussion with the proper attitude and, in particular, as a warning not to let oneself be confused by those empty techniques of arguing being proffered in the fashionable instruction of the Sophists and in obvious opposition to the philosophic community cultivated by the academy.

Only if one is clear about the function of the excursus, the propaedeutic locus of its exposition, can one attain the hermeneutically correct access to it. One knows then that in it none of the specific content of Plato's philosophy is to be expected —nothing of the ascent to the idea of the Good over the steps of knowledge, nothing of his dialectic of ideas, whose artful conceptual development we find mirrored in so many of his dialogues. As a matter of fact the so-called epistemological theory of the excursus is not a theory of knowledge at all but a theory of teaching and learning, the mettle of which is to be tested in didactic and eristic discourse.[11]

---

said of dialectic that "in any order in which a many becomes a unity, in the state and in the soul, in knowing and in the structure of the world, it sees the law of the One and the Many, of number and Being." (Incidentally Hegel's account of Plato in his history of philosophy is in essence hermeneutically correct on this point.) In my opinion there is no further need to explain why a letter of this political sort, especially one to the supporters of the assassinated Dion, who came from the circle of the academy, gives as little appearance as possible of being esoteric and never expressly mentions the doctrine of the ideas. On the other hand, I find it impermissible to interpret the reserve displayed in the excursus in regard to the doctrine of ideas as a renunciation of that doctrine. Interpretations of this kind, which would make the later Plato a critic of his own doctrine of ideas, are, even if the *Seventh Letter* is set aside, irreconcilable with the discussion in the academy as that has been transmitted to us.

11. In regard to 342 a, the παραγίγνεσθαι (to arrive at [knowledge]) presupposes from the start the spokenness of what is said. Only in this way does the significance of uttering the explanation of a word or concept become clear (343 b: ὃ νῦν ἐφθέγμεθα) ([the word] which we have just uttered). And similarly, the tacit assumption that the setting of what is said is within a question raised (343 d ff.) and that what is said could be re-

Knowledge — presupposes the (spokenness) of what is said " is spokenness limited to verbal (speech, writing ↄ oral) answers ? For dance + music and painting are "language"

A ridiculously simple example, knowledge of the circle, i.e., an object of mathematical investigation, illustrates the general theme that the media, means, *momenta*, in and by which insight and the communication of it are to be achieved, are not capable of compelling someone to understand. Aristotle's syllogisms or a deductive system, Euclid's geometry, for instance, can construct proofs which by virtue of their logical cogency compel everyone to recognize the truth, but this, according to Plato, is not to be achieved in the realm of the philosophy of ideas.[12] And it seems important to him to make that fact clear from the start to anyone who wants to participate in the communal seeking and inquiry which lead to the ideas. Thus the question raised here implies philosophy's criticism of itself. Why does the possibility of compelling someone to understand in the way mathematics can, for example, not exist for philosophy? Are not all the means which we apply in factual discussion and argument used for the precise purpose of bringing the other person to understand? And would not the ideal argument be intrinsically compelling and secure against the attacks of anyone who would speak against it? Plato wants to show that in fact this ideal cannot be realized. To this end he examines the means we use to make our meaning clear to someone who would understand us. He distinguishes among three components in any insight we might have about a thing,[13] three means in which our knowledge about it is

---

futed (343 c) also becomes clear. All refutation presupposes speakers and listeners. The striking ἐν λόγοις ἢ γράμμασιν ἢ ἀποκρίσεσιν (in oral statements, writings, or answers) (343 d 4) can be explained—as can d 7—by the fact that a written statement by Dionysius is the occasion for all that is said here. But it is hardly possible that a literary polemic specifically against written expositions of Plato's philosophy is intended here. By nature, speech as well as writing belong in the same category as the oral answer since any exposition of the *eidos*, whether spoken or written, will have to counter the objections of those who have no eye for the eidos.

12. 341 c: ῥητὸν γὰρ οὐδαμῶς ἐστιν ὡς ἄλλα μαθήματα (for it cannot be stated in any way like other forms of learning may be).

13. In regard to 342 a, τῶν ὄντων ἑκάστῳ ([belonging] to each existent thing): the dative is significant here. The question is not how one communicates his knowledge of a thing but how the thing communicates itself—how the *thing* is, i.e., what kind of reality it has, when knowledge and communication take place. *Logos* and *epistēmē* are always understood relative to the thing. Cf. *Euthydemus* 285 e: εἰσὶν ἑκάστῳ τῶν ὄντων λόγοι (there are *logoi* which pertain to every existing reality). The "thing" (*Sache*) is the noetic object, or, as Plato would put it, the idea, as that which is truly real. Hence the word order, which gives

to be communicated. To these three he appends a fourth,
namely, the knowledge itself produced by the first three. Here
we have four ways in which the thing known may be said to be
"present" for us, and obviously, the reality itself, the knowledge
of which is under consideration, is distinct from all of these. It is
the fifth in this series. The four means of communicating the
thing are as follows:

(1) name or word (*onoma*),
(2) explanation or conceptual determination (logos),
(3) appearance, illustrative image, example, figure (*eidōlon*),
(4) the knowledge or insight itself.

Now Plato asserts that all four of these provide no certainty that
in them the thing itself (*die Sache selbst*) will come to be known as
it truly is. He makes this point using the example of the circle.
    That, certainly, is a good choice. Plainly no previous knowl-
edge of the doctrine of ideas or of the dialectic of concepts is required to see that a circle is something different from the circular things which we call round, curved, oval, orbicular, etc., and
which we can see with our eyes. It is clear to us that the figure
which we draw to illustrate a mathematical relationship visually is
not the mathematical relationship itself, and clearer still that the
circular objects in nature are not to be confused with the circle of
mathematics. It takes no effort at all to understand the sense
here in which Plato speaks of a "true circle." This turn of speech
is understood immediately if it is used in distinction from everything circular which we encounter in our experience. A true circle is obviously something different from all of that.[14]

_____

emphasis to the ὄντων (existing, real). Of course there is no mention here of "things" but
instead only of that reality of which alone we can have knowledge according to Plato.
This fact also establishes that logos means explanation according to essence.
    14. It is striking that naming (and the corresponding conceptual explanation) oc-
curs so often here in the context of mathematics. Evidently that is because the concern is
with producing constructs which are not found anywhere else. Hence their conceptual
determinacy precedes, as it were, the designation of them with a name. That Eudemos
singles out Plato's contribution in his history of mathematics, namely, to have distinguished between name and concept (Simplicius, *Physics* 98), points in the same direction.
The mathematician is the protagonist for those who seek to leave the κατ' ὄνομα διώκειν
(search for a name) behind. In regard to 342 b, the distinction between *onoma* and logos
is also to be found in the *Laws* at 964 a (cf. also 895 d). At all events it is striking that

Neither, however, is the circle what Plato calls an idea in the strict sense of that concept. On the contrary, it belongs to the category of mathematical constructs which constitute a kind of intermediate world between the sense-perceived and the intelligible. There are many true circles and not just the one circle, and when represented by a figure, we can recognize all that can be known about the geometry of the circle in any one of these. Geometry requires figures which we draw, but its object is the circle itself. For that reason such mathematical entities as the circle are especially suited to illustrate the transition to pure thinking, which in Plato's opinion is the way to true knowledge and which he thus speaks of as the "turn" to the idea. Even he who has not yet seen all the metaphysical implications of the concept of pure thinking but only grasps something of mathematics—and as we know, Plato assumed that such was the case with his listeners —even he knows that in a manner of speaking one looks right through the drawn circle and keeps the pure thought of the circle in mind. Thus the example which Plato chooses is one of those mathematical entities which according to him have a propaedeutic function in regard to philosophical thought. They school one's vision for that which is thought purely. They raise the soul, as it were, to the level of pure thought in that they turn it away from all that is encountered in sense experience or in conversations where mere opinions are exchanged. He who does not complete this turn to that which is thought purely, he who does not complete this abstraction, can never attain the insights and knowledge which we call mathematics.

Obviously the circle is an instance of the knowledge of *all* those things which one can know through thought alone. The circle demonstrates that one cannot communicate his knowledge unless one knows a name for it and is able to explain the word with which one names it by means of a conceptual determination. It is evident, then, that one must have in mind the appearance of that specific sort of thing. The word comes first, of course, but obviously various words give linguistic characteriza-

---

Aristotle in pursuing a similar argument (*Physics* A 1, 184 b 11) also uses the example of a circle. Could it not be that this passage reflects an argument used frequently by Plato?

tions of the circular, e.g., round, curved, orbiculate, circular, and so on. The clarifying conceptual determination or definition which Plato provides—"everywhere on the periphery equidistant from the center"—says exactly what a circular line (the periphery) actually is. The example shows us precisely what Plato means by the logos: not just any statement at all but the essential determination, the statement which defines. But here, of course; there is no reflection on the logical structure of determination, i.e., the differentiation according to genus and species elaborated in the well-known doctrine of dihariēsis, which Plato again and again calls the core of the art of dialectic. That there is no such reflection is in keeping with the propaedeutic style of the whole.

Third on the list is the figure, and indeed the mathematical example chosen involves something of this sort. Clearly this third item on the list must be taken in a most general sense and it must be left open to just what extent the communication of knowledge involves artificially produced figures such as are drawn in mathematics or illustrative phenomena themselves or even illustrations used in talking—the "example," in other words. Evidently all of these may be thought of as *eidōla*. Plato's point of departure here is the circle one sketches in the sand or erases and also the circle turned on the lathe. In both cases the model is destructible. But the circle itself cannot be destroyed. Both the phenomenon given to the senses in which one cognizes (Plato would say re-cognizes) something and the illustrative example are thus essentially different from what becomes discernible in them. But there is something else which they have in common. Despite their difference from the circle itself, the circle is somehow present in both these forms of eidōla just as it is in the word and the concept.

Fourth on Plato's list is knowledge, insight, and true opinion. Insofar as all of these have their place neither in sounds uttered nor in the bodily and tangible but in the soul, this fourth is different from the other three. Nevertheless it too is not the thing itself. For the circle itself is not in the soul. It is something distinct; it is *one* thing identical with itself and different from everything which occurs in the soul. For in the soul *many* things occur. If seen in this light, it makes sense to place the insight together with the other three means of communication. Insights too do not belong to true reality, but to becoming (*genesis*). They are part of our intellect's stream of life. They emerge and recede. Our opinions change. This is true even of mathematical insights. To be sure, something like the Pythagorean theorem is one and the same invariant state of affairs to a much higher degree than the points of view which different people have about a thing. To know this theorem, to be the master of its mathematical intelligibility, its derivation, its demonstrability, is certainly something different from remembering the mere words and phrases in which its proof is given or remembering the particular figure which one happens to use for the proof. If I really know how to prove it, I am no longer dependent upon the different possible figures or drawings which are used in the proof. Even so our grasp of a mathematical theorem in our thought is not independent of our intellect. It is part of the latter and it is not certain that I can reproduce the theorem in my thought even if I do 'know' it. Like any thought, it takes part in coming-into-being and passing-away and in being other than itself. Unlike the thing itself, science in the soul is not timeless.[15] Closest to the thing itself is obviously that moment of insight in which suddenly everything which contributes to the intelligibility of the internal relationship of the thing to itself is present to me all at once: the steps of the proof, the auxiliary construct, which was so hard to find, and its function in the proof, and so forth. More than anything else this evidentness, which makes one want to say, "I've got it!," contains the intrinsic relationship of the mathematical structure as such. Plato calls this evidentness *nous*. He quite rightly distinguishes it from the science which I have attained when I master mathematics. And with even more justification he distinguishes it as well from a mere correct opinion in which nevertheless (if it is correct) this thing itself is also there as "disconcealed."[16]

15. Cf. the *Symposium* 208 a.

16. *unverborgen*. The word, of course, is Heidegger's. The theme in Heidegger which Gadamer appropriates here is that any insight which we can have emerges in finite human discourse and therefore, only partially. It is clearly "there," but all the

Despite all the differences among these four there is some-thing common to all of them which makes it possible to group them together. They all must play a part if one really wishes to grasp the thing. They all make a thing present in some way or another; in the word, the concept, the illustration, and, above all, in the luminousness of an insight which comes to us out of all of these, the circle itself is there. Thus besides these four which "are" the circle, the circle itself is the fifth. Plato's simple enu-meration which concatenates things apparently so diverse is not without its justification.

And now Plato begins to demonstrate the point toward which the whole exposition had been leading. These four are in-deed indispensable for true knowledge. But they are of such a nature that if one avails oneself of them, one can never grasp the thing itself with complete certainty. One can never be sure that with these means the thing itself is displayed in its full, "disconcealed" intelligibility. This is the basic experience in every philosophic endeavor, in every philosophic discussion: words, words, only words, and nevertheless these words which are just words are not supposed to be mere empty talk. They should be capable of constructing the thing meant in another person, erecting it so that it is there in him. What is the reason that the means, whether taken individually or all together, are actually incapable of compelling someone to understand? What is wrong with them? What is their weakness?[17]

The question has been raised why in this analysis of the *four* means Plato stresses only the weakness of the logoi. For as a mat-ter of fact not only word and speech but also figure and the in-ternal state of mind are numbered among these four. But who does not see at once that this process of attaining and com-municating understanding always takes place entirely in the me-

---

while embedded in what is not clear, in what remains concealed. Our insights, in other words, are limited by our discursivity. What is given to us to know is given from hidden-ness (λήθη) and in time lapses back into it. Thus our human truth, ἀ-λήθεια, is never ab-solute. For the origins of this thought in Heidegger see *Sein und Zeit* § 9 B on *Rede* (speech, talk, discourse) as a "letting show forth from," i.e., ἀποφαίνεσθαι. The later ideas of the *Lichtung* (clearing, lighting) and as disconcealedness are contained here in embryo. (Translator)

17. ἀμῶς γέ πως (somehow or other) (342 e) expresses Plato's concern here.

dium of one person's *speaking* with another? Plato leaves no doubt that even knowledge of the ideas, although it cannot merely be derived from language and words, is still not to be attained without them (*Cratylus* 433 a, 438 b).[18] The weakness of the logoi, which is the weakness of all four, is precisely the weakness of our intellect itself which depends upon them. They themselves offer no assurance that the thing itself is there in its true "disconcealedness."

Again it must be kept clearly in mind that Plato's exposition of this weakness is designed for those with no previous education in philosophy. He emphasizes not once but repeatedly[19] that each of these four means has a tendency to bring a reality of a specific sort to the fore instead of the reality of the thing itself which was supposed to be displayed in word or discussion, intuition or insight. They all have an intrinsic distortion-tendency, so to speak. In the process of bringing something else into (presence) they would assert themselves as whatever particular thing they are instead of fading out of view.[20] For they all are something besides the thing they are presenting. They all have a reality of their own, a character which differentiates them from that thing. The word *circle* is not the circle itself, nor is the statement which defines what a circle is, nor is the circle which is drawn. My opinion regarding the circle and even my insight into that which a circle is, is not the circle itself. Plato's thesis is this: all these means assert themselves as whatever they are, and in pushing to the fore, as it were, they suppress that which is displayed in them.

This is easiest to see in regard to what we referred to as figure. And it is not coincidental that Plato alters the sequence here (343 a) and begins by establishing that every circle drawn is the complete opposite of what it is supposed to be. At any given

---

18. In *Wahrheit und Methode* (pp. 384 ff.) I have elaborated on my thesis that the *Cratylus* points beyond its final *aporia* (439 a ff.) to the path on which the ideas are to be sought.

19. Repetition as a meditative (in Descartes and Husserl's sense), pedagogical device is something which we find often in Plato. The recapitulatory definitions of the *Sophist* and the *Statesman* come to mind in this regard.

20. In regard to 343 c, the distinction between τί (essence) and ποῖόν τι (quality), which obtains at all four levels of knowing, has to be understood as simply as possible.

point it is somewhat straight while the circle itself displays not the least bit of its opposite, straightness. There is no perfectly drawn circle—every figure is somehow deficiently round. Nowadays this example does not make immediately evident why that should jeopardize our insight. That the representation of the circle, in which there is always an element of straightness, obviously fails to attain true circularity does not seem to be of any consequence. While using the drawn circle, one can still mean the circle itself. Where is there supposed to be a deception or falsification or concealment of the thing? How is the straightness in the drawn circle supposed to push itself to the fore and assert itself?

However, if we keep in mind the state of mathematics in Plato's time, for which Plato's insight into the ontological difference between sense-perceived reality and intelligible reality was not at all so obvious, then the example makes very clear what Plato means. It is precisely the classical problem of the squaring of the circle to which he is referring—a problem which appears to be solvable if one departs from the deficiency of any drawn circle. To us it is obvious that it is impossible to transform a circle into a quadrangle of the same area by circumscribing polygons, each with a greater number of angles than the previous one. However, if one forgets the distinction between the figure and the thing and attempts to solve the problem using the figure, in that one draws smaller and smaller chords in the segments which remain, then it will appear that the polygon fully coincides with the line of the circle. As a matter of fact we do have substantiation of such attempts to solve the problem of the squaring of the circle mathematically, and it is quite right to say that these pseudoproofs are the result of the straight asserting itself in the curved. Even Protagoras is said to have contested mathematics because it takes what is not straight for straight and what is straight for curved.[21] Only after Plato were Greek mathemati-

---

21. In regard to 343 a, Protagoras' book on mathematics seems to have made much ado about exactly this behavior of the mathematician, who takes the crooked to be straight. This is established by Aristotle, *Metaphysics* 998 a 3, and, most illuminatingly, 1078 a 19, *Physics* 993 b 35, and *Metaphysics* 1089 a 21. That it was possible at all to argue in this way makes clear how difficult it was then for a mathematician to provide

cians in a position to see clearly why such proofs are not mathematical proofs at all. The point is wholly evident to Aristotle and he specifically refers to such proofs as nonmathematical.[22]

But it is not so easy to explain why the weakness of words and conceptual determination which takes place in words, i.e., in the medium of uttered sounds, should be that they bring to the fore that which they themselves are and conceal what they are supposed to represent. Plato says only that there is nothing constant and dependable in them because all designations of a thing are somewhat arbitrary and, given a different convention, could just as easily designate something else. That the sound of the word reveals nothing of the thing were it not for the *meaning* of the sound, is made clear enough in the *Cratylus*, much to the amusement of all. Furthermore it may certainly be assumed that Plato's listeners, who were prepared for what he said, were immune to the linguistic tricks which played such a large part in the Sophist teachings of the day. Of course nowadays we would again counter that the fact that all words are conventional and not firmly attached to the thing designated does not in itself produce *pseudos*. The arbitrariness of naming and of agreeing to call something something does indeed indicate how little the sound of the word as such contains the thing itself. But especially when the word is understood, not as an image or copy but as a sign arrived at by convention, it is hard to see how its own being, the particular being of the sound, is supposed to assert itself and conceal the thing. The intelligibility of the sign lies precisely in

---

justification for himself and his method. This situation can be detected in the background of the *Theaetetus* when Theodorus seeks to avoid ψιλοὶ λόγοι (derisive words) (165 a 1) and when Theatetus is only led up to the aporia and no further. Of course no one claims that the real mathematician knows nothing of the difference between the figure and the thing itself and that he is thus necessarily misled by the figure into a mistake. Here too the critical point is not the correctness of one's own insight but its ability to withstand a 'logical' argument which would refute it. Similarly in Aristotle the case of obfuscation of a geometric truth by auxiliary lines or constructions is not treated in the analytics of language but in the "logic of probability" (*Topics* A 1, 101 A 5 ff.). It seems significant to me that in applying the concept of the atom to mathematical problems—in defense against Protagoras' attack (?)—Democritus displays no knowledge of Plato's distinction between the noetic and what is perceived by the senses.

22. Aristotle, *Physics* 185 a and the commentary of Simplicius (special edition by F. Rudio [Leipzig, 1907], pp. 103 ff.).

the fact that it points away from itself and *does not* assert itself as
an independent reality but merely serves its function. Still Plato's
argument is valid. The fact that the sound of a word can bring
something else to the fore which does not represent the thing
meant results from precisely the fact that, insofar as it is a sign, it
depends upon a particular convention. The possibility of
renaming, which is implied in any giving of a name and
designating with signs and to which Plato points here, demonstrates that the sound by which the word names the thing does
not carry its meaning in itself unambiguously. What Plato has in
mind is obviously that this ambiguity of words allows a word to
let something else be there instead of presenting the thing
meant. In this age of artificial, logical languages this point needs
no further elaboration. As we all know, the reason for the invention of mathematical symbol-languages and their perfection in
the last hundred years was that conventional language was incapable of compelling someone to understand something. Instead,
because of its imprecision and ambiguity, conventional language
entangles us in pseudoproblems; ergo logic's claim to have rid us
of this kind of error by perfecting an artificial system of signs.
Such a perfected sign language would accomplish what Plato argues natural languages could not. Each individual sign would
designate one thing exactly and unequivocally. Still, given the
fact of mathematical artificial languages, one could ask whether
it is this means of word and concept itself which is too weak. Is it
not rather more the case that only its use, i.e., the convention
which underlies the natural use of words, is not established with
sufficient ingenuity and precision to ensure the comprehension
of what is intended by the sign or word?

Things become perplexing here, especially since Plato does
not stop once he has said that the word has nothing fixed and
certain about it. He goes on to characterize the definitional
statement (*logos ousias*) as just as weak, precisely because it is
made up of words. This sounds strange in many respects.
Clearly the ambiguity of a word is reduced directly by its posi-
tional value in the context of what is spoken. Having seen that,
one might well proceed to a critique of the whole idea of an
unambiguous coordination of sign and thing designated. The as-

sumption that a perfected instrument of designation exists by which everything that one means and thinks precisely could be designated—and this would be the ideal logical language—is a nominalistic prejudice, the untenability of which has in my view been convincingly demonstrated in Wittgenstein's logical investigations.[23] Thus one might think that the transition from single words to the whole of speaking would suffice to overcome the weakness which lies in conventional designation as such, and one would like to believe that Plato's dialectic does justice precisely to this consideration in opposing the *logos*, as the *koinōnia* of the ideas, to the fruitless undertaking of defining things atomistically. And as a matter of fact it seems to me that here we have the answer to the question of why Plato rejects the definitional statement with the same argument which he used against the single word. To be sure, the weakness of the word as such is overcome by the logos. It is in fact its purpose, as the clarifying conceptual definition, to transcend the artificiality which lies in the ordinary use of language with its mere naming of things. By determining the concept, it lets the thing itself be present as it is determined eo ipso. Insofar as one has established the definition, one seems to be beyond any mistaking of one thing for another, be it of the meaning of one word for another or of a figure for the thing itself. So what danger of things being obscured should be concealed in the conventional character of what is formulated in language?

Plato's *Parmenides* seems to contain a good answer to this question. As in the *Seventh Letter*, no logical insight is presupposed which one could have attained only at the end of some Platonic course of instruction. Rather the point of departure is the dialectical experience which everybody has from the start. Similarly there is good reason that the definition of the circle which Plato gives in the *Seventh Letter* is spelled out with no recourse at all to the genus–species schema. If one wants to describe the dialectical experience of thought, one may not just presuppose this systematic doctrine of classificatory concept formation. Instead one must display how the very procedure of

23. Ludwig Wittgenstein, *Schriften* (Frankfurt, 1960), 2: 289 ff.

conceptual definition itself contains something arbitrary and uncertain, for the genus under which a thing is to be subsumed obviously lacks singleness of meaning.[24] The variations in the conceptual determination of the sophist with which the dialogue of
the same name begins,[25] as well as the corresponding considerations in the *Statesman*,[26] make that fact completely clear. Viewed
logically, the ideal might be to portray the arbitrariness of such
possible definitions against the background of the "system of all
ideas" which supposedly lies behind Plato's doctrine of ideal
numbers, and thereby to eliminate this arbitrariness. But it
seems highly questionable to me whether the principles of the
One and the Many upon which this system rests are really meant
by Plato to guarantee that we can attain unequivocal meaning in
a classificatory structure. The traditional account of Plato's esoteric doctrine argues against that possibility, and there are indications of ineradicable ambiguity in the dialogues too. The
interweaving of the highest genera in the *Sophist* and, even more,
the dialectical exercise which the young Socrates is put through
by the elder Parmenides lead only to the *negative* insight that it is
not possible to define an isolated idea purely by itself, and that
very interweaving of the ideas militates against the positive conception of a precise and unequivocal pyramid of ideas. To be
sure, what the principle of such an order would be, the depend-
ency of one thing on another, can be shown very nicely using
Plato's prime example of systematic ordering, the relationship of
line, point, plane, and volume. But are the ascent leading
through the sciences of these to the highest insight into the Good
and the descent from this insight anything more than an ideal
program? Is it not always the case, as Plato so effectively teaches
us here, that as human beings we can perceive the order of good
and bad, the order of reality as a whole, only in finite, limited
attempts? Perhaps in the final analysis the indeterminacy of the
Two is meant precisely to imply that for us there exists no clear,
unambiguous structure of Being.[27]

24. For that reason Plato's dihairēsis necessarily proved unsatisfactory when measured by Aristotle's standard of *apodeixis*.
25. *Sophist* 221 c–231 c.
26. *Statesman* 258 b–267 c.
27. The manner in which each particular exposition is dialectically founded in the
Timaeus (even the exposition of the χώρα) seems to support my argument here.

In any event the dialectic to be experienced here is of exactly the same sort as the one demonstrated in the exercise in the *Parmenides*. It too results from the multiplicity of respects in which something may be interpreted in language. In this regard one might be reminded of the first hypothesis in the *Parmenides*. There that multiplicity was not a burdensome ambiguity to be eliminated but an entirety of interrelated aspects of meaning which articulate a field of knowing. The multiple valences of meaning which separate from one another in speaking about things contain a *productive* ambiguity, one pursued, as we know, not only by the academy but also by Aristotle with all his analytic genius. The productivity of this dialectic is the positive side of the ineradicable weakness from which the procedure of conceptual determination suffers. That ever contemporary encounter with the logoi of which Plato speaks[28] is found here in its most extreme form. It is displayed here as the experience which we have when the conventional meaning of single words gets away from us. But Plato knows full well that this source of all aporia is also the source of the *euporia* which we achieve in discourse.[29] He who does not want the one will have to do without the other. An unequivocal, precise coordination of the sign world with the world of facts, i.e., of the world of which we are the master with the world which we seek to master by ordering it with signs, is not language. The whole basis of language and speaking, the very thing which makes it possible, is ambiguity or "metaphor," as the grammar and rhetoric of a later time will call it.[30]

Only if one has this immediate and fundamental dialectical experience in mind does one understand what Plato means when he describes the ultimate possibility of knowledge as a lingering with all four of these means—a lingering which passes back and forth from one to the other. All attempts to read an ordered ascent into this series of means, a graduation of them which would correspond to the ascent of the soul over the whole system of knowledge up to the idea of the Good, are completely mistaken.[31]

28. *Philebus* 15 d: τῶν λόγων αὐτῶν ἀθάνατόν τι καὶ ἀγήρων πάθος ἐν ἡμῖν (an experience which never dies nor ages which we have of the logoi themselves).

29. *Philebus* 15 c.

30. Cf. Aristotle, *Soph. El.* 1 165a 7–17.

31. Cf. n. 3 above.

Still there is a difficulty here. Whereas the weaknesses of the first three are pointed out in detail in the discussion of the weakness of the logoi, there is seemingly no mention of the weakness of the fourth, of the state of the soul when it recognizes or knows—at least not in plain words. And the state of the soul which we call knowledge or insight into the truth must also be of such a nature that it asserts itself and thereby conceals the thing itself. As a matter of fact it seems to me that the demonstration of this point is not expressly given for the sole reason that it is implied to a certain extent throughout the whole exposition. For when there is mention made in what follows of the "bad upbringing" of the soul, when the helplessness of the individual soul in the confrontation with the dialectical techniques of the opponent is described, and when well-intentioned refutation and uncontentious questioning and answering are called for, an indirect indication is given of what Plato has in mind. In knowledge and insight there is distortion too. In an argumentative discussion the distortion, which any knowing implies and which it can push to the fore, is the obstinacy which makes us refuse to acknowledge that someone else might be right. For what is that obstinacy other than the opinion which I advocate, or have advocacted, asserting itself as *my own* position to such an extent that I am no longer able to follow the objective counterargument of the other person? What tend to block the path to objective truth are, in the first place, the fact that an opinion or insight is always my opinion or insight and always has such and such a particular character and, in the second place, the fact that I, since I am so taken with myself, am prejudiced generally against the opinions of others. How the soul must be disposed in order to avoid this self-assertion is treated with sufficient detail in what follows in the text.

To sum up, if one stays with the phenomenon, the thing itself, one can see that the weakness of all four is the same. And one can apply Plato's logic to make quite clear why this weakness cannot be overcome without Plato's actually having stated the reason. All four means are trapped in the dialectic of the image or copy, for insofar as all four are intended to present the thing in and through themselves they must of necessity have a reality of their own. That which is meant to *present* something cannot *be* that thing. It lies in the nature of the means of knowing that in order to be means they must have something inessential about them. This, according to Plato, is the source of our error, for we are always misled into taking that which is inessential for something essential. What occurs here is a sort of falling away from what was originally intended, i.e., from the orientation of all these four means toward the thing itself. Plato says expressly that this happens to all of us and that it fills us with confusion and uncertainty.

The significance of the fact that the inessential pushes itself to the fore can be shown easily in regard to the mathematical example. But it is not only the case there. One must constantly keep in mind that from the first to the last word this so-called theory of knowledge in the *Seventh Letter* refers to the community which exists among people speaking to one another. It raises the question of how an insight can become comprehensible and present for me and for you, or, put another way, how a thing can be there in what is said in such a way that it is truly there: disclosed and not to be confounded by any objections. Greek culture in the age of sophism, however, had gone through the eerie experience that in discussion any insight can be confounded and that even mathematics could be discredited by the sophists' shadowboxing. Plato's dialogues are full of satirical sideswipes at the sophists, which were meant to ward off their meaningless babbling, babbling which in the guise of an art of rhetoric and argumentation had intoxicated the youth of that era. When Plato says that usually we are content with that which the means of presentation bring to the fore because for the most part our "bad upbringing"[32] has left us unused to seeking the real thing

___

32. In regard to 343 c, ὑπὸ πονηρᾶς τροφῆς (by bad nurturing, upbringing), the difficulty of the phrase lies in the fact that it is inserted. And were it not for the insertion, the exposition here would concur fully with what is said in the *Republic* at 523 a ff. In accordance with the latter passage it would be the contradictions themselves which lead us beyond sense perceptions and which "force" us or "summon" us to thinking. That a perception which is in agreement with itself and free of contradiction could "suffice" for someone is certainly not a sign of his "bad upbringing." So what is the meaning of this addition? In my opinion it can be understood in relation to the two essential topics

itself, he is referring to the whole realm of everyday experience within which we find ourselves under way, trusting what everybody says and the opinions and points of view which everybody has. When he goes on to say that one actually does not appear ridiculous at all even in such cases when the arguments of the other person tie one in knots of contradiction, we are supposed to be reminded of more than the comic scenes in Aristophanes which demonstrate that fact exquisitely. This also brings to mind the sovereign manner in which Plato's own dialogues display just how contemptible and vacuous the sophistic arts are.

But things are different in those cases where there is no factual certainty of the life-world to immunize us against babbling,[33] i.e., in those cases where we are really concerned with the truth itself and in which, accordingly, we compel one another to get clear about what is right and to put up an argument. One should note that the text does not say "be compelled" but uses the active form, "compel."[34] This way of putting it expresses the solidarity which binds us to one another in such cases when we all, as

---

specifically stated to be under consideration here: mathematics and aretē. That the mathematician cannot content himself with the picture or image he uses, but instead only with the true "self," was made clear above. Thus for a mathematician it is bad upbringing when he does not insist upon holding to the fifth item in the list, i.e., the thing itself, with appropriate noetic rigor. The same thing also holds, however, in the sphere of our moral life. He who does not content himself in this realm with the image of aretē proffered, with what is passed around as bona fide in the world of moral maxims and social conventions, or, as Plato would put it, he who does not content himself with *doxai* but insists instead upon what is truly just and unjust—such a man differs indeed from the *polloi* by virtue of his upbringing. It is that ἕξις τῆς ψυχῆς εἴς τε τὸ μαθεῖν εἴς τε τὰ λεγόμενα ἤθη (the state of the soul with regard to learning and so-called morals) spoken of a few lines later (343 e) which explains the ὑπὸ πονηρᾶς τροφῆς.

33. Babbling, here *Geschwätz*, reminds one of Heidegger, of course (cf. *Sein und Zeit* § 35 on *Gerede*), but it reminds one of Wittgenstein as well. The point is that philosophical talk (*Rede*) runs a risk which more concrete, pragmatic "language games," say, that of laying bricks, do not, for it is always possible that the former will become sophistic or, as Wittgenstein puts it, that it will "go on a holiday." But unlike Wittgenstein, Gadamer is willing to take that risk. He argues that philosophical discourse, though far from being instrumental in getting something done, can still be valid. It can display, albeit finitely, the "what it is" of the subject matter or thing under discussion. Cf. my "Gadamer's Hermeneutics and Ordinary Language Philosophy," in the *Thomist*, Spring 1979 and n. 15 above on ἀποφαίνεσθαι in language. (Translator)

34. In regard to 343 d, there is a similar use of ἀναγκάζειν (compel) in the *Parmenides* at 133 c, the *Cratylus* at 432 c, and the *Republic* at 523 d ff. The latter passage generally parallels the distinction made here.

mathematicians for example, refute an unmathematical argument on the squaring of the circle. But above all it is in the momentous matters of living rightly, of right decisions in life, where we have such solidarity with one another that our concern is solely with "the thing itself," i.e., with that which is really good.[35] Here too someone can always overturn the answer given using the newly learned wrestler's holds of the sophistic art, i.e., that someone emerges as a 'victor' and thus makes it seem as if the other person who asserts something "in speech or writing or plain discussion" has understood nothing of the thing itself. It sometimes looks that way to all present, for they fail to grasp that the "soul" of the person who has said or written something, which is to say the sense and intent of what he has said or written, is not thereby refuted, but instead only the weakness of the four means is displayed.[36] Plato repeatedly makes it clear in his dialogues that in his eyes, not the one who is defenseless against such techniques is ridiculous but rather the young people themselves who are so proud of their empty skill.

Let us take an example. Examples, of course, are one of the necessary media in which true knowledge is presented. They belong to the class of the eidōlon, and in the realm of moral considerations and justifications their role corresponds in a certain sense to the role of the figure in mathematics. They themselves are not what is meant, but that which is meant becomes visible in them. They are what one points to in order to make clear what is actually meant. They are, in other words, *paradeigmata*. Now the example. He who asserts that promises must be kept, for that is the moral precondition of our living together as human beings, and he who seeks to justify this assertion, must certainly present

---

35. The most important passage in this regard is the *Statesman* 286 ff.

36. In regard to 343 ff.; the repeated use of the word ἑκάστου (of each) in the text here shows that it does not refer to the soul of the one who speaks or writes, i.e., that it is neuter, not masculine. Moreover, the subject matter itself is such that the concern here definitely cannot be with individual people. On the contrary where people are concerned, their overall identity and solidarity with one another is the characteristic constantly stressed. Note the "we" form at 343 d ff. and the πάντ' ἄνδρα (every man) (343 c 6) etc. On the other hand, the concern *is* with the four individual modes of the *thing's* Being, each of which individually pretends to present the thing itself. But each by itself is inadequate, and only with the greatest effort does the movement back and forth from one to all the others bring about the "birth" of insight.

evidence concerning the order of human society, e.g., the mutual need that people have of one another, the necessity of planning ahead, of being able to rely on one another, and so on. In so doing it may also be possible to penetrate to the depths in which human obligation has its foundation and in respect to which all pragmatic concerns can be seen to be secondary. This, for instance, was accomplished magnificently by Kant in his moral philosophy and by Plato no less so in the utopia of his *Republic*. Even so there is no means of compelling someone to see the truth who does not want to see it. Not only is it possible for him to point to what "everybody" says or does in order to evade unpleasant obligations. He can justify his evasion theoretically by placing moral obligation as a whole in question, as Thrasymachus and Callicles do. He who has no sense of propriety and obligation, he from whom no response is drawn when recourse is had to these concepts, will never understand what they are about. But worse than that, he will in fact be of the opinion that he knows better than anyone else and will seem to be the one who sees through the naiveté[37] of all those inhibited by such 'morality.'

For this reason the knowledge which we require of one another of the fifth thing, the thing itself, is constantly endangered, and it is among Plato's keenest and most marvelous insights that this danger has its source in the weakness of the logoi, the weakness which the new paideia in the age of sophism exploits. It may well be that the great masters of the rhetorical and argumentative arts of this new paideia at first thought that they were advancing the cause of knowledge and justice. But it is convincing and logical that Plato selects as preeminent in the circle of its disciples a series of questionable personalities for whom justice is nothing more than a word to be used in duping the dim-witted.[38]

Now the moral example which we have used makes clear at once what is meant when the text says that he who is himself

37. ἠλίθιος: *Gorgias* 491 e.
38. ἀλλότριον ἀγαθόν (someone else's good): *Republic* 343 c ff. See my analysis of this section above in chap. 4.

supposed to get a vision of the thing itself or he who would en-
gender that vision in another must have an "affinity" for the
thing besides having the intellectual gifts of comprehension and
memory. The purpose of the Socratic art of conversing was to
avoid being talked out of the fact that there is such a thing as the
Just, the Beautiful, and the Good. Plato holds to this aim, but he
goes beyond it here. What is sought and made available in the
back and forth of proper discussion is much more. Plato maintains that he who would understand what is truly good and truly
bad must at the same time understand the "falsity and truth of
the whole of reality." There can be no doubt what "the whole of
reality" means, i.e., that it does *not* mean an intact whole of any
specific thing being talked about. Rather this all-inclusive expression is meant to point beyond single opinions about any one
thing.[39] This intent is demonstrated by the developmental structure of the text as a whole. The movement of thought had long
since passed beyond the specific example from which it had
taken its departure, i.e., the true circle. Without expressly saying
so, but obviously enough, it had made the transition from the
mathematical virtue which in all speaking of the circle aims at
the circle itself, to true virtue and vice in general, and it had
thereby uncovered the indissoluble unity of the whole as the
foundation of its insight. Thus true knowledge can never be
reached in anything partial. One will recall that it was a structural principle of an entire group of Plato's dialogues that the

39. In regard to 344 b, τῆς ὅλης οὐσίας (of the whole of reality); the phrase reminds one of the *Phaedrus* at 270 e: τῆς τοῦ ὅλον φύσεως (of the nature of the whole),
where to be sure, it is open to debate whether "nature of the whole" is meant in the sense
of the All or in the sense of an organism. Still the interpretation of the passage at hand
can be given independently of this question. For however it might be resolved, Socrates
actually applies this phrase in a quite general sense in the *Phaedrus*. There the concern
appears to be only with the right knowledge of the nature of the soul, i.e., that knowledge which would enable one to scientifically apply the right logoi to it—as if knowledge
of the right logoi, i.e., knowledge of *dialectic*, were not presupposed by the whole
discussion! Cf. in this regard Archytas, 47 B 1, (Diels, 2: 432) περὶ γὰρ τᾶς τῶν ὅλων
φύσιος καλῶς διαγνόντες (having differentiated nicely in regard to the whole of the universe). Here in the *Seventh Letter* the important distinction in the *Phaedrus* between a
technē and a *tribē* (knack) is also implied. Essential for a technē is that it knows not only
the true, but the false τὸ ψεῦδος ἅμα καὶ ἀληθές. One is reminded in this regard of the
Hippias.

question of this or that virtue always was reduced to the question of the unity and entirety of virtue. Ultimately the magnified constellation of this entirety took shape in the heavens of thought as a political utopia, and the way through the whole of knowledge to the idea of the Good was sketched out as the true form of education within this true state. Thus the *Republic* provides a mythological picture for precisely that insight as a whole and insight into the whole, of which Plato speaks in the *Seventh Letter*.

If we keep this background in mind, we can determine more precisely what Plato might have said in the single, long discussion which he tells us he had with Dionysius II, i.e., the discussion which the aspiring young prince had attempted to put down in writing—without authorization from Plato and quite inadequately. At 344 d 4, a virtual title for Dionysius' technē is given: περὶ φύσεως ἄκρα καὶ πρῶτα (the highest and first [principles] of nature). The word *physis*, which is used in a similar way at 341 e, is the subject which is actually under consideration, the *pragma*. The insight into this subject, the letter tells us, cannot be expressed in the way mathematical insights may be expressed. The best that can be hoped for is a meager "indication" which could illumine the thing only for someone who has the prerequisite nature to understand it. This indication, as Plato had given it in his discussion with Dionysius (and in his dialogues) and as he continued to give it, is said to be of such a nature that the insight which it awakens completely fills one. One could never forget it; indeed, one discovers that it is perpetually preserved. Now obviously we are not dealing here with an extended, wide-range exposition. This is to be deduced from the fact that it was a single talk of Plato's which enabled Dionysius to write about the whole matter. Also it is specifically stated at 344 e, πάντων γάρ ἐν βραχυτάτοις κεῖται (for it lies in the very briefest statement). There can be not doubt that Plato considers the doctrine of the One and the indeterminate Two to be the real subject under investigation and that he declares a written exposition of that doctrine to be impossible. It is, as we know, precisely this doctrine which Aristotle above all represents and criticizes as Plato's actual philosophy. And as Aristotle tells us, this doctrine of the *archai* can under no circumstances be separated from the doctrine of ideas. The doctrine of the One and the Two is not a step beyond the doctrine of ideas which would negate the latter but a step behind it which expresses its actual basis. That can be deduced with sufficient clarity, I think, from Plato's *Parmenides*. The assumption that there are ideas remains for Plato an inescapable conclusion to be drawn from the nature of discussion and the process of reaching an understanding of something. But this assumption as such is not Plato's actual philosophy. It is not by accident that in the *Phaedo*, i.e., where it is presumably given its first literary articulation, the assumption is characterized as "old hat" (76 d). For far from being Plato's philosophy itself, the assumption occasions his real philosophical endeavor. As the *Parmenides* shows, a single idea by itself is not knowable at all, and here is the source of the error which the young Socrates makes. In any insight an entire nexus or web of ideas is involved, and Plato's actual questioning is in regard to the constitutive, organizational, structural principles of this interconnectedness of the ideas. Just as the exemplary system of the mathematical sciences provides a unified continuum extending from the number to the point, the line, the plane, and the solid (from arithmetic to stereometry), so too the ascent and descent, oneness and multiplicity, the merging of what is disparate into an astonishing and transparent unity of many far-reaching implications, is the law which in fact governs progress in philosophic insight within the whole of discourse, the whole of the logoi. It gives the appearance of rigid schematizing when one takes the numbers, the One and the Two, to be the generative principle of all insight and the structural principle of any discourse which properly reveals the thing under discussion. And this appearance of rigidity may be the reason that Plato thought it ill advised to put this doctrine down in writing. What this doctrine actually describes, I contend, is the felicitous experience of advancing insight, the *euporia* which the *Philebus* says (15 c) happens to the person who proceeds along the proper path to the solution of the problem of the One and the Many—the way of discourse which reveals the thing being discussed. It is this very dialectic of the One and the Many which establishes the finite limits of human discourse and insight—and our fruitful situation halfway between single and multiple meaning, clarity and ambiguity. Plato is not interested in any alternative, say elevating Socrates' *docta ignorantia* to a dialectic of reflection (Hegel) or erecting a structured universe deriving from a first, highest principle—although the latter sort of Neoplatonic idea of structure might be traced back to the academy and the thought of Plato's disciples. Even if it can be, and even though the transcendence of the Good does indeed have religious implications and at the very least makes it possible for Plato to build upon popular religion, the fact that the transcendence of the Good can be philosophically explicated in the doctrine of *two* principles, the One and the Two, creates problems for a Neoplatonic interpretation. In Plato the "principles" of the One and the Many are not advanced as a foundation for genealogical tales such as those told by earlier thinkers. Rather his concern is with the meaning of Being (*der Sinn von Sein*) as that meaning displays itself in its unity and multiplicity in the logos. And it is this question of the meaning of Being which leads him to the One and the Two, an entirety of the logoi in which reality, according to its ordering principle, both unifies and unfolds itself. The entirety of the logoi is a true entirety but one which is given to finite human knowing only in its basic structure and only in concretizations of it in specific contexts. What is, is as the whole of the infinite interrelationship of things, from which at any given time in discourse and insight a determinate, partial aspect is "raised up" and placed in the light of disconcealment.[40] Even the visible cosmos, whose order reaches down into the disorder of our terrestrial human world, is situated between the intelligibility of the ideas and an element of resistance. The way the *Timaeus* is constructed shows us how much indeed this intermediate status defines the mode of being of the realities of our world. The "new beginning" which opposes *anankē* to the ideal order clashes in no way with the ideal conception behind this cosmic genealogy. On the contrary, it actually amounts to the reassertion of a qualification which had been presupposed from the start[41]—a qualification which is ob-

40. *ins Licht der Unverborgenheit.* See n. 16 above. (Translator)
41. *Timaeus* 48 e and 28 a ff.

lecture as a ["shared inquiry"] which never ceases to more sharply define a word, concept, intuition in respect to another, yielding to the play of question + answer, and leads to thought

viously implied in the Pythagorean doctrine of opposites on which Plato is elaborating here.

Plato's cosmology, however, is no simple variant of Pythagoreanism. It is based on the doctrine of ideas and presents the genesis of the world in a mythical tale according to which the demiurge makes things in looking to the ideas as his model. Thus Plato wishes to show that the ideas are the foundation of the whole world order and for that reason he must apply the technē model to nature as a whole. It follows that otherness, the unbounded, must now appear as the resistance of the substance in which the building process builds. It is clear that this juxtaposition of idea and Necessity is a correlate of the duality of *tautotēs* and *heterotēs*, which also appears in the *Timaeus*. This point is decisive, i.e., that *the opposition is actually an opposition in the structural concepts of the logos: its origin lies not in cosmology but in dialectic.* Just as resistance is inevitably encountered in the ordering and shaping of the world, so too is it inevitably encountered in any discourse which would display the thing under discussion, i.e., in that discourse which provided the sole access to knowledge in Plato's philosophy after the "flight into the logoi" in the *Phaedo*. The labor of dialectic, in which the truth of what is finally flashes upon us, is by nature unending and infinite. And that infinitude is displayed in the impediment to understanding in the human realm, the impediment which corresponds to the function of the receptacle of all becoming in the *Timaeus*. Plato's Pythagoreanism is not a Pythagoreanism of the world but of human beings. The Many, the unlimited Two, sustains (and restricts) both the order of the world and, equally, the possibilities of human knowing.

There is no mention of all this within the context of the *Seventh Letter*, but nevertheless it underlies Plato's exposition there. He describes how insight can still be attained, even within the given limitations and finitude of our human existence. The shared inquiry which never ceases in its effort to more sharply define one word, concept, intuition, in respect to another and which willingly puts all individual opinions to the test while abjuring all contentiousness and yielding to the play of question and answer—that shared inquiry should make possible not only

Goal of this Dialectic is that ... (see p. ...)

Nature of Plato's dialectic

insight into this or that specific thing, but, insofar as is humanly possible, insight into all virtue and vice and the "whole of reality".[42] What Plato describes here as the untiring movement back and forth through the four means of knowing is in fact the art of dialectic—a perpetual passing from one thing to another which nonetheless perseveres in the single direction of what is meant and which, for want of cogent deductive proofs, remains in proximity to what is sought without ever being able to reach it. In just this way the old Parmenides forces Socrates back and forth, up and down, from the single concept to its conceptual implications, drawn on as they are by ever-recurring visions of the truth, in order then to allow the One to submerge in the Many and the individual thing in the whole. Thus Socrates' "leading" in discussion, his "guiding" talk as the earlier dialogues portray it, and the dialectic of dihairēsis presented in the later dialogues, have the identical purpose. And so does the dialectic displayed in the *Parmenides*, the unfolding provisional theses and countertheses without knowing the "what" of what is being talked about (Aristotle). For they all serve to make one more "dialectical," to educate one's vision for the thing itself, which of course is not this particular thing, the circle, but the whole of the ἄκρα καὶ πρῶτα. All four means of presentation are required for this education and in all of them there lurks the same danger of producing sophisms. Thus it can be seen that the program announced in Plato's *Seventh Letter* fully accords with his lifelong concerns and with his literary explication of these concerns in the dialogues. The philosopher and the sophist are all too easy to mistake for each other. Hence it must be the task of philosophy to separate them and to separate itself from the impurity of sophism within itself, a task which creates the perpetual tension in which philosophy has found itself since Plato's time.

Socrates' question was a new one, i.e., the question of *what* something is. It was based on the suspicion and the experience

---

42.   In regard to 344 c, cf. *Laws* 968 de. There too it is emphasized that only success can show whether one has learned something at exactly the right time, for insight too occurs in the "interior of the soul": "For it would not become evident to the students themselves why what they learn is taught at a certain time, until insight into what is learned has developed in the interior of the soul of each."

that he who says something does not always know what he is saying and that it was precisely the art of rhetoric and the general
acceptance of mere opinions which made this ignorance dangerous. Thus there had to be a new art which would promise deliv-
erance from this danger, and this new art was that of leading a
discussion in such a way as to remove the risk that all knowledge
and insight would eventually be confounded. That any insight
can be confounded has always been and still is the experience we
have in discourse, in which medium alone, however, all philosophy must take place. Philosophy had to put itself on the very
same basis from which the danger of sophistic verisimilitude
arose and therefore finds itself in the constant company of its
shadow, sophism. As dialectic, philosophy never ceases to be tied
to its origin in Socratic discussion. What is mere talk, nothing but
talk, can, however untrustworthy it may be, still bring about understanding among human beings—which is to say that it can
still make human beings human.

6

Plato's Unwritten Dialectic

The works which were produced by Schadewaldt and his followers at Tübingen have served to remind us of the importance of the indirect tradition, the secondary accounts of Plato's philosophy in interpreting Plato's thought. These works are devoted to a sharply disputed question about which even classical philologians are not at all in agreement. Their lack of unanimity is displayed most strikingly by the extreme case of Cherniss, who goes so far as to question Aristotle's account. But philosophers too have found their attempts to reconstruct Plato's doctrines, as they might be disclosed in the indirect tradition, contested—and for several reasons. For one thing, the results of the reconstructions made by the Tübingen school sound much too much like the *Schulphilosophie* of the eighteenth century. And for another, whatever can be discerned of Plato's doctrines in following their approach to reconstruction remains singularly skeletal and meager.

The controversy which has developed here has a long history. One source of it has been the fact that we have come a long way in the last fifty years by using the methods of *Formanalyse* on Plato's dialogues, an approach which classicists have learned to apply in an ever more refined way. It is natural, however, that such analysis, which stresses the form in which something is said and the context, would favor the direct tradition over the indirect. Ultimately this preference can be traced to Schleiermacher, who was inspired by the Romantics' emphasis on dialogue as such, and who consequently, in his dispute with Herrmann, focused his philosophical interpretation of Plato on the dialogues.

But there is yet another longstanding historical tendency whose effect on the present controversy is no less important: the dispute in principle with systematic philosophy. This dispute has its origin in the late Romantic period, and Kierkegaard is perhaps the one who represents it best. It played an important role once again when neo-Kantianism collapsed at the end of World War I and it may be said to have influenced German Plato research at the time when classicists in Germany came to emphasize the so-called political Plato. The latter trend began with the Plato studies of Wilamowitz. Wilamowitz made his point of departure the political content of the *Seventh Letter*, which by that time was again considered to be authentic, and he was followed in his approach by many (Kurt Singer, Paul Friedländer, Kurt Hildebrandt). Coincident with this research in classical philology was Paul Natorp's and Nicolai Hartmann's philosophical rejection of any attempt to evaluate Plato's thought as systematic philosophy. In a sense, Julius Stenzel's investigations of Plato's dialectic represented a sort of mediation between the two extremes, i.e., the philological and philosophical approaches. But it was precisely Stenzel who called our attention to the literary character of the dialogues, and as far as his *philosophical* interpretation was concerned, he remained a neo-Kantian. Thus it came to pass that more and more, philosophers, in taking note of the dialogical character of Plato's work and of the inherent inconclusiveness and open-endedness of dialogue, turned against establishing any doctrine of Plato's. This tendency went to an extreme, and on that count my own Plato book at the end of the 1920s must also be faulted. Using the tools of phenomenology, it attempted to tie Plato's dialectic to Socratic dialogue, but in so doing the basic theme of Plato's doctrine was pushed all too much into the background.[1] Our task now must be to shed some light on this controversy.

In order that we might secure a point of departure and find a reasonable direction in which to proceed, let us completely exclude from our discussion such concepts as esoteric doctrine or even secret doctrine. These formulations unduly stress the contested points in the problem we are investigating. We can certainly agree that in general Plato gave oral instruction

1. *Platos dialektische Ethik.*

only to those who belonged to the intimate circle of his "school" and that he exchanged his thoughts with them alone. Unquestionably, the majority of the literary dialogues are different in this respect since they were intended to reach a wider audience. As Plato himself knew, what is written must of necessity be exposed to misunderstanding and misuse, for it must fend for itself and do without the assistance in achieving proper understanding which the speaker can provide in a discussion. Having seen this, Plato developed and consummately mastered the literary form of the dialogue, which observes the laws proper to what is written. Oral instruction, however, stands under a different law. Above all, it preserves a far-reaching continuity with what is said before and after, and it does so even when it is not in the form of a series of lectures. As a matter of fact the lecture format, insofar as we can speak of lectures at all in this context, must be for the most part excluded. For surely it would be strange indeed if the skilled architect of the literary Socratic dialogues and the critic of the μακρὸς λόγος (long speech) had not greatly preferred didactic discussions. Even if there were actually complete lectures, as the case of the lecture περὶ τἀγαθοῦ (*On the Good*) teaches us, I would hold that the essential core of Plato's doctrine was presented in ongoing didactic discussions which engaged the participants for whole days at a time and established a living community among them.

But however that may be, it can be agreed that there is an enormous difference in type between the contents of Plato's oral teaching and what is presented in the form of the dialogues. This view could not be disputed by anyone who is serious about the matter. The question which results is what, in that case, we should make our point of departure. How might we achieve the best results if our aim is an interpretive exposition of Plato's philosophy? That must be the preliminary methodological question, and like Aristotle we all know an answer: ἴσως οὖν ἡμῖν γε ἀρκτέον ἀπὸ τῶν ἡμῖν γνωρίμων (*Nichomachean Ethics* A 2, 1095 b 3)—which happens, coincidentally, to be in reference to Plato. Unquestionably, "we must begin with what is known to us." And it can also hardly be questioned that the dialogues must be given the methodological priority which not we but our situation in the tradition dictates. They are there, and they are not the product of some reconstruction.

This certainly does not mean that the direct tradition of the dialogues is the only tradition we have to take into account. Obviously we must bring to bear every traditional source which is in the least way reliable. Especially because of the one-sidedness of the German Plato research in the 1920s and 1930s we are indebted to the works of the Tübingen classicists for emphasizing the fact that the dialogues are intentionally reserved in what they purport to communicate. Actually this should have been made evident to everyone by the reading of a single one of them. The question can only be in regard to what this reserve means. Does it imply a withholding and reserving of the "doctrines" for instruction in the limited circle of those properly prepared for it? Or does this reserve persist in the lectures too, such as περὶ τἀγαθοῦ, and even in the oral didactic discussions? The Tübingen school has demonstrated most thoroughly and convincingly something which had been evident to me for quite some time: that according to their literary type, the dialogues belong in the genus *protreptikon*.[2] As important as this insight is, it leaves open the methodological question of how far one can and must project beyond what is said in the dialogues expressis verbis when one attempts to think them through and to interpret their deeper meaning or, put negatively, to what extent the prohibition against doing so, stated in the *Seventh Letter*, applies to all Plato's thought.

With that I have arrived at the actual hermeneutic question derived from the preference which unavoidably must be given to the literary dialogues over the doctrines constructed from the indirect tradition: the former *are a whole of discourse*. The priority of the dialogues in the tradition is of decisive methodological significance, as can be made evident by a brief hermeneutic observation. Like all knowing, philosophical knowing is identification of something as what it is and has the structure of recognition, or "knowing again." But the object of philosophy is not given in the same way as the object of the empirical sciences.

---

2. Konrad Gaiser, *Protreptik und Paränese in den Dialogen Platons* (Stuttgart, 1955).

Rather, it is always reconstituted anew, and that occurs only when one tries to think it through for oneself. This means, however, that any indirect tradition is in principle inferior insofar as this act of constituting the object, as the thinker has carried it out for himself, is not contained in that tradition and cannot be reconstructed from it. The thesis that only the person addressed really understands, it seems to me, hardly needs justification for students of Plato. After all, who else but Plato said that Socrates, whatever he might begin to discuss, ultimately demands an answer from the individual whom on any occasion he has right in front of him, and that he forces the latter to account for what he is saying? The methodological primacy which the literary form of the dialogue has for an interpretation of Plato's philosophy derives from the same principle. In these dialogues we ourselves are the ones (thanks to the lasting effect of Plato's artful dialogical compositions) who find ourselves addressed and who are called upon to account for what we are saying. We understand because *we* are given to understand.

This of course does not mean that the indirect tradition is of no concern to us. But in the sense which I have just explained, it is to be understood only on the basis of what is known to us. If philosophy can only be understood as carrying out the construction of the object in one's own thinking for oneself, then we—starting from Socrates' art of discussion—must make it our goal to clothe the indirect tradition in living flesh, i.e., if I may be permitted such an image, to fill out this clattering skeleton. And, if I might hold on to this metaphor for a moment, it is certainly clear to everyone that this skeleton provides only a very limited vision of the living thing. Thus it might well be that even in regard to Plato's philosophical "doctrine" the skeleton which can be reconstructed is not the essence of his teaching.

For the philosophical task of understanding Plato's philosophical thought one other question seems to me to be of the utmost importance, a question which the Tübingen school has brought into sharp focus by their reconstruction of Plato's indirect teachings. It is the question of Plato's so-called development. There is in this regard a conventional point of view shared by many which would have it that there is an early Plato who taught the doctrine of ideas in a form which he later found problematic and which was subjected to criticism by the "elder Parmenides" in the latter's discussion with Socrates in the *Parmenides*. According to this theory a crisis in the doctrine of ideas arose with the extended application of it beyond mathematical and moral ideas to universal matters, a crisis which led subsequently to the later Plato's dialectic of dihairēsis. And this dialectic in turn, it is suggested, may have even evolved into the doctrine of ideal numbers.

It is Julius Stenzel to whom the credit is due for having worked out this point of view, one which has dominated Plato research ever since.[3] Opposite this schema of "development" stands the thesis which I have been advocating for more than 30 years now and which I should like to put forward here although only as a hypothesis. It is the thesis that from very early on in the dialogues there are references to what in a word might be called the *arithmos* structure of the logos. This idea was first elaborated by J. Klein in his investigations concerning "Greek Logic and the Origins of Algebra," and his work had pointed my own research in new directions at the time when I was with him at Marburg.[4] As I see it, the works of Krämer and Gaiser have served to give new weight and relevance to this thesis which opposes the "development" theory precisely because they have devoted themselves to interpretation of the indirect tradition. To be sure, I am of the belief that we still have a long way to go in reaching a philosophical understanding of how things stand in regard to that tradition, and it is my belief that it can be fully illuminated only if one departs from Plato's dialogues.

There should be no dispute that the indirect tradition is insufficient without the dialogues. Porphyry knew that it was.[5] He declared that the copies of Plato's lecture "On the Good,"

---

3. Julius Stenzel, *Studien zur Entwicklung der platonishen Dialektik von Sokrates zu Aristoteles* (Breslau, 1917). This book has the revealing subtitle, "*Aretē and Dihairesis*," which in itself is already an articulation of the "development" hypothesis which the book will present.

4. "Die griechische Logistik und die Entstehung der Algebra," in *Quellen und Studien zur Geschichte der Mathematik, Astronomie und Physik*, sec. B 1934, vol. 3, no. 1.

5. Cf. Simplicius' commentary on Aristotle's *Physics*, 453 f.

upon which the whole of our indirect tradition is based, were inscrutable, and he confessed that he could not make a thing of them without the *Philebus*. And we too, I suggest, can make nothing of the indirect tradition without the *Hippias Major*, the *Phaedo*, or the *Republic*, book 4. Even when it is a matter of doctrines like that of the ideal numbers, a doctrine we know of solely through the indirect tradition, we must not lose sight of the fact that for the methodological reasons adduced above the way through the dialogues remains the *via regia* to understanding Plato.

To begin with, I would like to illustrate in two respects how I envision the solution of our problem, i.e., closing the gap in the circle of the indirect and direct traditions. The fact that Aristotle's account is the only part of the indirect tradition related to us within the context of a unified philosophy in its own right which deals explicitly with its own set of problems, gives that account a definite priority over the remaining sources. And it seems to me to be demonstrable that his account of the two principles, the One and the Two, develops a schema not entirely foreign to Plato. Such appears to be the case not only if one begins from Aristotle's side but from Plato's too. In Plato, to be sure, the expression archē is not yet the concept which we know from Aristotle. Using the *Sophist*, the *Philebus*, and the *Seventh Letter* as a basis, we may assume that Plato's accustomed expression was τὰ πρῶτα καὶ ἄκρα (the first and highest) (344 d). I cannot believe that the expression τὰ μέγιστα (341 b) περὶ ὧν σπουδάζω (the most important things with which I am concerned) (341 c) has the specifically technical meaning which Krämer assigns to it. On the contrary, a passage like 285 d ff. in the *Statesman* shows that this expression has as its reference the general realm of the ἀσώματα (bodiless things), i.e., the ideas. There is adequate evidence for τὰ πρῶτα, however, and furthermore it fits with what Aristotle refers to in his account as the two ἄρχαι, the ἕν, and the ἀόροστος δυάς, the principles of the One and the indeterminate Two.

Now it can be shown that from very early in the dialogues the concept of the *hen* is quite closely connected with the concept of the *agathon*. The concept of the hen is to be found above all in the context of the problem of aretē as that is discussed beginning with the *Protagoras* and explicated positively in book 4 of the *Republic*. I have had something to say about this in my article "Prefigurations of Reflection"[6] and would only repeat here that for the most part the problem of the four cardinal virtues has been taken hold of by the wrong end in the research to date. It is common knowledge that Wilamowitz held a verse of Aeschylus (Sept. 610) to be inauthentic because he was of the opinion that before Plato there could not possibly have been any mention of the four cardinal virtues. Thanks to the work of Werner Jaeger, however, that position has since been abandoned. And as I tried to show, the actual truth of the matter is precisely the opposite. Far from creating the four cardinal virtues, Plato took them from the tradition and dissolved them. Following Socrates, he transformed and interwove them. In book 4 of the *Republic* he demonstrated that all these classical concepts of virtue imply essentially the same thing, i.e., knowledge, and that this knowledge is knowledge of the one, which is the Good. Thus from early on Plato sees the problem of unity and multiplicity. Even in the large-scale model of the utopian state developed in the *Republic* this problem is the theme: it is not the differences among the three classes which are distinguished from one another here but their agreement and *oneness* with one another which constitutes the ordered state. Correspondingly it is the true nature of the soul to be one in all multiplicity. *Harmonia*, *homologia*, or whatever expression might be applied, all point in this same direction.

In my estimation this provides a firm starting point from which we ourselves can begin to think through and understand the question of how the concept of the hen is connected with the concept of the agathon as the μέγιστον μάθημα (most important doctrine)—albeit there is obviously nothing implied here of the Neoplatonic conception of unity. Dönt's recent contribution, which brings the *Laws* to bear on this question, points in the same direction as my own research insofar as he has established

6. "Vorgestalten der Reflexion," in *Subjektivität und Metaphysik, Festschrift für W. Cramer* (Frankfurt, 1966), pp. 128–43.

that the concept of the One can be found in the content of the exposition in the *Laws* too.[7] This is certainly not to say that the concept of the One in the form in which it is thematized in Plato's early dialogues, e.g., in the *Protagoras* at 329 ff., can be equated with Aristotle's concept of the hen as he formulates it in his account of the Platonic principles. Nevertheless it must be kept in mind that, as opposed to Neoplatonism, wherever the One becomes a problem, the problem of the Many is present as well. The *Protagoras* provides initial evidence for that fact. *The thesis, then, which I would like to propose for discussion is that the problem of the Many is from the very beginning the problem of the Two.*

A sure proof for my contention is to be found in the *Hippias Major*, which develops the well-known theory of the "participation" of what is in the idea. According to that theory the idea is what the particular existences have in common, and each of the latter may be said to be what they are to the extent they participate in the idea. And *besides that relationship* the quite different relationship is developed of the number "common" to the different units in a sum (300 ff.).

Now that which a certain number of sum or things may be said to have in common, that in which their unity consists, is quite distinct from that which unifies the members of a genus. For there are remarkable attributes which may be predicated of the sums of things but precisely not of the units, the things themselves of which the sum number is made up. The sum number is a specific type of number, e.g., even or odd, rational or irrational, and these attributes are properties of numbers which may be predicated of the unity of a number of things but not, in contrast, of the units which constitute that number. Immediately the question arises: Does not the unity of discourse also have a certain determinate property not found in any of its component parts (letters, syllables, words) and is this not exactly the point? At the conclusion of the *Theaetetus* the logos or account which purports to explain something by listing its component parts and which thus claims to be knowledge, is reduced to an aporia. This

7. Eugen Dönt, "Platons Spätphilosophie und die Akademie," in *Jahrbuch der Österreichischen Akademie der Wissenschaften*, vol. 251, essay 3 (1967).

aporia, in turn, leaves us in a dilemma. Either the syllable consists of the collection of its letters or it is an indivisible unit with its own special property. Here, I suggest, the true relationship of the One and the Many, which gives the logos its structure, is made evident in the analogy of the meaninglessness of the syllable and the dilemma with which it confronts us.

Anyone can see, of course, that the thing which unifies a genus may also be predicated of each of the exemplars of that genus and to that extent the one is many. Plato emphasizes again and again that when rightly understood, *this* unity and multiplicity, the unity which makes it possible for the many particulars to participate in the one idea, does not lead to any fruitless entanglement in pseudocontradictions. But can this argument be advanced in support of the unity of an insight, that is, the unity of that which is said and meant in the logos? One suspects that the latter is more comparable to that other form of being in common: that it has the structure of the sum number of things which precisely as that thing which all of them together have in common cannot be attributed to any of them individually. And indeed the sum of what has been counted is not at all something which could be predicated of each of the things counted.

There is no mention of all this in the *Hippias*. But is the distinction made there between what is had in common by the members of a genus and what is had in common by things counted in a sum, entirely coincidental? The topic here is the Beautiful. And is it not unsatisfactory to view precisely the Beautiful—or the Good, for that matter—as a universal in the sense of a κοινὸν γένος (common genus)? And does that not hold equally for "τὸ ὄν" (Being) and all the "highest genera," which do not gather together the content of a class but rather, as the "vowels" of discourse, make discourse possible in the first place? We call such things as these "concepts of reflection"[8] or "formal" concepts, meaning the formal concepts of logic. Obviously their mode of parousia is essentially different from that of "material" or concrete ideas, and there is a great deal, it seems to me, which

---

8. Cf. Hegel's *Wissenschaft der Logik*, book 2, chap. 2, on the determinations of reflection, Identity, and Difference (Leipzig, 1934). (Translator)

indicates that Plato was sensitive to this distinction⁹—and a great deal in precisely those places where the Beautiful is thematic. At the very least it must be said that the path of love shown to us by Diotima leading to the αὐτὸ καθ' αὐτὸ μεθ' αὐτοῦ μονειδὲς ἀεὶ ὄν (itself by itself, always existing in one form with itself) (*Symposium* 211 b) is not identical to that which occurs in the formation of any concept, i.e., the συνορᾶν εἰς ἓν εἶδος (seeing [the many] together in one form), where one always abstracts from the accidental particulars. For the Beautiful is experienced again and again in each thing as something whose beauty is distinct and unique unto itself; it is experienced in the *sum* of all the stages of the ascent from bodies to souls to institutions to insights, as immanent to them all, and therefore no "looking away" (ἀπιδεῖν) from any of them is implied. Thus it emerges as more like the ubiquitous presence of the day at any place, an analogy which Socrates employs in the *Parmenides*. And does not the interrelationship of the Good and the Beautiful as that is developed in the *Philebus* in the "three" of κάλλος, συμμετρία, and ἀλήθεια (beauty, symmetry, and truth) fit into this analogy as well? One senses the character of number and measure in the Good and the Beautiful, and this indeed implies that what is "in common" in the genus is not what is "in common" here.

Thus perhaps the most striking aspect of the idea of the Beautiful is that the indivisible unity of the essence is *not* paradigmatic for thinking it. Rather it is *the number* which serves as a model. For it is in fact the mystery of the number that one and one together are two without either of the units, which are each one, being two, and without the two being one. Theopompus, a contemporary of Aristophanes, makes that clear in a comic verse—at Plato's expense:

9. To be sure, it is said in the *Sophist* at 255 e that the *heteron* pervades everything and that any given thing is not heteron according to its own nature but rather by virtue of its participation in the idea of the heteron. However, this does not mean that each thing is heteron because the being of the heteron itself comes into view as a unitary eidos. Nor, conversely, is the specific thing which is different in view if the concern *in reflection* is directed to the being of the heteron.

> "For one is not one at all.
> And two? The two can hardly be one as
> Plato says."[10]

This puzzle, if I view the matter correctly, is first presented in the *Hippias Major* without any positive conclusions being drawn from it. It is used solely in criticism of an attempt to define something. Must one not assume for this reason that Plato, in referring to the special structure of number as a sum, was alluding to something of greater significance in another context? And was it not perhaps even then the arithmos structure of the logos which he had in mind. Merely seeing the participation of particulars in *an* idea does not yet constitute knowledge or insight. In my opinion any theory of the doctrine of ideas which made the latter look like Eleatic atomism was always inadequate and Plato himself seems to have recognized that at an early stage. Someone understands what cognition, knowing, insight, is only when he also understands how it can be that one and one are two and how "the two" is one.

In Plato the problem of the Two and its relationship to the One appears early and repeatedly within the development of the themes which are decisive for him. I would remind the reader of the puzzle in the *Phaedo* regarding how the number two is to be arrived at—by adding something to something else or dividing what is one—a puzzle which is said there to have forced Socrates to have changed his thinking and to have occasioned his famous flight into the logoi (96 e ff.). There the *hypothesis* of the idea is developed precisely out of the question of what "two" is. Furthermore the problem of the relativity of sense perception, which is of such crucial importance in Plato, also seems to imply some sort of connection with the problem of the Two. In the

10. Incidentally, one might ask what significance this evidence has in establishing the time sequence in Plato's thinking. Does it not imply that the mystery of the number was sufficiently well known at that time to be a preferred theme of Plato's so that one could understand the allusion to it in this comic verse written for Attic theater? And are we really to assume that references in the written work like this one in the *Hippias* or even the famous passage in the *Phaedo* are responsible for its being so well known? Or is it not rather more likely that Plato alludes in his written work to something already quite well known by his readers?

Phaedo at 96 de, for instance, the problem of the Two appears in the context of the problem of relativity, and in book 7 of the *Republic* the question is raised quite specifically whether the "large" and the "small," which can be attributed to the finger between the middle and little fingers, are two or one. The answer is that, contrary to what we perceive, *in our thinking* we must distinguish between them. For obviously each by itself is one and together they are two (*Republic* 524 bc). What a triviality! Or is it perhaps a first indication of the structure of the two-one which shows up later as the large-small or as the more-less (μέγα καὶ μικρόν μᾶλλον καὶ ἧττον) (the large and the small, the more and the less). For whatever the answer, the problem of relativity, which leads us here to the relationship of One and Two and thereby to the archai of the hen and the *dyas*, is precisely what calls us "to wake up and think," and that famous call initiates our way to the ideas. In our thinking we are able to overcome the contradiction in which the testimony of the senses involves us only if we distinguish between the two which one thing is, its being large and being small. This implies, of course, that the coexistence of contrary aspects of the same object is no real contradiction at all. But the hidden implication beyond this is that these aspects, which can be so distinguished from each other only in thought, are, insofar as they are ideas, actually inseparable from each other and belong together, two as one—something which, in fact, becomes the explicit theme of the *Parmenides*. It seems to me that Plato research has not yet sufficiently taken note of the fact that the relativity of sense perceptions, one of the earliest themes in Plato, implies everything which is subsequently explicated as the participation of the ideas in each other—everything which leads us to the arithmos paradigm which we refer to as Plato's doctrine of ideal numbers.

But even if we set the question of the relativity of *aisthēsis* aside, the problem of the participation of the multiplicity of things in the one eidos still leads one to the multiplicity of ideas and their correlativity and interconnectedness. That it does is demonstrated in the *Parmenides* by the way in which the One necessarily transforms into the Many and the Many into One. For what essentially is the being of the Many? This much can be said at least: The Many has only an adulterated form of the pure being of the eidos as the latter exists separately, in itself. The reason, however, that the paradigm becomes impure when it appears in the Many can only be that something *other* than itself now attaches to it. But this "other" which is in the Many is not nothing; rather it too is a reality: τἆλλα τοῦ ἑνός (the other of the One).[11] Thus there is more present than just the one eidos with nothing besides itself. Where the one eidos is, there must "be" some other reality, and not only must that reality "be" as the Many, but also it must "be" as the determinations which are mixed into the individual phenomena. To be, however, means to be idea. Thus in the *Philebus* the problem implied in positing the one eidos, viz., how the one eidos can at the same time be many, is no longer discussed in reference to the unlimited multiplicity of perceived particulars. Instead it is said that the dialectician must learn to see distinctions, i.e., to discriminate among the many different levels of unity which can be distinguished in the one. This implies, however, that the multiplicity of the many is a multiplicity of ideas. Now the classic examples of the systems which organize letters and harmonic intervals show how it is precisely the arithmos model which makes possible the solution of the problem of participation of ideas in one another. The determination of the indeterminate by a number, the establishing of the μεταξὺ τοῦ ἀπείρου τε καὶ τοῦ ἑνός, the "between" the unlimited and the One (16 e 1), is said to be the crux of dialectic: ἐάσαντε αὐτὸ τε καὶ τὸ μέτριον ἐν τῇ τοῦ μᾶλλον καὶ ἧττον καὶ σφόδρα καὶ ἠρέμα ἕδρᾳ ἐγγενέσθαι ([they]) allowed it [quantity] and measure to develop in the abode of the more and the less, the harsh and the gentle) (24 d).

It is true, of course, that it is not until the *Parmenides* and the *Philebus* that the *methexis* problem is developed so radically that the participation of the many particulars in the one idea converts

---

11. *Parmenides* 157 b. This way of putting it points to the "ideal" nature of the "counter-one" which becomes quite explicit at 158 c, where it is called τὴν ἑτέραν φύσιν τοῦ εἴδους (the other essence of the eidos). This "other" is present in any eidos as a constituent in the latter's own being. Although it itself is Unlimitedness, it allows an eidos to delimit itself from what is another: ὃ δὴ πέρας παρέσχε πρὸς ἄλληλα (which, however, provides the demarcation from others).

into the participation of ideas in one another. *However, the role played by the hypothesis of the eidos in the argument of the* Phaedo *implies this very solution.* There it is shown that "soul" is always together with "life" and never with "death," "two" always with "even" and never with "odd," "warm" always with "fire" and never with "snow." In the *Parmenides* just as in the *Philebus*, the problem of methexis, i.e., of the participation of the many in the one idea, is developed dialectically to the point where apparently insuperable difficulties result in order that the participation of the ideas in each other might then emerge as the solution. For the latter alone makes clear what knowledge, and what the logos is.

To properly assess the significance of this point one must first rid oneself of the assumption that it is the *principium individuationis*, individuation in space and time, which the participation of the ideas in each other is meant to explain. That assumption has its origins in Hegel's and Fichte's systematic conception of philosophy and in the neo-Kantian interpretation of the later dialogues, an interpretation which has dominated our thinking since Natorp. On the basis of this assumption Nicolai Hartmann, for instance, developed his theory of "descending participation."[12] As a consequence the problem of the ἄτομον εἶδος (indivisible form) which accepts no individuation was looked upon by him as a dogmatic limitation which Plotinus first recognized as such and succeeded in overcoming. Such a view neglects, however, that *science in antiquity was not primarily empirical science but mathematics, pure eidetic knowing.* "The problem of *methexis*," I wrote in 1931, "is thus not solved, but transformed into another problem and then solved as that other problem."[13] And today I would add that this solution implies the arithmos structure and that the *momenta* of that structure not only surface in Aristotle's account as the two "principles" but also underlie the four genera of the *Philebus*.

These four genera or eidē of the *Philebus* are obviously not a random selection from the totality of ideas; rather they are the eidē basic to all ideational determinacy. In 1931 I was able to

12. "absteigende Methexis": *Platos Logik des Seins* (Giessen, 1909), to which Natorp specifically refers in the second edition of this *Platos Ideenlehre* (Leipzig, 1921).
13. *Platos dialektische Ethik*, p. 78.

display how complex the distinction in the *Philebus* is between the genus of the limit, on the one hand, and the genus of that which is limited, on the other.[14] Today I would add that in this distinction one discovers one of the most important innovations in Plato's thought. For thinkers before Plato, Pythagorean categories of limit and the unlimited were applied indiscriminately to what *is determined* in the factual world and to what *determines* mathematically, and no distinction was made between the two. One can only see that what is a limit is something ontologically different from what is limited, when one has first seen that forms such as number and measure have a different being from that which they determine. And to have clarified this point is the great accomplishment of Plato's thought—one known to us from the *Republic* and the *Theaetetus*. The naive conflation of distinct kinds of reality basic to Pythagorean arithmology is here analyzed into the components of the ideal order of number and measure, on the one side, and the world of phenomena which the former encloses and determines, on the other. Only after such a distinction has been made can that which is a mixture of limit and the unlimited appear with its own mode of being opposite the ideal world of what does the limiting. It seems to me that the speculation regarding the *aitiai* in the *Philebus* is meant to provide an ontological account of the orders of being which have now separated from each other, an account which is elaborated upon at length in the *Timaeus* later on. That which we see ἐν ἡμῖν, "in our world," in the finite action of the *technitēs*, viz., the production of an intelligent ordering of something, makes evident in reverse that there must also be an intelligent cause for the order of the cosmos which surpasses all earthly ordering. When the *Philebus* distinguishes between mixed being, e.g., the fire ἐν ἡμῖν, and the pure being, Fire, it simultaneously links the reality of the world which we experience with the ideal cosmic order. The conceptions which Plato develops here are obviously designed to dispel the illusion of any unbridgeable gap between the ideal and the sense perceived. These conceptions by no means imply, however, that Plato had distanced himself from the

14. Ibid., pp. 103–13.

doctrine of ideas. On the contrary, they are an attempt at theoretical explication of that doctrine. We know of other proposed solutions to the *chorismos* problem, and Plato's attempt displays a remarkable similarity to the doctrine of ideas in Eudoxos' theory, as that is recounted by Alexander. But I have already gone beyond the testimony of the dialogues to the indirect tradition. It is methodologically warranted to do so, I believe, despite the attendant risks. Any interpretation of Plato's thought true to his intent must make use of what the dialogues only hint at without actually stating. However, this necessity by no means obviates the requirement that the content of the dialogues be understood as accurately as possible. Indeed, it is only in this way that the requirement can be met.

*   *   *

It seems to me that the proper method is to interpret what can be surmised from Plato's dialogues by correlating it with the subsequent development of Platonic thought in the academy. In reconstructing Plato's oral teachings it indeed is an important philological task to separate, as much as possible, that which may be attributed to Plato himself from that which his students, in particular Speusippus, Xenocrates, and Aristotle, developed on the basis of these teachings. But ultimately *there is also no evading the opposite task of making this later development clear using Plato's doctrines as a basis*. In fact the latter task may even be said to have a certain priority. Although Konrad Gaiser's careful evaluation of Aristotle's testimony in *De anima* (404 b 16–17)[15] might lead us to the conclusion that Plato himself and not Xenocrates is being cited as the proponent of the numerological interpretation of the world-soul, and although we might therefore venture that here we have an oral teaching of Plato's, it remains of secondary importance to the question of how Xenocrates' doctrine of the self-moved number (frag. 60, R. Heinze) can be understood in relationship to the doctrine shimmering in the background of the *Timaeus*. For no one could fail to see that the doctrine of the self-

15. Cf. Stobaios' reply in Gaiser, op. cit., frag. 67, VIII.

moved number goes back to the world-soul in the *Timaeus*. But the theme which we first find disclosed in the *Timaeus* itself, with its mythically tinged, iridescent doctrines, actually goes back even further. It derives from the doctrine of nous as we know that doctrine from Anaxagoras. There too nous is the source of motion and, consequently, of the separation of all the many shapes of things within the original mixture—just as mind also perceives, recognizes, and comprehends within itself the distinctions in that which has been separated. And even after Aristotle, this double function of differentiating and moving (*krinein* and *kinein*, *De anima* A III a 4) is said to be the essence of the psychē. This coupling of both functions which is already implicit in Anaxagoras' nous doctrines, the intrinsic connection between the two, must be grasped prior to attempting any interpretation of Plato's doctrine of the *psychē*.[16]

What Xenocrates means by world-soul or better, by the arithmos which moves itself, must be viewed against precisely this background. Plato's and Euclid's well-known definition of the sum as a πλῆθος μονάδων (plenum of ones) already implies the mysterious nature of the arithmos insofar as in the sum number a multiplicity is gathered together in a unity of a special sort. The "plenum of ones" is at the same time a unity of many. Thus the implication which lies in the concept of a sum is that numbers are an unfolded multiplicity which, although extending infinitely, are gathered together into a unity in any definite sum. If, in abstracting from the process of counting, one thinks of a series of discrete numbers being run through, then one thinks of the sum as tallied units moving past the one who counts them. In this we have precisely the structure of *kinēsis* which Plato attributes to the heavenly bodies being counted each time they come around again. The order of the heavens has bestowed upon man the greatest of the gods' gifts: knowledge of number.[17] That is the real Promethean fire of which the *Philebus* speaks (16 c). It also makes clear to us the meaning of Xenocrates' definition of the soul. "Soul" is the movement of the

16. Cf. my "Vorgestalten der Reflexion," pp. 138 ff.
17. *Timaeus* 39 b, *Epinomis* 976 e ff.

heavens; or better, it is the sequence of numbers which is forever unfolding itself in the heavens and closing itself together again: the repetitive sequence, that is, which constitutes time.

We may draw specific conclusions from this about the significance of the world-soul in the *Timaeus*. Let us start with the assumption that soul is to be thought of as it had been at first in the earlier Greek tradition, i.e., as expressing the essence of life. What does that yield? In the first place, it implies that soul, in distinction from visible bodies, is invisible. This is pre-supposed as self-evident in the doctrine of the *Phaedo*, for instance. This invisible being which is soul integrates the living thing into a visible unified living being. The soul is that which integrates the scattered multiplicity of the bodily, and therefore its diminution is the onset of bodily disintegration. But this means, in the second place, that the soul is spread out every-where throughout the body—at least in the sense that the great sensitive skin which clothes all bodily things belongs directly to the soul. For after all, the skin with its five senses passes on whatever it feels to the soul. Accordingly, in the *Theaetetus* (182 d) this area of the soul, which knows with the aid of the senses, is juxtaposed to older doctrines, which take knowing to be a colli-sion of existents, "like" with "like" or "unlike." And thus it obvi-ously makes sense to say that the soul must be spread out every-where. Even our own anthropology has made it evident that the nature of the animal differs from that of the plant at least as far as the animal relays back to itself all the stimulations which the senses experience. It is not surprising, then, that the *Timaeus* portrays the world soul as spreading out over everything.

There is just as little need to explain why the soul moves it-self, for it is precisely motion which distinguishes the living body from the inanimate body left after death. This ancient and con-vincing observation regarding that which distinguished the living from the nonliving and the no longer living leads us to think of the soul as the archē of kinēsis. And thus it becomes clear why Plato calls the soul the essence of physis (*Laws* 892 c). For self-evidently the order constitutive of nature, the order which it displays in its preservation of itself throughout all changes, is found in every existent being which has a soul, in every organism. And in the most highly evolved organisms the soul is so constituted that it displays both its own embeddedness and the embeddedness of everything else in the circular course of being as a whole.

This puts us in a better position to ascertain the precise meaning of the world-soul in the *Timaeus*. For even if one were to seize upon nothing more than the general statement therein that the soul is "earlier" than the body, the way is pointed out for interpreting the dialogue. When the soul is described as being spread out everywhere and enveloping and permeating everything, we have the graphic way of stating that behind the All as it presents itself to our senses there is an invisible, prevailing order—a sort of celestial mathematics and music upon which both the segmentation and the unity of the whole are based.

Now the fact that Plato makes the concept of mixture (*mixis*) the point of departure for his definition of the world-soul determines the entire construction of the mural of the *Timaeus*. The soul is said to consist of a mixture. For those familiar with the *Philebus* or the *Statesman*, this comes as no surprise. "Mixture" is one of the basic models in terms of which Plato conceives of Being. In the *Philebus* the being of what is either gauged by measure or fixed and determined by number is said to be a "mixture of limit and the unlimited." And "mixture" is again paradigmatic in the *Timaeus*, where it is said that the three ingredients of the world-soul are Being, Selfsameness, and Difference (37 a b). On the surface of it, that sounds very odd, for the latter two are *logical* concepts, concepts which express the nature of the logos. But the logos is of such a nature that whenever anything is meant by it, that thing is meant as identical to itself and, at the same time, as different from other things. Thus Selfsameness and Difference are always present in anything which is and is recognized as what it is. Only the interweaving of Selfsameness and Difference makes an assertion (logos) possible. In any assertion something which, in *being* what it is, is *identical* to itself, is linked to something *different* from itself. But it does not thereby lose its selfsameness. Hence the mixture of Being with such "logical" constituents can easily be seen to express the structure of the logos although, to be sure, metaphorically.

The only problem lies in the fact that the order of the movement in our universe *as that presents itself to the human eye* is also
described in terms of this mixture. The famous X woven from
the circles of Identity and Difference is meant as something real.
It does not originate in our thinking and speaking and exist only
there; rather it mirrors the order of movement in the universe
itself. It is an image of the ecliptic, the tilt of the earth's rotation
on its axis in relationship to the orbit of the sun. The
significance of this tilt was evidently recognized at an early date
by the Greeks. The periodicity and shape of all things on our
earth were seen to derive from it and, as Aristotle says, it is the
cause of coming-into-being and passing-away insofar as it is the
cause of the rhythm of the seasons.

When the *Timaeus* portrays the soul, i.e., the true reality of
the self-moving All, as the intertwining of Selfsameness and Difference, we can perceive in the background the general doctrine
of motion which we know from the *Laws*. There a mode of
movement is depicted which seems entirely determined by
Selfsameness: the stable movement of something spinning on its
axis while standing still. This movement is so much identical to
itself that no differences are visible in it at all, not even those
which are intrinsic to movement as such.[18] But the movement of
the universe portrayed in the *Timaeus* (thanks to the tilt "woven"
into it) is not like this, for it displays its motion and the widest as-
sortment of differences.

But the invisible basis of the constancy and alteration in the
cosmos, which Plato calls soul, is *also* meant to be *knowing* soul.
And the doctrine of the soul in the *Timaeus* expressly demands
of us that we think of the soul as knowing. The mixing together
of Being, Selfsameness, and Difference leads, if one is oriented
toward the Same, to knowing in the form of insight and science,
and, if oriented toward the Different, to knowing in the form
of opinions and convictions (δόξαι καὶ πίστεις) or perception
(*Timaeus* 37 b). This would imply that Selfsameness and Difference have the same basic significance for reality which they have
for knowing. The question must now be just how these two—the

18. The *Sophist* also alludes to this "standing" movement (256 b).

differences which are in reality and thé differentiation which the mind carries out—correlate.

The exposition in the *Timaeus* explains how the constant order of motions in the heavens of our universe, though always selfsame, nevertheless brings about the manifold phenomena and processes which keep the world we know in motion. And because the constellations are ever repeating their regular revolutions amid constant alteration, it is natural to think of the complex mathematical order governing stellar movement as the true essence of the world. It is also evident why that which is present throughout the All in this way, and which pervades it in precisely the way in which the omnipresence of life, the psychē, pervades and constitutes the organic, living thing, should also be called psychē. For the being of the living thing, the unity of its self-motion and the constancy of its organic functioning, plainly rests upon just this invisible reality which enlivens it. The circulation of the living thing and the circulation of the heavenly bodies have the same form and point to a common ground.

But how does one get from here to the other definition of the soul as not merely that which moves but also as that which knows? This must be understood against the background of Plato's doctrine of the logos. We must analyze the nature of Difference, once again using Anaxagoras' anticipation of Plato as our guide. Difference is based upon something's differing from something else. But this sort of differing always implies the emergence of differences not present as such in what is at first undifferentiated. That emergence can be thought of as a *real* process like that which Heraclitus tells us occurs in the settling of a liquid, e.g., a barley drink whose ingredients separate.[19] But we can describe the process from another perspective. Differences which have emerged are simultaneously differences which have been brought out. The emergence of differences implies that the differences have been separated from one another so that they emerge *for* something for which they are different. Thus separation is always at the same time differentiation and implies something which knows the differences that have emerged. Or we can

19. Diels, op cit., frag. 125.

say to *be* different is to be *known* as different.

This, it seems to me, is the evidence to which Plato is averring in his analysis of the structural complex of Oneness and Multiplicity, Selfsameness and Difference, the evidence which supports his whole thinking on the matter. Differences are possible relationships. The separation of them according to their nature—like the "severing of a deer carcass at the joints"—is the essence of knowing, or dialectic, as Plato calls it. The True is what is brought out in such distinctions. Even more, knowledge itself is nothing other than the existence of what has been brought out in this way. From this vantage point we can see in what sense the movement of knowing is implied in cosmic movement. To the extent that there are always new differences which are brought out in this way, which is to say, assembled in their "disconcealedness" (ἀλήθεια), the knowing which knows them is forever changing. This gives the doctrine of the *Timaeus* its precise meaning in regard to Selfsameness and Difference. Knowing occurs as the self-presentation of the thing which is known. Such self-presentation is a process full of movement. The aspects of the existent thing, the views which it offers of itself, shift and at the same time the points of view or opinions which the human soul develops also shift, in that they refer to the thing in different respects.

If we should ask ourselves what conceptual means Plato might apply to grasp the special character of the soul which knows in this way, it seems eminently reasonable that he would have recourse to the *number as a sum*. That is the proper paradigm. One need only recall that in his analysis of time Aristotle determined the latter to be the enumerated sum of movement and he adds, as if it were an incidental point, that the enumerated multiplicity of motion which time is, is dependent upon the soul (*Physics* IV 14 223 a 21 ff.). In essence Plato had put the relationship of idea and soul on this same foundation in the *Phaedo*, and the connection between idea and number, as we have seen, appears to be present very early in Plato. For we have observed in the example of the *Hippias Major* that Plato was sensitive to the mysteriousness of the number. This is by no means to say that behind this early dialogue (which, to be sure, is among the latest of its group) there already lies the doctrine of the generation of the numbers out of the principles of the One and the indeterminate Two, in the form in which the indirect tradition tells us Plato taught it. Nevertheless a preliminary indication can certainly be found here of the continuing mystery and ontological difficulty with which Plato saw his analysis of knowledge and the logos confronted. The doctrine of the idea as the one real existent in opposition to the multiplicity of arising and fading sense appearances which participate in it, does not yet suffice to elucidate what knowing actually is. Such a "having in view" of the idea is only a precondition and presupposition in all knowing. In that I have the idea in view, I can subsume the appearances under the eidos common to them, or perhaps better said, I can identify the appearances with their eidetic universality. This is the reason for the assumption that there are ideas. But it is obviously of no concern to Plato which concept one uses to envision the relationship of the appearances to an idea—participation, koinōnia, *synousia*, parousia, mixis, *symplokē*, or whatever. For him the problem does not lie there at all. Instead it lies in the *logical* question of how it is possible in the first place that one can be many and many, one. What is said of a thing is supposed to be different from the thing and nevertheless it is supposed to be attributed to it. What a thing is supposed to be in truth is supposed to hold for each of its appearances and yet the appearances are supposed to be different from the thing itself. Plato uses the number to illustrate what he finds puzzling here. The number consists of units each of which by itself is one, and nevertheless the number itself, according to the number of units it includes, is not many but a definite "so-many," the unity of a multiplicity bound together: ἀμφότερα δύο ἑκάτερον δὲ ἕν (both two, but each one) (*Theaetetus* 185 ab). Every logos has this formal structure, however puzzling that structure may be.

Plato's example of "writing" serves nicely to illustrate the state of affairs here. We have letters, syllables, words, and sentences. Now even the coarse difference between the meaning of words and that of letters will suffice for our purposes. What each letter means by itself it no longer means when it is combined with others to form a word. For the word has its meaning not as the collection of the meanings of the letters but as the one whole which it is. This schema can be applied—as Plato often does apply it—in defining the nature of dialectic and discourse. And as the *Philebus* emphatically declares, the secret of all technē, i.e., of all real knowing in the sense of prior acquaintanceship with a thing, lies in the proper solution to the problem of the One and the Many. Every logos contains the unity of an opinion which results from the multiplicity of words and concepts bound together in it.

An example like that given in the *Sophist*, i.e., "Theaetetus flies," over which a stream of ink has been expended, can, in the final analysis, be explained only if one thinks of the essence of this statement using the model of the number as a sum. The context necessitates that we think of the problem here as an incompatibility in ideas. The universal idea of "man" is implied in the name "Theaetetus," and that idea excludes the idea of flying. Thus the putative *one*ness in the relationship of things asserted here, the oneness constituted grammatically by the interweaving of noun and verb, must be false. These *two* ideas cannot be combined with each other. A correct assertion, on the other hand, presupposes that the ideas expressed in it are indeed compatible with each other and that they can be combined. (Even so this necessary condition for the truth of an assertion need not be a sufficient condition, as is shown by the judgment of perception.) Since the number is paradigmatic here, it follows that the concern in the case of this sample sentence from the *Sophist* is not at all with the predicative structure of the judgment, the structure which figures fundamentally in Aristotle's logic and doctrine of categories. Here no specific *hypokeimenon* is presupposed to which a determination is added as a predicative attribute. On the contrary, in Plato the logos is thought of essentially as a being-there-together, the being of one idea "with" another. In that they are taken together, the two of two separate ideas constitutes the one of the state of affairs expressed. And that is even true of judgments of perception, which can be true only when that which is tied together in the thing perceived can also be thought together in the logos. But it is most clear that the "interweaving" of genus–species determinations is constitutive where it is a matter of stating the essence, a matter of the definitional statement (logos ousias).

The definition is derived in Plato by the procedure of dihairēsis, which as Stenzel saw decades ago, provides an indirect confirmation of the paradigmatic function of the number. For every dihairēsis is a dividing in *two*. (In the *Philebus* division into three is also mentioned, evidently in reference to specific rational systems.) In Plato the definitional logos is formed by the addition of the definitions run through in a dihairēsis and then counted up—yielding a collected multiplicity which as such constitutes the unitary essence of a definite thing. Thus precisely insofar as it is arrived at by the procedure of dividing, the definition displays the role of the number. The compatibility of all definitions in a genus with one another, or what is more, the necessity of their coexistence with the final determination common to all of them, is what constitutes the unitary nature of the thing. This means that the statement of the essence, the definitional statement, is the collected sum number of all the essential definitions which have been run through, and as such it has the structure of number.

This explanation, I think, gives us at least the outlines of how the paradigmatic function of the number which is indicated in the dialogues can be correlated with the doctrine of the ideal numbers known to us from the indirect tradition. There is an overall structural parallel between number and logos. It also seems to me that we can explain the lack of clarity in the reports of how the doctrine of ideal numbers was worked out and what specific content it was applied to as follows. Let us begin by saying that the real problem in the logos lies in its being the unity of an opinion composed of factors or items which are distinct from the opinion itself. Now as we know, *logos* is a mathematical term that means "proportion." Toeplitz, who has pointed out the sense of proportion contained in the logos concept, took as his point of departure 251a in the *Sophist*, where it is said specifically that the search for the proper concept of Being and Not-being can be carried out only by pursuing the proportion of one to the other. And as a matter of fact, the power of the logos to reveal the being of what is derives from the intrinsic interwovenness in it of Being and Not-being, which are to be taken as Selfsameness and Difference, respectively. This is the doctrine which the Stranger from Elea is supposed to communicate to us. The doctrine, however, implies the structure of number. I would point to *Theaetetus* 185 ab. The soul, it is said there, which thinks purely and deals only with itself (185 e, 187 a) also knows the numerical constitution of what is, in addition to knowing Being and Not-being, Similarity and Dissimilarity, Selfsameness and Difference: ἔτι δὲ ἕν τε καὶ τὸν ἄλλον ἀριθμόν (but also one and the other number) (185 d). In this there is an allusion to the mysterious character of the number, viz., that something taken together is two while each of the two is only one (185 b 2).

But that is not all. Characteristic of a proportion is that its mathematical value is independent of the given factors in it, provided that they keep the same proportion to one another. The same relation can exist even when the numbers in it are changed. The universality of the relationship as such transcends its components. One must keep that in mind when one discovers how sparse, indefinite, and contradictory the substantive content is which we have of Plato's doctrine of ideal numbers. The hierarchical structure of the mathematical sciences proceeding in the sequence of dimensions from point to line to plane to solid, which Gaiser has so splendidly worked out for us, is very likely only one specific application of the more general numerical relationships of the ideas and their configuration. The same configuration of ideal numbers can evidently prefigure other sequences; for instance, according to the *De anima* text, it prefigures the sequence of modes of knowing, nous, epistēme, doxa, aisthēsis.[20]

20. Both sections of the account in *De anima* I, 2 404 b 13–30, which are divided from each other by the ὁμοίως (similarly), point back to the *Timaeus*. Αὐτὸ τὸ ζῷον —perhaps nothing more than an expression for the world-soul (?)—is also mixed with the body in the *Timaeus*, the difference being that in Aristotle the three dimensions are listed. Similarly the *Timaeus* differentiates among the performances of the soul in knowing, specifically in reference to the circle of Selfsameness and the circle of Difference, except that there two double groups are given while in *De anima* the count goes from one to four. Can the authenticity of such an account be questioned—especially if compared with the analogy of the divided line in the *Republic*?

Thus the reason that Aristotle and our other indirect sources in the tradition say nothing precise about which numbers are to be coordinated with which ideas can hardly be because they were uncertain about it. On the contrary, Aristotle obviously has good grounds for saying that the correlation of numbers to specific ideas is of no importance (*Metaphysics* 1090 b 24). For similar reasons Aristotle points (1084 a 12) to the limit of ten, set by Plato. This is not a vestige of Pythagoreanism (the *tetraktēs*). It makes plain sense that according to the nature of the decadal system any forming of numbers beyond the first sequence of ten is merely repetition. *Precisely for that reason the sum number proffers itself as the prototype of the order of Being and the ideas. And it claims nothing more for itself than to be such a prototype.* The lack of specificity in the coordination of ideas and numbers results from the nature of the matter itself—from the nature of human knowing, which, as human, is incapable of comprehending the entire order of being and ideas *uno intuitu*. Instead it is capable of uncovering only limited ordered sequences as it goes through the ideas one by one and must then relinquish these sequences again to a whole without internal differentiation (cf. *Philebus*: ἐὰν εἰς τὸ ἄπειρον [let fall into the unlimited-indefinite]). It is exactly like that in counting.

The analogy between knowledge of the ideas and the generation of numbers can also be illuminated in the following way. Inconclusiveness and endlessness is obviously characteristic not only of our finite, discursive penetration of the ideas in knowing but also of the generation of a series of numbers in counting. Both "generations" depend on the principles of the One and the indeterminate Two. Thus, the endlessness and inconclusiveness of dialectic are not in the least qualified by the doctrine of numerical principles, of which Aristotle tells us, or supplanted by some dogmatic teaching on these principles. For Plato the decisive point to be made clear in the doctrine of the generation of numbers is that *they can be continued indefinitely*. Although each number is definite, counting goes on indefinitely "into infinity," and that fact implies the equal involvement in counting of both the dyas and the hen. All the attempts to give the dihairetical generation of the numbers a wider meaning than this, such as have been made by Stenzel and Becker et al., seem to me to bog down in arbitrary constructions. It is my contention that Plato's concern is not with achieving a unified system of dihairetical generation but only with the fact that the principles of the One and the Two are able to generate the series of all numbers—*just as they make all discourse possible*. The entire series of numbers, the even as well as the odd, can be explicated according to these principles, though of course not by strict dihairēsis. This special status of the One and the Two giving them the character of principles could be what is indicated by the ἔξω τῶν πρώτον (outside of the first) in that famous Aristotelian text.[21]

If we are indeed forbidden to seek a fixed system of deduction in Plato's doctrines and if, on the contrary, Plato's doctrine of the indeterminate Two establishes precisely the impossibility of completing such a system, then Plato's doctrine of ideas turns out to be a general theory of relationship from which it can be convincingly deduced that dialectic is unending and infinite. Underlying this theory would be the fact that the logos always requires that one idea be "there" together with another. Insight into one idea per se does not yet constitute knowledge. Only when the idea is "alluded" to in respect to another does it display itself *as* something. Heidegger revealed for us the constitutive significance of this hermeneutic "as," and in *Metaphysics* Theta 10 Aristotle arrived at the correlative conclusion that the simple (ἁπλᾶ', ἀσύνθετα) essences permit no error; rather they are either hit upon (θιγεῖν) in thought or not. Now it is clear that any given idea can also coexist with ideas besides the particular one with which it has been said to coexist. Departing from Aristotle's analysis of the structure of predication, we can say that we can make a statement about a thing in different respects—even categorially different respects. As a consequence of the point of view chosen, any particular assertion singles something out from

21. πρώτων (of the first), of course, must be filled out with ἀριθμῶν (numbers). But perhaps the effects of Plato's specific usage πρῶτα for "principles" can still be felt in Aristotle's account. In any case it seems to me that these principles are what is meant and not the odd numbers, as Alexander believed, or the prime numbers, as one is wont to think today. The modern reading in the technical sense of prime numbers seems to have resulted from a false understanding of what the dihairetical production of numbers is meant to accomplish (*Metaphysics* A 6, 987 b 34).

that about which it is made, and in making the assertion, it "raises" the particular thing asserted into our awareness. Only as a relationship thus "raised" into our consciousness is the relationship actually "there," i.e., placed in the openness and obviousness of what is present in our believing and knowing. This general theory of relationship, it seems to me, is responsible for the fact that in his dialogues Plato fails to deal adequately with the problem of pseudos. For pseudos does not lie in falsely speaking of one thing as another but only in speaking of it as something which it is not. The being of Not-being lying in "difference from," which is displayed in the *Sophist*, provides only the formal prerequisite of the actual pseudos. The being of the ideas, precisely in their interweaving of Being and Not-being, consists in their displaying of themselves and being present in a logos. However, that does not provide an ontological foundation for the false appearance of something and pseudos. Nonetheless it *is* made clear that the realm of ideas with their limitless interweaving with one another implies an element of Not-being, namely, the incompleteness characteristic of all human thinking.[22]

Hence it is true of dihairēsis too that in the determination of the essence or definition of a thing, a variety of possible "deductions" suggest themselves. This certainly does not imply that the selection of an acceptable common basis, the genus with which the deduction of the thing being questioned begins, is merely gratuitous. But neither is it the case that a completely

22. The point here is one which Gadamer made in his Heidelberg lectures on Heidegger. How a thing may "show" itself deceptively is not accounted for by Plato, who in passing over the equifundamentality (*Gleichursprünglichkeit*) of Being and Not-being, truth and falsity, authenticity and inauthenticity, and so forth, in existents, as these display themselves, proceeds to logical not-being as *heterotēs* or difference, the "is not" of "a is not b." But Gadamer points out here that nevertheless Plato knows "existent" not-being. That he does is demonstrated by his sensitivity to the inevitable finitude which characterizes human discourse and understanding, and to the resultant perplexity which accompanies any human insight. In Plato anything which "is," i.e., is disclosed "there" in human discourse, is "there" only partially and never in its entirety. Thus it "is not" insofar as it always exceeds the horizons of what is "there" at any given time. It is this concommitance of the ineradicable "is not" with any "is" which makes a systematization of the ideas impossible. Since our insights are only partial, the view of the whole, which alone would make a systematization possible (Hegel), is never given to us. (Translator)

unequivalent, fixed classificatory system exists which would prescribe a definition. The basic consensus which sustains every fruitful discussion and without which the latter could not begin, can take many different forms. There is a presupposition of some kind in any choice of the perspective from which the deduction is to be carried out, and Plato's discussions often lead to the discovery of a hidden *mis*understanding here insofar as the initial proposal was accepted although it actually should not have been. The *Sophist* and *Statesman* dialogues in particular attest to this fact in their quite humorous and comical way. And is not Plato's lecture on the Good supposed to have argued the essential incompleteness of the dialectical endeavor? Throughout all of what Plato attempts to derive from these two principles, the One and the indeterminate Two, the element of indeterminacy or indefiniteness in our thought is plainly implied. This, it seems to me, is the reason that one of the two determinants is precisely indeterminacy. Plato's system of ideational relationships could be so structured that each individual relationship possible within it can be brought out and expressly posited at some given time, but a simultaneous positing and being present of *all* relationships is fundamentally impossible. Plato can hardly be said to have subordinated the realm of ideas to a divine mind like Leibniz's central monad, in which everything is present which *is*, everything which can be true. And that he did not have any such thing in mind seems to me to be exactly what is implied in Plato's so-called doctrine of "principles" as well as in the kaleidoscopic play of assertions in his dialogues. Plato thinks of the finite, searching human being in terms of the latter's *discrepancy* from the knowing god, and that he does has more than religious significance. It bears on dialectic as well. But although human thinking and knowing can never be complete—any more than anything can which exists on this earth—the wondrousness of the path of this human knowing, which, as human, is always directed into the open-ended, is in no way diminished.

There is a variety of evidence that Plato thought along the lines which I have indicated here. The *apeiron* "cause" of the *Philebus*, for instance, is obviously meant to restrict the success of human life. Because of the apeiron, human life can never be absolutely successful; rather it always runs the risk of miscarrying and must forever be wrested from its tendency to sink into a measurelessness even so extreme as that of the unconscious and torpid life of an oyster (*Philebus* 21 d). It appears that it is *the* human task to constantly be limiting the measureless with measure. And the role which Necessity plays in the abstract, intellectualized world structure of the *Timaeus* seems to me to point in the same direction. Necessity assures that the order of existences formed by copying the ideas is a real order precisely because it must be asserted *against resistance*. When Plato, in transforming the Pythagorean apeiron, discovers in the Two a new categorial version of the earlier Pythagorean concept, he does not just use another word; rather he grasps and defines more precisely what the logos is in essence. Using the Two as a basis, he correlates the intelligible world of the ideas and numbers, sense appearances, and the structure of human knowing; he thereby establishes a splendid system of correspondences. For in spite of its indeterminacy, this Two is the principle of all differentiation and all differing, which is to say that it codetermines reality. The indirect tradition which informs us of the principles in Plato's doctrine is not evidence of some dogma which lies concealed behind Plato's written work and which could possibly undermine our understanding of Plato's dialectic. On the contrary, it articulates and confirms the limitedness of all human knowing and shows why the highest possibility of such knowing must be named not sophia but philosophia.

7

Idea and Reality in Plato's *Timaeus*

If we intend to study and interpret any one of Plato's puzzling dialogues carefully and with real concern for what is said in it, it is essential that we become aware of the hermeneutic preconceptions which have given us our image of Plato. That alone would clear the way for us. With a persistence bordering on the absurd, the prevailing form of interpretation in which Plato's philosophy has been passed on to us has advocated the two-world theory, that is, the complete separation of the paradigmatic world of ideas from the ebb and flow of change in our experience of the sense-perceived world. Idea and reality are made to look like two worlds separated by a chasm, and the interrelationship of the two remains obscure. Indeed, the sole historically significant account of their interrelationship is the Neoplatonic translation of the two worlds into hypostases of the grand process of emanation, in which the One prior to all determinations externalizes and displays itself in a hierarchically segmented universe. Nowadays, however, the prevailing view among Plato scholars is one which has developed in positive or negative response to Aristotle's criticism of the separation of the two worlds, and this although the intent of Aristotle's almost malevolent dialectical exposition of Plato's theory of ideas is still being argued.[1] Sooner or later we will have to approach Aristotle's critique of Plato with concepts of critique and polemics very different from the ones we are used to. For the most recent research with its deeper philosophical interpretation of Plato's and Aristotle's thought has provided us with enormously strengthened evidence of the continuity of Platonic thought and has allowed us to see Aristotle

1. Compare my own attempt to clarify this matter below (chap. 8).

more and more clearly as a Platonist. Given these circumstances, the meaning of Aristotle's criticism of the doctrine of ideas remains debatable. Presumably, we must get far more used to relegating the polemics of ancient philosophers to the realm of argument and dialectic and far less to seeing it as the statement of a position in contradiction to someone else's.

But the third version we have of Plato's two-world theory must be placed in question too, i.e., the genetic-historical account of it which dominates modern Plato research. This theory asserts that in the course of his intellectual development Plato himself recognized that the dogmatic assertion of the doctrine of ideas was untenable and that he then sought by means of dialectic to overcome the gap between the two worlds. Even today the prevailing opinion is that the criticism in Plato's *Parmenides* which the head of the Parmenidean school directs at the young Socrates, i.e., that the latter had proposed the hypothesis of the ideas too soon, is in fact Plato's criticism of himself. According to this view the paradoxes displayed here in the "participation" of the particular in the universal are reflections of the crisis in Plato's doctrine of ideas. The new dialectic of the later dialogues, it is said, confirms that the "dogmatic" doctrine of ideas was modified, and in respect to the tradition of philosophy what emerges is seen to point in the direction of the systematic thought of Fichte or neo-Kantianism.[2] Only most recently are voices of those who would loosen up this genetic schematization to be heard. For instance, the Tübingen school (Gaiser, Krämer) has given new support to the suspicion that a doctrine of ideal numbers was always implied in Plato's dialogues, a suspicion which had already surfaced here and there earlier. Certainly it

2. I have in mind, for example, Nicolai Hartmann's theory of "declining *methexis*" in *Platos Logik des Seins* (Giessen, 1909) and the later Academy treatises and the trend-setting works of Julius Stenzel. Patzig and Kamlah—after a considerable struggle—are also of the opinion that the earlier doctrine of ideas foundered on the problem of methexis and was shunned by the later Plato. Kamlah must make quite an effort to erase the traces of that doctrine from the *Timaeus*. I would raise the counterquestion, whether it would not be proper to trust Plato himself when he says that the *chōrismos* was intended only to characterize one aspect of that which defines the new dimension of the logoi as a whole. If so, it is quite possible for him to go on speaking of the chōrismos in the mythical style, for example, of either the *Timaeus* or the *Phaedo*.

cannot be disputed that there is a change in the character of the dialogues, which at first present Socrates as the negative dialectician who confounds his interlocutors and later as the man who reveals and bears witness to a dialectic which is meant to be taken positively. But that need not indicate a change in Plato's thought. A dialogue like the *Hippias*, which must surely be considered authentic, obviously alludes to the doctrine of ideal numbers, and one does well not to make light of the issue here by seeking to avoid it with some genetic-historical hypothesis concerning Plato's supposed development.

Compounding our difficulties is the fact that for us the *Timaeus* occupies a singular position on the periphery of the works of Plato. That it does is due in large part to our critical disposition toward it, which has its origins in Aristotle's physics and which has led us to believe that the tale of the demiurge who makes the world is nothing but an empty metaphor. Since Aristotle we have grown accustomed to viewing Plato's "physics" as secondary, something lying on the periphery. But our view of the *Timaeus* can also be traced to the all too strong sympathetic vibrations which its mythical tale of the creation of the world stirred later in those holding the Judeo-Christian beliefs on creation. Although it was already open to debate in ancient times whether this portrayal of the creation of the world was purely didactical, and although in the *Timaeus* there is plainly not the faintest hint anywhere of a divine will which decides to create a world, the interest in the *Timaeus* was to a great extent interest in what was taken to be its anticipation of Christian beliefs.

To be sure, all this changed with the awakening interest of modern physics in the *Timaeus*. Galileo, Kepler, and the atomists of the seventeenth century all rely not so much on the idea of creation in the *Timaeus* as on its mathematics. And the atomists in particular were justified in their recourse to the *Timaeus*. But even that does not change the fact that the *Timaeus* remained on the periphery of Plato's works and, more specifically, that its mythical narrative was not integrated into what, properly speaking, may be called Plato's dialectic. Thus a task is precisely set for us. We must make up for what has not been done and, in penetrating behind the form of the myth, we must make clear its relationship to Plato's dialectic as a whole.

However, in just this regard the *Timaeus* poses a specific methodological problem which relates in a special way to the general problem that confronts us in interpreting Plato today, i.e., the problem of the as yet unclarified relationship between Plato's fictional dialogues and his "doctrine," which is known to us solely through the indirect tradition of secondary sources. It took one and a half centuries of intense investigation of Plato's texts for us to fully comprehend the literary character of his dialogues, which Schleiermacher and Schlegel correctly sensed from the start. And even now there still exists the overwhelming countertendency to interpret the dialogical compositions critically as statements of a doctrine. One could learn from the precedent which Aristotle sets in this regard, but as I have noted above, Aristotle also seems to present a problem since in our approach to him we continue to be governed by our modern preconception of what scientific criticism ought to be. The methodological problem is clear. We must establish the philosophical significance of the *scene*, the setting of the dialogues, of the relationship of the speaker to what is spoken, of evolving meaning as it unfolds in live discussion. And we must apply what we can learn thereby to understanding the philosophical questions which Plato puts to us. Here too the *Timaeus* poses a special problem. To be sure, there is a charming dialogical prelude in which a previous conversation about the ideal state is recalled and a historical background disclosed in a sort of fairy tale. And without doubt this political frame, across which the story of the genesis of the world is stretched, is not coincidental. But the actual narrative, for which Timaeus is the speaker, has no more "scenic" interludes and for long passages at a time the text can be read as a self-contained treatise.

Of course the tone in which the story is told here has something quite distinctive about it, and the truth which the narrative claims for itself is explicitly limited to what is "probable" both in respect to what is presented as a story (mythos) and in respect to what is presented in rational argument (logos). So we are indeed faced with the methodological problem of extracting the substantive content of the narrative, extracting its rational themes from a kind of story which, in fairy tale fashion, is peculiarly loose, incoherent, and allusive. The incoherence is especially obvious in the way the natural sequence in which a narrative would usually unfold is interrupted by regressions, corrections, repetitions, and abrupt new beginnings. Not only is the portrayal of the ordering of the universe suddenly broken off in an odd way and the construction of the world-soul repeated, a construction which, as we are told in an explicit correction (34 bc), precedes the construction of the universe, there is also that most opaque relationship between the genesis of the cosmos as it is recounted and the genesis of time, which only occurs "after" the genesis of the cosmos has begun. And there is above all the suddenness with which the narrator, absorbed as he is in his zealous accounting of the particulars of human perception, interrupts himself and allows that we ought to view things after all in the light of anankē (46 c, 48 a). This new, second start, which is specifically singled out as such, lies somewhere between being an ongoing *story* of the premeditated action of the demiurge and a logically consistent *explanation* of the cosmic order in rational terms—only to issue at the end into a concluding piece of narrative.[3] Thus we are confronted with the specific methodological problem of digging out the factual value of what is stated from behind Plato's facile way of telling it with all his puzzling vacillations and touches of irony. And having accomplished this task, we must relate the *Timaeus*, despite all its stylistic peculiarities, to the whole of Plato's dialectic.

Timaeus' actual speech begins with a sort of methodological

---

3.   69 a. The outstanding English interpreters, Taylor (*A Commentary on Plato's* Timaeus [London, 1928]), Cornford (*Plato's Cosmology* [New York, 1957]), and Crombie (*An Examination of Plato's Doctrines* [London, 1963]), from whom we have all learned a great deal, seem to me to be alike in one respect, however much their hermeneutical principles may differ. They all fail to pay sufficient attention to the shifts from the narrative to the expositional mode of discourse in the dialogue, and as a consequence, for example, they misunderstand the insertion of the "atomic theory" in the narrative as a continuation of the story of the ordering activity of the god. Insoluble problems arise from that mistake, and the provocative central question of the *Timaeus*—how teleology and necessity relate to each other—is lost from view.

proem. A series of "axioms" is set up from which conclusions are drawn and in accordance with which the epistemological claims of the ensuing narrative are specified. The distinction between Being and Becoming is introduced right at the start as fundamental. Note, however, that this well-known distinction of Socrates' and Plato's with which Timaeus begins his presentation is supported in an entirely Platonic way by the correlation of one side of it with thought (*noēsis*) and of the other with opinion (doxa), as the latter is mediated by the senses. Note too that this distinction is introduced by Timaeus with an explicit "in my view." And as a matter of fact, the distinction here in modes of being is one which only such a "Pythagorean" is actually capable of making who has already been alerted by Plato or Socrates to the difference between noetic being and being for the senses, and who has abandoned the naive identification of the being of number with the being of reality as a whole, an identification which was typical of Pythagorean thought.

Then, in a second step demarcated by αὖ, there is mention made of the thing or things which have come to be, i.e., that which no longer continues in the previous indeterminacy of Becoming in the sense of constantly becoming other than it was (28 a). In speaking of such a becoming, one necessarily looks to that which it has become. And as a becoming-something it raises the question of its cause. Such a cause would imply, however, that the thing which becomes something becomes precisely that something which was somehow envisioned for it. Thus the demiurge and his envisioning of the end of Becoming are made the determining cause. Whether that which becomes a certain thing is beautiful or not, whether it is constant or transient, is dependent upon the envisioning of the demiurge. However, by nature the envisioning of the maker remains ambivalent. It can aim at that which "always is" (the constant) as its paradigm, or at that which is formless and lacking in constancy. But when that which has become is "beautiful," the envisioning must have been aimed at the Beautiful, and as an obvious consequence, "beautiful" always implies constancy.

The possibility of knowing something about the world as an ordered whole rests on precisely this two-tiered structure of Becoming, i.e., on the constant noetic order behind the surface. For the cosmos as a whole, which has the character of Becoming, is accessible per se only to the sense experience of seeing. But since the cosmos, as Becoming, must derive from something which causes it, and since there is no doubt, given the beauty of the world, that he who makes it looks to that which always is, i.e., the self-identical, it is concluded that what we perceive is not mere *gignomenon*, i.e., "always other" than it is, but instead the copy of something fixed and determinate. The possibility of really knowing something of this world of Becoming is founded, accordingly, in the copy structure of things. Of course this knowing of what becomes can only take the form of probable, credible assumptions (29 c 8). Hence the world order which displays itself to the senses can be portrayed only in a story which is told. A knowing which went beyond that "story" would be incommensurate with our human nature (29 d).

These, then, are the first results of the introductory proem. In addition it contains something like axiomatic presuppositions for the ensuing narrative which are completely reasonable, i.e., in accord with logos. Observe that nowhere is any question about the beginning of motion or Becoming asked.[4] Taken by itself, the mode of being which characterizes Becoming does not raise the question of a beginning of Becoming or of a cause of it. Only becoming-something makes this question necessary. Thus it is the envisioning of the "what" of what is being made, which is to say its being ordered, which raises the question of the cause (28 b; γίγνεται ἐξ ἀρχῆς τινος ἀρξάμενος [it comes to be in having begun from some principle]). The unordered and transient (κινούμενα is "simply there." It follows from this fact that the fundamental differentiation of modes of being with which the

---

4. Cornford, to whom in many respects a methodologically important advance beyond the enormously learned A. E. Taylor must be credited, creates a multitude of difficulties for himself by importing this question into the discussion. For Plato mere motion as on-going confusion has no "cause" at all and least of all a living one, the soul, which would never "cause" wild, chaotic movement but only circularity, rhythm, and order! In viewing the *psychē* as the source of all movement (a theory which sounds indeed like Plato's as well as Aristotle's) one may never dissociate it from the special, orderly character proper to the movement of what is *alive* and thereby reduce its work to mechanical *causality*.

exposition begins is at first not based in any way upon a paradigm–copy structure. Only secondarily when things are viewed in terms of "making" and the envisioning which guides the process of making, does the concept of the paradigm enter in. Accordingly an act of making something and of having it come to be can be guided just as easily by a bad paradigm or bad projection as by a good paradigm and a projection toward the Beautiful.

The beginning of the narration proper has a distinctive style. It has a certain hymn-like solemnity to it, but at the same time it stops short of actually mythologizing. The demiurge, who at 28 c has already been characterized as a "maker and father," is referred to here only as a producer of something. To be sure the expression "wanted to" occurs (ἐβουλήθη) (29 e) but not as an indication of a decision made at some time, and not at all as an indication of some reason for making the world. The actual motive for his productive action is never stated at all. Only the manner of his making is deduced, and deduced in a way which is odd in itself. Because he is "good," he knows no *phthonos*, no possessive, jealous hanging on to something which only he has or is. On the contrary, he wants everything to be like himself as much as possible. Obviously any speculations of the later theological sort about this maker of the world are misspent. Plato's portrayal of him can perhaps be better used to understand the Neoplatonic physics of emanation, which is similar at least in its attempt to give a purely ontological and not theological account of the genesis of the world. In any case, the demiurge of the *Timaeus* symbolizes nothing more than the conversion of a condition of disordered movement into a condition of order.[5]

But something else of significance follows from the beginning which Plato makes here. The god, because he makes something which is good and beautiful, must bring something into be-

5. In my view Cornford was right in defending this theory against Taylor. One must keep the function of the demiurge in the argument completely separate from the question of how far Plato's theology succeeds in providing an explication of popular belief on the one hand while, on the other, conforming to the demands of rigorous thinking. Precisely *this* making of the world order, the "creation" of the world, is far removed both from popular belief and from the mystery religions. Cosmogony is in essence the most extreme opposite of creation, or demiurgy.

ing which has nous. As was the case in the *Sophist* at 249 a, it is emphasized without question and apparently as self-evident that nous cannot exist without psychē, i.e., life, and further, that the god thus puts the soul (psychē) into a body. This deduction from the envisioning of the god is characterized expressly as an *eikōs logos*, which is to say that the justification for it is not a religious one which relies on traditional authority; rather, it is thought to be a matter of logical insight available to anyone that our universe is a living and reasonable being. The assumption that what lives is better, i.e., more "good" than beings of a lower level of organization, is without doubt an ontological presupposition which has not yet been justified in the dialogue. By way of explanation one might adduce that what lives is held to be better precisely because it is unified to a higher degree and has the highest awareness of its unity, which is to say that it has reason. This presupposition dominates all of Timaeus' exposition of the world entirety. A self-contained order of a Pythagorean sort, which would have the character of a mere mathematical harmony, appears not even to have come under consideration. Now just what is the status of this presupposition? Is it logos or mythos?

Whatever it might be, the constitution of "our" world is derived here from the paradigm of the ideal, unified, living, all-encompassing being. This ideal universal being includes every idea of living beings within itself, and hence it is concluded that the being of the concrete world produced by the demiurge must be equally inclusive. The conclusion is explicitly drawn that the copy must be as comprehensive as the model and that it therefore can only be one of a kind. The deduction here is a source of no small perplexity. Certainly there is nothing to prevent making repeated copies of even the most ideal paradigm, especially since an "ideal copy" is a *contradictio in adjecto*. But as a matter of fact the argument that the paradigm as such can only be one is not based upon the copy-structure which governs here but upon the idea of all-inclusive. If there were a second all-inclusive being, there would have to be a third which would include the first two and which would be the single paradigm for the genesis of our world (31 a ff.). In essence this is the well-known "third man" argument. Here it functions, not as it does in the *Parmenides*, i.e., as a paradox which militates *against* the hypothesis of imitation in general, but as an argument *for* a single model. But although the paradigm must be single, why must an imitation which only presumes to be similar be single too? Why might it not be as all-inclusive as possible? Why might it not be caught up in an approximation to the ideal of the universe? It would be convincing that the copy should be single only if one views the demiurge mythologically as a master who gives his best performance on the first try.

A closer examination reveals, however, that there is still some ancient Ionic reasoning to be heard in this argument, albeit in Eleatic form: Being, reality, is one. For the concern here is with the *unity* of the inclusiveness. If the copy is to be similar to the all-inclusive living being, then a being-alive is implied which is self-contained movement, a regular alternation or exchange completely independent from anything else. This is the basic thought, and it can be actualized in the All only if the latter has the organic nature of life. It is not necessary to pursue the consequences of this reasoning in detail, viz., the reconciliation of opposed elements among themselves achieved through mathematical proportion, the perfection of this being of the whole, its spherical form, and its self-contained circular motion.

Equally unnecessary—especially after Cornford's precise commentary—is yet another detailed investigation of how the construction of the world-soul is carried out, i.e., the principle of life and motion which, to be logical, must precede the making of the body of the All out of the elements. The description of a two-stage mixing of Selfsameness, Difference, and Being, from which the world-soul, which is to say the patterns of star motion in the heavens, is deduced has been acknowledged since ancient times to be the most mysterious and difficult section of the whole work. In part this mysteriousness may have its source in the deficiency of our knowledge of Pythagoreanism in Plato's day. Even so one should not forget that in principle such an artful literary composition as the *Timaeus* must have a certain immanent logic to it. This, of course, is completely lost sight of if, like Proclus, one bases one's understanding of the soul on the know-

ing which characterizes it rather than on the *autokinēsis* characteristic of what is alive. That the latter is the primary property of
the soul in Plato's view is demonstrated by the context. The concern at this point in the dialogue is with the *movement* of the
whole. Only secondarily (37 a) and on the basis of this first description of how the world-soul is mixed together out of the
three components, is anything like knowledge and true opinion
attributed to this soul.

Now it is indeed both understandable and significant in
many respects that the autokinēsis of the All, i.e., of the world-
soul, implies Selfsameness and Difference.[6] The function of
Selfsameness and Difference in the soul is described explicitly
(36 c), first in the movement of the fixed stars in the sky, and,
second, in the six-part division of that other astral movement,
i.e., of the sun, moon, and planets—the ecliptic, in other words,
to whose significance for the periodic changes of nature the
Greeks were singularly sensitive. And certainly it is logical that
every periodic motion must be grasped as a combination of
Selfsameness and Difference. All that remains unclear is why the
constitution of the world-soul, from which the courses of the
stars are deduced, is not produced by one simple mixing of
Selfsameness and Difference but by a carefully elaborated two-
stage process of mixing. It helps here to pay close attention to
the description of the first mixing process. It is plain that this
description is to be seen in relationship to the distinction made at
the start between *on* and *gignomenon*, what is and what becomes, for participation in both is attributed here to the psyche.
Now given the movement, activity, and life which already characterize the paradigm of our world, it is completely logical that the
psyche should participate in both. The only difficulty is that Becoming has been defined as perceivable by the senses, and Being in its selfsameness as comprehensible in thought alone. The
psyche, naturally, must be taken to be invisible. However, the intermediate status of the psyche becomes evident precisely in the
fact that since it is the thing which gives life, activates, and

6. The question of identity and difference and its relationship to motion are dealt
with extensively in Gadamer's *Hegel's Dialectic*, chap. 1. (Translator)

moves, it itself is indirectly visible in the movements of the body. And to this extent it participates in both realms. Proclus is right on this point (cf. Cornford, p. 64 ff.) and the text does indeed state clearly enough that the demiurge placed this third entity, psychē, exactly in the middle between the ideal and bodily worlds (κατὰ ταὐτὰ συνέθηκεν ἐν μέσῳ [35 a]).

But now, surprisingly, the ousia found "in" (*peri*) the bodies, the ousia which "becomes" and in which the psychē indirectly participates, is further specified as "divisible" (*meristē*) and the ousia of the selfsame, correspondingly, as "indivisible" (*ameriston*) (35 a). This is a clear reference to the extentionality which underlies all motion, as is, even more clearly, the expression, *skedastēn* (scattered) (37 a), which later is similarly juxtaposed with *ameriston*. Let us put the question aside whether, as many ancient commentators have held (e.g., Xenophanes), precisely the One and the indeterminate Two lie behind this first mixture, that is, the sources of all numbers. Whatever the case here, their significance for the constitution of time, i.e., in the establishment of the periodic rhythm and the articulation of the celestial movements, certainly becomes obvious in what follows. At 39 b it is said specifically that these movements display to mankind their participation in number and thereby show mankind what time is: counted motion. It is typical of the style of the *Timaeus*, however, that even later on, the number doctrine as such remains in the background. In any event one cannot fail to recognize an implication of this mixing process in which the psychē is engendered and which precedes the making of the heavenly bodies and mortal beings (an implication that points to the addition later of a third mode of being—spatial extension—to the two already given). That this middle thing, the psychē, then causes the specific selfsameness and difference in the periodic motions of the heavenly bodies, i.e., that it knows and participates in diverse ways in both, is made clear by Timaeus in his description of the new mixture. Difference or Otherness here becomes a necessary constituent in the periodic ordering.

The curious story of the two-stage mixture which produces the world-soul and its celestial functions has a sequel just as curious, which for the most part the commentators glibly pass over. I

mean the assigning of nous and knowing to the domain of
Selfsameness, and of opinions and firm convictions to that of
Difference. Two other texts veritably force themselves upon us
here: on the one hand, the dialectic of ideas which the *Sophist*
founds primarily in Selfsameness and Difference, and, on the
other, the corresponding distinction between the modes of human knowing in the *Republic*, for instance, which shines through
clearly here from beneath the surface. In the *Timaeus*, however,
it is the universal living being embracing all other living beings
which is under consideration. And this universal living being has
as little need of the senses as it does of nourishment or limbs.
Mention is made only of its knowledge and opinions. And if one
wants to be precise, it must be said that it can only be a matter
here of the relationship of motions "within" this universal living
being and of their being reported, as it were, to the whole of the
soul (πᾶσαν τὴν ψυχήν, 37 b). It is indeed an odd extrapolation
which proceeds from the experience of the world, had by the beings of that world, to the experience which the world has of itself. And what a peculiar logos which without sound or voice, as
it were, makes something known, evidently by nothing save its
being moved (*pheromenos*, 37 b). We are then told that this logos
serves as proof to all that such movement can happen only in the
"soul," and thus, as a sort of afterthought or appendix, the active
life and soul of the universe are confirmed. How everything is
stood on its head! Certainly anything which perceives or thinks
must be alive, and certainly Selfsameness and Difference are
part of knowing: something can only be identified *as* something,
i.e., as something different, when as itself it is identical to itself.
This fact we all know from the *Sophist*, and as a rule the commentators tend to rely on the relevant insights provided by the
Sophist. But what they fail to observe is that the *Sophist*, with an
unaccountable insensitivity to fundamental distinctions, places
Rest and Motion in the sequence of Selfsameness and Difference. And can it be said that this passage in the *Timaeus* provides
any better explanation of this peculiar fact? As a matter of fact it
might after all.[7] Existent, real Selfsameness, for example in the

---

7. For the general implications of *kinēsis* and *stasis* and their close relationship to the
heteron and the *auto* see the recent research, especially Gaiser, op. cit., p. 190.

rotation of a "standing" circling-around, and existent, real Difference, for example in the always-being-somewhere-different of a body in a circular path—perhaps these are indeed the preconditions for thinking of Selfsameness and Difference and consequently for all thinking. Thus we might well say that the order of celestial movements—in which constant relationships result, such as occur in the revolution of the heaven of fixed stars, together with the varying but not disordered or irregular relationships, such as occur in the paths of the sun, moon, and planets—are indeed the preconditions of being able to think of Selfsameness and Difference. The world offers us an example of the reliable selfsameness of the same, on the one hand, and of the varying but not irregularly shifting opinions, on the other; and it offers these, as it were, primarily to itself. What we have here is the reasonableness of the world's own order of being and motion as the world experiences it in a kind of self-awareness. But the world also offers these to the thinking observer of the heavens. That is its ἀληθὴς λόγος (true logic). Here, fortunately, we are not forced to rely on our own speculative fantasy. On the contrary, it is stated in the course of the narrative itself that the engendering of time or, in short, the revolution of the heavens, teaches man *numbers*: i.e., time, which is specifically designated as ἅμα (coeval) with the ordering of the heavens (37 b) and the illumination of the world by the sun (39 b). And later, when the mortal beings are created by the lower gods, the endowment of mortals with vision is accounted for by saying that only that gift makes awareness of time and the desire to know the physis of the universe possible. In this way the mythical narrative establishes the logical connection between movement and knowing which we inferred above.

Thus it is indeed appropriate that at this point, where the φιλοσοφίας γένος (genus of philosophy), the human desire to know, is shown to be a natural potential in man, a new theoretical, scientific element intrudes into the narrative.

And with that we have come to the real problem of the *Timaeus*. Although the Pythagorean science of number which underlies its mythical astronomy has served as a model up to modern times (cf. Kepler), the crucial question is not really in regard to the astronomy of the *Timaeus*, i.e., its celestial mathematics.

Rather, the essential problem lies in the fact that right in the middle of a detailed description of the mortal living being contained within the All, the surprising concession is made that up to this point only half of the whole has been dealt with. The first hint of this deficiency occurs at 46 cd, where it is said that the exposition has become mired down in secondary causes while the primary cause, i.e., that of the rational and logical ordering of the whole, should have been emphasized all along. Therefore the discussion of human vision, which begins in a most detailed manner, now suddenly turns to the question of the rational purpose of vision: Vision makes possible the perception of time and consequently all the other modes of knowing. But at 47 e the eventuality is squarely confronted that besides the rational purpose which determines all things there is that other cause which had been mentioned previously as Necessity (anankē).

Henceforth Plato's interest is concentrated entirely upon this secondary cause, and surprising new lines of questioning are introduced which change the whole course of the exposition. One must concede that this new orientation which Plato now demands and which he specifically characterizes as the search for another, more fundamental beginning cannot be inserted straightaway and unobtrusively into the story being told. *The entire passage 48 a to 68 e has a completely new look to it.* To be sure, mere probability is claimed for this section too and, as before, the limits of human insight are stressed repeatedly. But it is pointedly emphasized that the new explanation goes deeper than the previous one and this fact gives us an indication that it will be logically comprehensible, reasonable.

Thus we are faced with the task of following not only the mythical tale but also the theoretical explanation "for you," i.e., "you" who are mathematically trained and who can therefore follow the *logic* of the argument. We must sort out mythos and logos as they intertwine in the exposition which follows here. To all appearances there is a casual intersubstitution of mythical and theoretical elements in the text, an intersubstitution no less conspicuous than the casual, jumbled chronological back and forth in the previous narrative. Precisely this mélange of different modes of exposition is of special methodological concern to us.

As a hypothesis for our inquiry I propose that Plato deliberately put things together in this way and thus I would challenge the interpretation that Plato worked foreign ideas into his line of thought because he was incapable of doing otherwise and that he worked them in in such clumsy fashion that they are readily discernible to the critical eye. The painstaking critical investigations into the sources of Plato's thought coming from the Wilamowitz school (I. Hammer-Jensen, Eva Sachs et al.) presuppose that Plato in fact wrote so badly that one could see through his composition, as it were, and reduce it to its very poorly assimilated components. This assumption seems to me to be rather hard to reconcile with the high degree of artistic sensitivity which Plato displays throughout his work.

In his criticism of Anaxagoras in the *Phaedo* Socrates had already worked out the thought that along with the cause aimed at a reasonable purpose there is a secondary cause or, better said, coeval cause. The matter is handled in the *Timaeus* in exactly the same way (46 de). The secondary cause is what we would call the *conditio sine qua non*. Here it is redefined within a distinction between what happens "by Reason" and what happens "by Necessity." The becoming of the world is characterized as a mixture of both. That is nothing new as such. What is new, however, and different as well, is that in the *Timaeus* Reason *persuades* Necessity to bring most of what comes into being to the best conclusion possible. Thus Necessity is explicitly subordinated to the persuasion of Reason.

The introduction of "persuasion by Reason" gives the causality of Necessity an entirely new significance. As a matter of fact, the reader learns right at the start of the new beginning made here that it is a beginning which concerns (1) the nature. of the elements before the genesis of the universe and (2) the conditions preceding these elements. Attention is thereby drawn to the construction of the elements out of the elementary triangles and to the regular solids made from them. And with especial self-assurance it is announced that "No one until now has revealed how these bodies are generated" (48 b). To be sure, it is emphasized immediately thereafter that the one giving the account will accomplish his task only within limits and that, just as before, he claims nothing more than probability for what he says. (In this pronouncement and in the further course of the exposition as well, there is an implicit reference to an even more radical founding which one might quite correctly take to be Plato's number doctrine with its principles of explanation, the One and the indeterminate Two.) Still, the new beginning is not meant to be less plausibly justified than the earlier axiom distinguishing the two kinds of being, perceived and noetic, an axiom which may be said to underlie the entire exposition here. It should in fact—if I have emended the text (48 d) correctly —follow more logically from that axiom than from the preceding section. It will turn out that the proposed reduction of the elements as we know them, to that which precedes them, is to be grasped precisely as a consequence of the beginning of the dialogue.

Nevertheless, this new beginning at first appears to be related in no way to the deduction which had been promised before. On the contrary, a further distinction is made according to which the previous two types of being are now differentiated from yet a third. This third being, which is to be presented here, is an impenetrable and obscure eidos—something like a nurse who takes all that becomes up into herself. This abbreviated formulation at 49 a is more precisely explained in a number of arguments which follow (49 a ff., 50 c ff., and 51 b ff.). Only at 52 d, it might be said, is this presentation concluded.

The first argument is specifically introduced as a preliminary discussion dealing with fire and the like. Evidently the concern is to show that the elements here are not at all the stable and unchanging elements which usually figure in cosmology. Neither fire nor water is sufficiently enduring that one could say of them that they *are* this or that. The phenomena being alluded to are above all shifting aggregates and the only thing here which is truly stable and which can accordingly be designated as a "this," is the thing in which these elementary phenomena occur at any given time and from which they disappear.

In a second argument (50 a ff.) a further clarification is given. In an analogy to gold, this "in which" is now defined as an "out of which": It is that "out of which" one can make the most varied things. It assumes any form desired, since it itself has no form, and is therefore characterized as being like stuff (*ekmageion*). The problem of how individual things taking form therein can be imitations of that which truly is, the classical problem of methexis, in other words, is spoken of as a difficult question and put aside for the time being. The absence of quality and form in this third thing is illustrated by comparing it with an oil suitable for the base of an ointment. Like the oil, it is something invisible and formless, something which absorbs anything and which can be "thought of" only with the greatest difficulty (μεταλαμβάνον ἀπορώτατα τοῦ νοητοῦ) (51 b). This "something" is encountered as fire, water, earth, or air depending on the amount of what is mixed with it.

We must keep in mind that these arguments regarding the idea of the "in which" or the "out of which" underlying all appearances are explicitly designed to bring out the appearance-character and changeableness of the four elements. But in the third argument, which begins at 51 b, the consideration widens to more general matters. And only now does the differentiation of the self-identical eidos from the varying homonymous appearance of it to the senses prove to be basic for the supplementary exposition of the third *genos*, i.e., space as the seat of all that is. We see now that the determination of this third kind of being is in fact specifically founded upon the basic ontological differentiation of the first two kinds.

The interesting thing here is that once again the example of fire is made the starting point, and the question is raised again whether one must assume that fire has some sort of pure eidos. It will be recalled that fire plays a special role in Greek cosmology and in Plato too insofar as it is not only light and flame, i.e., gentle and destructive fire, but something present everywhere there is warmth. In every warm living thing there is fire. When Plato, using precisely fire as his illustration, emphasizes that the pure eidos accessible only to thought must necessarily be distinguished from the changing points of view in which something is given to the senses, he has deliberately chosen a sharply disputed example—as is also indicated in the *Parmenides* at 130 c, where fire and water are mentioned. Can anything be purer fire than the flame which bursts out of something heated? Or even purer than the light which beams from a steady flame? Is not the assumption of an eidos here a vain duplication? Is it not empty, as Aristotle often critically remarks—in words in the *Nicomachean Ethics* at A 4, incidentally, which are reminiscent of the *Timaeus* at 51 c?

In any event, the exposition of the third genos, space, which follows in this third argument may be termed the most logically precise of all. It is said of this *chōra* that it may be "touched," so to speak, in a kind of inauthentic thought, but this does not mean that it is reached by the senses. Evidently what is meant is that the pure "that" of any given thing is something which we experience as space, much as in first touching something we hit upon it without being able to identify it *as* what it is. Plato calls this way of becoming aware of space (as a consequence of which everything which is for us is at a place and takes up room) dreaming, and he alludes to something else which is similarly encountered as its "sibling." Number and size seem to be meant (cf. Diels, Archytas, frag. 1). What, however, does dreaming as opposed to waking mean here? In the text one finds that when we are awake, we are not able to differentiate properly as long as the dream still has hold of us. That which we are not able to differentiate properly and which evidently only the truly awakened, the philosopher, can differentiate is the inner segmentation of existing appearances, an inner segmentation which allows us to call the outward appearance a copy or image. (Cf. the *Republic*, 476 c, where dreaming is called taking τὰ μετέχοντα for αὐτὸ, the things participating in the form for the thing itself). An image does not exist by itself; rather it exists in pointing to something. It always makes something else evident. However, precisely because it brings something other than itself to the fore, it must be distinct from that other thing. A picture can be a picture only to the extent that it is not the same thing as what it pictures, but something on its own. On the other hand, a picture is a picture only if it does not visibly assert itself but instead brings only what it pictures to the fore. Using this dialectical structure of the picture as a basis, Timaeus is able to isolate the mere "in which" or "out of which," respectively, in which the being of any image comes to be. The image must be *in* something and made *out of* something other than that of which it is an image. Otherwise it cannot be a picture or an image at all. In distinction from true being, which always is what it is, i.e., which either is this *or* something different, an image is always simultaneously one and the same thing *and* two different things (52 d).

Note what this difficult and compressed discussion demands of us. We must think of the third genos, i.e., space, the pure "in which" as such, precisely by thinking of any thing which shows up in it, any thing which appears not as the thing itself but as the copy or image of a paradigm. What we have here is thus not a new thought which overcomes the difficulties of the paradigm conception of ideas but, on the contrary, a deeper discussion of precisely the copy-paradigm relationship itself, a discussion which forces us to postulate this third genos, the chōra. The analogy of the *eikōn* structure given here fully deserves to be termed "reasonable indeed" (λόγῳ μᾶλλον). Cornford is right when he says (p. 196), "In this passage Plato comes nearer than anywhere else in the *Timaeus* to the problem of the *eidōlon*." The important basic structure of the eidōlon, its being precisely that which it should not be, is fully brought to light here. And the reasoning here is truly a δι' ἀκριβείας ἀληθὴς λόγος (logical argument valid because of its accuracy) (52 c): The eidōlon is simultaneously one and two. This is the clearest reference to the doctrine of the Two which I can find in the *Timaeus*. Cornford is correct (idem) in citing Gorgias: δύο γενήσεται τὸ ὄν τόπος τε καὶ σῶμα (Being will become two: place and body) and the *Parmenides*, 138 a—both passages devoted as they are to the Eleatic aporia of the ἐν ᾧ (the "in which"). But what seems impossible for Being, as the Eleatic thinkers conceived of it, is what emerges positively here as the heterotēs structure of the eikōn. While it is the determining characteristic of Being to be what it is and nothing different, it is precisely the ontological characteristic of the copy, the mere appearance, not to be what it is. Its being, i.e., *what* it is, is in reality distinct from its spatial position. Thus along with Being and Coming-into-Being there is space. The exposition here seems logically convincing indeed and deserves to be placed alongside

the critique of the Eleatics found in the *Sophist.* But who could
foresee that this excogitation of the third mode of being, of the
chōra, paves the way for a deeper insight into the structure of
the being of the so-called elements?

After all, one tends to forget the announced goal of the
discussion, which must constantly be kept in mind: the elements,
as they appear to us, are to be traced back to something which
lies behind them. This is completely lost from view after the conclusion of the discussion of the third genos. At that point a description is given of how this third thing, receptive as it is to all
the given elements, takes them up in itself. But it receives them
in an as yet wholly unordered form and simultaneously is moved
by them and moves them. It shakes them, and shakes them in
such a way that prior to any world order a certain pre-ordering
of the elements is established "insofar as that can occur without
the god being involved in it" (53 d). One is led to expect, and indeed one finds in the text, that when the god himself puts his
hand to it, this pre-ordering will become the actual world order
"in accordance with form and number," as that actual order is
brought about by the god through the application of the geometrical proportion (31 b ff.).

At this point I diverge from the usual explanation of Plato's
line of thought here because I have been unable to arrive at anything reasonable by pursuing it. To me it seems obvious that this
difficult section can be coherently integrated into the whole only
if it is interpreted as follows. The mythological god does not participate in constituting the elements geometrically. He takes over
pre-ordered elements and creates the world out of them. This
does not become evident right away because here, just as later,
one does not expect that in the middle of "logical" explanation
Plato would again return to the mythical tale. One should not be
misled, however, by the fact that the turn of speech, "according
to form and number" (εἴδεσιν καὶ ἀριθμοῖς) is used later in reference to the constituting of the elements geometrically. On the
contrary, that it is, is precisely the point of what follows. Even in
the realm of the *necessary*, where everything moves as if it were
being shoved and bumped (cf. 46 e), the ordering principles of
form and number, which the demiurge has in mind, have the ef-

fect of making Necessity accommodating and amenable to the persuasion of Reason. In my view the previous explanations of this difficult section (Taylor, Cornford, and, more recently, Crombie might be named here as the most important contributors) fall short of reaching an accurate understanding of this text because *all of them fail to pay heed to the abrupt change in the mode of discourse here*. That may be because the relationship of the demiurge to the chaos with which he is confronted is thought of too much in terms of a creator to his creation (Taylor: cf. above on the distortions in the Christian interpretation) or because all of them make the god do mathematics in those places where it is we ourselves who can explain what occurs mathematically by an eikōs logos. Not only is it the case that demiurge does not create but instead merely puts what is disordered in order; the truly decisive point is that he orders what is pre-ordered. The crux of the argument here is that the god has to deal with a "mass" which is pre-ordered according to Necessity. To be specific, the initial chaos of the four elements is ordered in two ways. It is ordered by the automatic shaking movement. But beyond that, the fact that there are *four* elements derives from a hitherto undiscussed lawfulness of space whose necessity is *logically* understandable quite apart from any teleological intentions of a mythological demiurge. The privileged forms of spatiality, those which constitute regular solids capable of being circumscribed with a circle, make the elements possible and thereby give the elementary state of the world displaying the "first traces of order" a reality all its own. One must pay close attention to the fact that Timaeus nowhere makes the mythological god responsible for these processes preceding the elements; rather the god has delivered to him the coarsely pre-ordered elements from which the world is actually fabricated. He has evidently "persuaded" anankē to provide him with an appropriately pre-structured material.[8] But even if the god is not involved in the entire mechanical pre-ordering, he knows just how to put Necessity to use. To make that clear and to keep the focus on anankē in the analysis which ensues, Timaeus calls attention again to the general prin

8. More on the matter of the god's persuasion of anankē follows below.

ciple that everything which the god makes, he makes as beautiful and good *as is possible.*

I do not find anything here of the ensuing derivation of the elements from the triangles and regular solids.[9] The text provides nothing more than a repetition of the continuing theme that the reason of the maker brings about the beauty of what is made. But immediately after this repetition, which brings the mythical motif back into focus and which a modern reader would therefore hardly expect, we find something surprising and astonishing. The attempt is made to present the ordering (*diataxis*) and origination (*genesis*) of the elements themselves for "you," i.e., for you mathematicians who can follow the account given, and to present it "in an unaccustomed exposition" quite apart from any mythical tale (53 b, 54 a).[10] As specifically stated as this might be, the transition remains deceptively unobtrusive, and for that reason, it seems to me, it has never been dealt with precisely enough in the literature on Plato. The tone of what follows is noticeably different. Timaeus is no longer the narrator of a myth; rather he is now the exponent of a logical theory. It is also striking that Timaeus places great value on the propaedeutic mathematical training of those with whom he is conversing, and one sees right away that the concern here is not only with geometry but also with the latest accomplishment of the mathematics of that time, stereometry. As early as the *Republic* reference is made to stereometry (528 b), and the *Epinomis* at 990 d already uses the accepted term. Beyond this it is pointedly stated that the concern here is with a "logos with a plausible necessity to it" (53 d), a necessity evident not specifically to divine wisdom but to the speaker's own intelligence and insight in regard to certain mathematical matters. Accordingly, the following deduction is

9. Cornford is of course correct when he does not burden the elements, which are given a preliminary ordering in the shaking process, with the mathematical constituting of themselves. But he is mistaken in the belief that they are only subsequently constructed in this rational way by the demiurge. They are ordered proportionally by him after they have been pre-ordered mathematically by Necessity.

10. The text does not seem to me to admit of any other interpretation. The god orders the world and we know it *as well as possible.* But at this point (νῦν δ'οὖν, 53 b 6) the genesis of the elements themselves is to be considered, and the "unaccustomed exposition" now begins.

based upon the geometrical structure of the plane and, in particular, the plane geometry of the triangle. One sees too that an extraordinary feature of the corporeal per se now begins to play a role: namely, the mathematically demonstrable fact that there are five and only five regular solids and that their transformation into one another is possible because they are in part constructed of the same triangles. Still the connection of this exposition with what came before it is barely articulated. And oddly enough the question of how this mathematical account of the solids relates to the third genos, the chōra, is not stressed at all.

The fact that this transition is not emphasized—i.e., that the relationship between the doctrine of the third genos of reality, the chōra, and the constituting of the elements from the mathematical structures of the triangle and regular solids is never clarified though it was clearly said that it would be (cf. 48 b)—helps to explain why the irrelevant question of individuation is often introduced by commentators into the discussion of the chōra. Even if one grasps that space could only be the *principium individuationis* in combination with time and not by itself alone, one has still not picked up the actual line of thought. Plato has something entirely different in mind when he points out that the chōra is an inevitable implication of understanding the world in terms of copy or image. In the realm of that other cause, Necessity, something of a reasonable sort, although itself without active reason, was to be displayed, viz., the structural regularity of space which accommodates the demiurge in his ordering of the world and gives him a head start, so to speak. The question, therefore, is not how the individual thing comes to exist as individual. Rather the point is that the potential of anything to be an individual thing depends upon the overall *lawfulness* of space. The consideration of the chōra is motivated solely by the question of how within what is irrational and unreasonable, "reason," i.e., a logically understandable necessity, still prevails.

Of course the unobtrusiveness of the transition here reinforces the point that Necessity, as it is displayed in, and made comprehensible by, the theory which follows, is subservient to the higher purpose of the ordering of the world by the reasonable god. But one misses Plato's intent if one fails to see that for the following the mythological god is no longer the originator and orderer. That he is not is expressly presupposed for the whole realm which we now find ourselves investigating. Along with the divine cause there is that other cause, Necessity. In itself this is nothing new, but the surprising thing here vis-à-vis the *Phaedo*, for example, which also contains that insight, is that this Necessity is seen to favor the beautiful and that it forms figures (triangles and solids) which from the point of view of *Reason* are special. This favoritism, as it were, is what is to be displayed here.

Accordingly, the following theory is treated *as a theory*, i.e., as an eikōs logos, and for the time being there is no mention of the god. Only at the end of the derivation of the regular solids is it said abruptly that "there is, to be sure, yet a fifth figure, but the god makes use of that in pre-schematizing the All" (55 c). In respect to the chronology of the genesis of the world this is to be understood as follows: the god makes use *later* of the dodecahedron, which was left over.[11] What we have here is an anticipation of what comes later insofar as in this context only the construction of the regular solids is under discussion and not at all their application or distribution in constructing the cosmos. Obviously this anticipation is not wasted. It has the purpose of justifying the omission of the construction of the dodecahedron here. But it does not prove at all that the god is at work where the construction of the elements is concerned. Mathematics is indeed a divine thing, but it requires no god to do it.

One would have reason to expect that the actual application of the regular solids in making the transition from truths of rea-

---

11. Not, for instance, as one reads in the standard interpretations, that the fifth element had already been put to (that) use by the god. The dodecahedron is not actually constructed here because it is not necessary for constituting the four elements. The expression, διαζωγραφεῖν (sketching) is virtually a ἅπαξ λεγόμενον (onetime occurrence). It is absurd to relate it to the celestial circle of the animals (Plutarch 1003 d). But on the other hand, it is plausible that the workman develops an outline or circumspection, as it were, of the universe and makes use of that regular solid which best approximates the area of the circle. In support of the thesis that in δία the schematizing act of circumscription as in διαγραφεῖν is implied, cf. *Republic* 501 a, and Aristotle, *Topics* 105 b 13. With the word διαζωγραφεῖν, Plato does seek to remind us that it is a ζῷον (living thing) which is being outlined, namely, the universe.

son to contingent vérités de fait would be carried out by the mythical god, but even that appears not to be the case. Timaeus is not concerned with how the actual elements come to be out of the stereometric bodies. He simply states that they do, while presuming that there are plausible patterns in the process of their constitution. All this is argued as something which we mathematicians understand. The transition into the actuality of visible nature as such is never described. It is alluded to but one time. At 56 c it is said that *we* notice the regular solids in the form of elements only when the tiny particles appear massed together.

To be sure, at the end of this theory of the constituting of the world there is again mention of the god, who is said to put what exists together in correct proportion according to number, motion, and other *dynameis* (potentialities) to the degree that Necessity permits. I for one doubt that even here one should attribute preliminary insights into modern molecular chemistry to the god. If to anyone, it is Timaeus himself to whom they should be attributed. At 57 d the task of uncovering something like a molecular structure is specifically assigned to the natural scientist and there is no indication given at all that he would thereby be investigating what the god has designed. The following passages too are concerned exclusively with motion and such things *which are caused by Necessity*. Thus one must view the passages in which the god is mentioned as references to the mathematical, proportional rules which the *mythical* god brings into being subsequent to the *logical* pre-constituting of the elements by Necessity. The god is like man: Just as the latter first perceives the appearance of elements once their minute corporal components have massed together, so analogously, the god first orders them once they have been pre-ordered.[12] That is the way it had been described

12. The καὶ δὴ καί (56 c 3) and the following infinitive construction are obviously dependent upon the same δεῖ which governs the "massing" and "becoming visible." Thus the god is not involved in the original constituting of the elements but only completes that constituting by putting the elements together according to proportion. How the ὑπ' αὐτοῦ in the traditional text is to be tied in, escapes me. As an addition to ὑπεῖκεν? Or to ἀποτελεσθεισῶν, in other words, "under his aegis"? But even if one prefers to view διευχηματίσαιτο (59 b) as meaning that the god joins in the constituting of the elements—something quite possible given the ambiguity of the text—the dominant and clear separation of nous and anankē forces us to restrict the god's activity to persuasion.

at 31 b ff. and so it is described again in the recapitulation at the conclusion of this exposition of Necessity and its effects (69 b)—and, incidentally, with specific repetition of the guiding concept here, *analogia* (69 b and 56 c).

It follows, then, that the constituting of the regular solids and their correspondence to the four traditional (Empedoclean) elements is a product of Necessity—a Necessity which, of course, is reasonable, i.e., logically understandable and accommodating to Reason. To be sure, this entire exposition is only a theory in the modern sense of the word, that is, a hypothetical eikōs logos which by itself is not necessarily the ultimate truth. The narrator himself points this out repeatedly. He not only emphasizes it at the "new beginning" where Necessity is first treated (48 cd); also in founding the theory of the elements anew in the doctrine of the elementary triangles he leaves the question open whether a god, or for that matter a man loved by the gods, might know even more radically fundamental truths. There is a definite indication here (as in the *Republic*, bk. 6) that above geometry stand the numbers and in particular the "beginnings" of all numbers, the One and the Two. Finally another qualification is appended to the characterization of the regular solids. Their mathematical structure is not challenged; also not challenged is the fact that there are four specific elements among the visible bodies which correspond to them (53 e). However, the possibility of another construction in the constitution of the elements out of those particularly appropriate triangles is acknowledged. It is

---

The entire exposition which follows never mentions any involvement of the god. If one entrusts the god with the mathematical construction of the elements, as the interpreters of 53 b 5 are all wont to do, then one could indeed interpret Timaeus' statements here as the continuation of a homogeneous narrative. But I cannot figure out what the shaking of the elements and their being massed together would mean in this case, since the elements have characteristics of their own (ἴχνη μὲν ἔχοντα αὑτῶν ἄττα [53 b 2]). If fire exists already, it is already constituted as a pyramid, and only its distribution over the universe and the resultant massing, making it visible and nameable, have not yet occurred. In order to allow the demiurge his mathematical work, Crombie assumes that the prior condition of fire described at 53 ab is that of crude pyramids, which the demiurge refines according to "figure and number." But there is not a single word of this in the text, and it would be a peculiar idea indeed if the mathematical construction of fire particles were to be prepared in such a mechanical way. Cf. 56 c, where, after the completion of the construction of the elements, the massing of the invisible particles and, *subsequent to that*, the action of the god are discussed. 73 c also confirms my point here.

easy to see why. The mathematics of the time had proved the earlier point that there are only these five regular solids.[13] On the other hand, the characterization of the kinds of triangles suitable for the construction of these solids is obviously not founded upon any mathematical theorem (λόγος πλείων [extended account] [54 b]) regarding special triangles. The question of how these mathematical truths actually determine nature, that is, the elements and the differentiated constructions out of these elements, is never broached at all.

There is at the most one passage where one could find an explicit, substantive discussion of our contingent world, and that is in the restatement of the question of whether there is one world or a multiplicity of worlds (55 d). I am certain that the fact that five possible worlds are allowed derives in part at least from the thesis of the five regular solids and not primarily from ancient Pythagorean teachings, as many learned scholars have claimed. And beyond that, the regular solids are the only five bodily forms to be deduced from the geometry of the triangle which can fit within a sphere, that is to say, which can be applied as the inner structure of the perfect archetype of the universe, the sphere. It was specifically demonstrated earlier by an eikōs logos that "our" order is indeed the only one for us. This fact makes it all the more striking that other systems are said to be possible at all, and an indication of the contingency of our world might be found here.

However, that is of no consequence in our attempt to establish a clear distinction between the work of the god and the work of Necessity. According to what has been said and according to the deduction of 31 b, another construction of the world is conceivable only if it is out of the same elementary bodies and if another of the regular solids is used for the sphere-diagram. But what would that change? Should one imagine other distributions of the regular solids among the elements such that there would be another element? For instance a fifth element, such as we find in Aristotle? Idle speculation! The sole philosophical

13. It is unlikely that anyone nowadays would approve of Taylor's search for historical accuracy in Plato and would want to hold Plato to the state of science in 420 B.C. because of a discussion supposedly "played out" in that year.

significance of this odd suggestion of Plato's lies in the distinction made between "possibilities" and the single actual world. The stereometrical theory of space underlying this distinction is completely independent of any mythological "intentions" of the demiurge, and the theory could not be different in any other world. This is an insight of which Plato may justly be proud and which for the first time offers us something to juxtapose with the boundless contingency of the boundlessly many worlds postulated in earlier theories.

Certainly one must ask oneself here how the possibility of five worlds (55 d) is to be reconciled with the "logical" demonstration that this is the only world (31 a). The earlier argument seemed absolutely cogent: What encompasses must eo ipso be all encompassing and therefore single. Of course at 31 a this is demonstrated only for the *paradigm*. That it follows *mutatis mutandis* that our world can only be one, is, as has been shown, not logically convincing at all. Now in the later passage only the possibility is granted of looking *eis allo* (to other facts) and of then assuming that there are other worlds (*hetera*). It seems certain to me that these *alla* (others) are the other possible internal structures of a round, all-encompassing universe, i.e., that the other four regular solids are meant. At the same time it seems clear to me that the contingency of our world as *pephukota* (generated) is being described here, a contingency which is established by an eikōs logos. It appears, then, that the next passage is meant to be taken as follows. There are five possible structures of the world. Each of these could provide a structure for the archetypal spherical universe. In this way the logical argument deriving from the essence of the "all-inclusive" would be left untouched. Or, more precisely, although five plans for the universe are conceivable—which is to say not infinitely many worlds or plans—for us the dodecahedron makes the most sense. But however that might be, the existent universe is one and the framework for the elements can now be built into it: καὶ τοῦτον μὲν μεθετέον (and him [who looks to other worlds] we let pass) (55d).

Without doubt this passage is in response to theories (Democritus?) according to which the void, which is to say the empty structure of space, admits of any number of world formations. Against this thesis Timaeus argues that space admits of only five types of construction. Whether this view is meant as a counter to Anaximander's *ekkrisis* (separating out) or to Dem-, ocritus seems to me not all that significant. But it is important to understand why at this point where the genesis of the world is no longer being considered as a pure story (mythos) but as a process to be comprehended by reason, the possibility of re-peated geneses of the world is focused upon. Of course that means geneses "at another place" and not "at another time," for the latter would imply coming-into-being and passing-away, something which cannot be properly reconciled with the basic idea of physis as a cyclical, balanced order. However, the argu-ment on the all-inclusive character of the universe seems di-rected against any possibility of another genesis of the world. That argument is now reasserted as an eikōs logos and no revi-sions of it are called for. The ideal world is the only world. If the new argument is taken as a plan of construction of schematic or-dering, it proves to be quite compatible with the necessity that only one of these plans could have come to be executed. This in-terpretation is supported by the fact that at 31 a 2 and b 3 the word used is *ouranos* (heavens), and *kosmos* only at b 2, which in this context means the same thing as ouranos. However, 55 d follows directly upon the comment on the god's diazogram (i.e., the actual construction based on the dodecahedron) and its rela-tionship to the *pan* (All), and it obviously refers to the world "structure."

The five possible construction plans of the single universe could then indeed be reconciled with the designation of the do-decahedron to be that actual structure of the world which best approximates the space defined by the sphere. Thus one can say that the problem of the contingency of the world is the actual concern of the entire exposition here. The fact that it is the god who *makes use* of the dodecahedron for the construction of the world (a point specifically accentuated) confirms indirectly that the god is not immediately involved in the construction of the in-dividual elements.

If one keeps in mind the conclusion to which our analysis has led, i.e., that the mythical god is not at work everywhere in

the whole process but instead only takes over the result of a previous formation, the significance of the sole act attributed to
him becomes clear, the act, that is, of having "persuaded" Necessity. *That is the mythical way of stating the mathematical, rational truths
which the mathematics of the time had uncovered in the structure of
space.* Or is there some other way to understand the talk of "persuasion"?[14] One might take it to mean the whole of the god's
utilization of anankē in the task of producing the beautiful world
order. The result of this persuasion would then be that Necessity
allows itself to be worked into a design oriented toward the
beautiful—it obeys voluntarily, in other words, because it has
been persuaded. In particular the passage at 56 c could be understood in this way: ἡ τῆς ἀνάγκης ἑκοῦσα πειθεῖσά τε φύσις
ὑπεῖκεν (Nature as governed by Necessity has submitted, having
voluntarily allowed itself to be persuaded). But is it really the
case that a demiurge, even if it were a mere human one, would
find it necessary to talk nature and its "necessities" into allowing
him to make of them what he considers good? In the comparable
passages of the *Phaedo* and the *Laws* it seems to me that nous is
assigned no such diplomatic task. And in the *Timaeus* itself,
where the secondary causes are first introduced (49 de), there is
no mention made of such a task of persuasion and also none, incidentally, in the concluding general discussion at 69 a. Yet there
is mention made of it directly before the introduction of the
third genos (space) with all its consequences (48 a). And right
afterward, evidently as a consequence of the successful persuasion of anankē, comes the whole protracted story (introduced at
48 a by οὖν) of the chōra and the triangles and regular solids.
And again, only directly following this story and the assignment
of the elements to their places do we find something repeated of
the successful persuasion of anankē. This gives weight to the argument that the persuasion is not a matter of subordinating
anankē but of reaching a certain kind of accommodation with it.
If I understand it correctly, this accommodation consists in the
fact that anankē, since it includes the chōra within itself as the
necessary presupposition of the appearance of every thing, al-

14. I am indebted to Kurt von Fritz for the idea of this more precise exposition.

ready proves to be beautiful itself—this without any insight into
the use in the world order which the demiurge intends to make
of the beautiful regularities. Ananke itself has no "intentions"
such as those of a mythical god. Plato uses the metaphor of being
merely persuaded to express just this fact, and in my view, the
metaphor is most illuminating. He who is merely persuaded
gives in without seeing why. But he does not give in just pas-
sively; rather he does what he himself wishes to do: ἑκοῦσα . . .
ὑπεῖκεν. Ananke acts as if it itself wanted the beautiful when it
accepts those regular solids which can be constructed out of triangles: προαιρετέον οὖν αὖ τῶν ἀπείρων τὸ κάλλιστον (And
from the infinite number the most beautiful are to be chosen)
(54 a). If one interprets this particular persuasion of ananke in
this way, one will accept the mythical mode of discourse generally, without being disconcerted by the clear distinction between
nous and ananke. It was a triumph and a completely new insight
when one realized that the priority of the Beautiful exists not
only when someone makes something according to plan and with
a specific teleological intention for it, that is, not only when the
enduring forms of order, the νοητὰ εἴδη (noetic forms) are envisioned ahead of time by a maker. Among the rational, demonstrable spatial structures of the regular solids there are certain
privileged ones—per se and of Necessity. They are Plato's five
solids and these are constructed out of two selected privileged
types of triangles. Their ability to be so constructed is what gives
the new stereometry its mathematical rationality. Their bodies
derive from the geometry of the triangle. And not only that. At
least three of them (not, Plato says, the hexahedron and the
cube) can be constructed from the same type of triangle. Accordingly a construction of the Beautiful in special solids in space
made out of the same mathematical element, i.e., the triangle
specifically designated, is possible.

It has to be this fact which led Plato to the "physical" application of mathematics. The four elements, of course, were conceived of by Empedocles. But Empedocles' theory was inadequate to account for the shifting condition of aggregate entities.
If something fluid becomes solid—if water becomes ice, for
example—the transformation cannot be explained by a change

in the mixture of the elements. It is, after all, the same thing which is first water and then becomes ice, and then, upon melting, water again. It was Plato's concern, in constructing the three regular solids from a specific triangle, to find an intelligible model to explain what the mixture theory could not. Necessity accounts here for a visible process. Further, it is by no means an embarrassment that this possibility of construction from the same triangle is given only for the three solids subsequently assigned to fire, air, and water and that the cube alone, earth, can only be constructed out of an isosceles triangle. There is indeed evidence in nature for the special status of earth in the meteorological processes, evidence which would provide a defensible argument even against Aristotle.

Plato's "emendation" of the previous, all too general proposals of the dialogue increases the credibility of the explanation given and for that reason the "emendation" is made at this point (54 b).

In further elaborating on the mathematical pre-formation of the elements, Timaeus now adds details to the account which had begun with the shaking of the chōra—although only in what he himself calls a playful speculation (59 cd). In a prefatory recapitulation the argument is reinforced that the elements can be named only once they have first been arranged by the ordering hand of the god (69 b). I see no reason here to tie this arranging by the god to the mathematical construction of the elements. On the contrary, the reflections which conclude the exposition of anankē make as clear as one could desire that the demiurge *takes over* the products of anankē for his production of the universe (παρελάμβανεν [68 e]), that he makes use of them. However, it is repeated that the "good" in what happens (τὰ γιγνόμενα) comes from him (68 e; cf. 29). It is evident, then, that one must count among the effects of anankē the entire self-perpetuating meteorological process described in the previous section (cf., for example, 58 c). The difference between the two causes, the necessary and the divine, is obvious enough. The necessary is that without which what we want to happen would not be possible, while the divinely caused is always chosen only insofar as it helps in the attainment of a happy life. In short, in matters of Necessity there is no choice; the laws of necessity *must* be observed. Even when they are good and useful, they are not designed with that in mind. On the contrary, a number of possibilities can be thought of for anything which can be made using them as a basis, and among these possibilities the demiurge always selects those which are best for what he actually wants, i.e., the happy life. That holds for the universe as a whole; its form is described as that of a complete and perfect *living* being. It also holds for the "divine" star constellations and, beyond that, for the θνητὰ ζῷα (mortal living things) which the demiurge leaves to the lower gods. The lower gods do their best too although they must use a material incapable of immortality.

The remaining narrative is a well nigh impenetrable mixture of clever invention and ingenious adaptation of traditional theories.[15] The conclusion of the dialogue assumes the style of a hymn and is thus reminiscent of its august beginning.

*   *   *

I believe that the account which I have given here establishes the logic and internal coherence of Plato's exposition of the constituting of the four elements according to the tenets of his atomic theory as well as of his integration of that constitutive process into the ordering of the world by the demiurge. But prima facie, at least, the question of how this coherent theory in the *Timaeus* relates to the dialectic of the later Plato remains a problem. The *Parmenides*, with its reduction to an aporia of each hypothesis proposed, seems to have no relationship to what goes on here, nor does the unified theoretical and literary complex

---

15. Even so, the idea that the god himself only receives the mathematically prestructured (and mechanically pre-ordered) elements and purposively orders them, is maintained here throughout, as is shown indirectly by the (isolated) reference to the creation of marrow μυελός [73 b]). The god is concerned with mathematically prestructured elementary material. To be sure, he chooses the smoothest among the triangles by sorting them out from their *genera*. But since it is then said that he mixes them symmetrically (μειγνὺς . . . σύμμετρα), it is tacitly presupposed that he chooses elements made of the smoothest triangles and that from among all triangular elements he mixes these smoothest ones together to make marrow. Plato's way of putting things here can only be understood as *pars pro toto* and it does not justify naming the god as even a co-worker in constituting the elements stereometrically, and even less calling him a geometrician.

of the *Theaetetus*, *Sophist*, and *Statesman*. At the most it could be said that the meaning of heterotēs, of difference, is made clear (as was shown above) but only in the most general way and primarily in its cosmological function as the "circle of otherness." And there is no mention at all of the *dialectical* problems contained in the participation of things in the ideas and of the ideas in one another. Indeed, these problems are specifically set aside here. Insofar as it provides the basis for the mythical figure of the demiurge and all his activity, the doctrine of ideas is presupposed unabashedly, even for the things of nature, and not subjected to questioning at all. The hierarchical order advanced in the *Parmenides* in support of the supposition of the ideas—a hierarchy which places mathematical and moral entities at the highest level of credibility while "man" and "fire" are only reluctantly acknowledged to exist on the third level—plays no role in the *Timaeus*. Indeed, the mythical adaptation of the technē model for the ordering of the world seems evidently intended to dodge the issue of the ideas, as J. Stenzel pointed out.[16]

Nevertheless, one must ask what the consequences are of our "demythologizing" of the *Timaeus* and what connection the line of thought thereby exposed has with the dialectic contained in Plato's doctrine of ideas. In so doing one must avoid getting involved in that old and fruitless game played by scholars from Proclus to Cornford, the game, that is, of seeking correspondences with other dialogues. Plato's dialogues are each complete movements of discussion and thought, movements which one must enter into oneself and pursue to their conclusion. One cannot interpret them in departing from comparable individual statements which one finds in them. This must even be said in regard to what is without doubt the most obvious correspondence of the *Timaeus* to Plato's other works, i.e., to the *Philebus*. The correspondence lies in the fact that both dialogues directly apply the doctrine of ideas to knowing "our" world or "our" life. On this basis the *Timaeus* develops a physics and the *Philebus* an ethics, or practical doctrine. One should note that unlike the *Re-*

---

16. *Arete und Diairese, Studien zur Entwicklung der platonischen Dialektik von Sokrates zu Aristoteles* (Leipzig, 1917).

public, the *Philebus* does not inquire about the idea of the Good and its function as a paradigm for human life; rather its questioning is the opposite of that. It asks how the concrete life of human beings with all its contingency and impurity, and determined as it is by impulse and pleasure just as much as by knowledge and insight, can nevertheless be "good," i.e., can participate in the Good. Similarly, the world ordering described in the *Timaeus* is derived from the "axioms" of the doctrine of ideas, to be sure, but the task in the *Timaeus* is obviously to combine teleological and mathematical-mechanical causal explanation. Thus we do have a special case here which warrants seeking illumination of one dialogue by comparing it with another. As a matter of fact the *Philebus* provides what the *Timaeus* still owed us, as it were: an explicit linking of the problem of the dialectic of the ideas with the ordering of that reality which heretofore had been shunted aside as a mere adjunct to Not-being—specifically, the reality of our human life.

Of course no solution to the intricate problem of participation is offered in the *Philebus*. On the contrary, it is presupposed as self-evident that the aporia of participation arrived at in the radicalization of the dialectic in the *Parmenides* (viz., that no knowledge of the ideas at all is possible for human beings) is somehow wide of the mark. Indeed, all forms of knowledgeable ordering of reality systematize a multiplicity of eidē. Thus one can speak of knowledge of ideas only insofar as that means a determination of the indeterminate in which each idea achieves its full definition within the unity of such a system. This holds just as much for the system of vocal sounds as for the phonetic system of written letters and, finally, for the theory of modes and notes in music. These examples are instances of the scientific ordering of a specific field of reality, the conceptual underpinnings of which are to be found in the ancient Pythagorean categories of the *peras* and the apeiron. All systematic numerical determination establishes firm bounds and definition within the measureless and boundless. Thus ultimately even the idea of right living is reduced to the right harmonic mixture in which everything measureless receives its determination. However, this always occurs in such a way that the determinacy is sought and found within the measureless and indeterminate. Thus, where determinacy is not achieved or where it ceases to obtain, one must let the matter drop and leave it to indeterminacy (ἐὰν εἰς τὸ ἄπειρον).

Now one can also say that the creation of the world by the demiurge (or, to say the same thing, the knowing of the world by men) is every bit as much a kind of determination of the indeterminate, an ordering of the unordered. Certainly it is just as true in physics as it is in ethics that ordering is made possible by reason or, better said, that reason perceives the *possible* order and is therefore able to undertake bringing it about.

In a sense, however, the mythical portrayal in the *Timaeus* is meant to be a deeper founding than that which the Socratic reflection about right living in the *Philebus* can provide. Here, instead of man who learns to seek and produce order in himself, the constitutional order of the world itself is under consideration. Of course it is evident in the *Philebus* too that the Good and the order of reality as a whole are the real concern. Viewed from man's perspective, however, the indeterminate appears only as the realm which cannot be subjected to determination, into which one "lets the matter drop." Now the given order of the world presents the demiurge, who exercises the proper "practice" which one calls "nature," with a general limitation. He can only do what is possible. *But the "possible" does not restrict him; rather it is more like an ontological opportunity.* Only because of the reason already displayed in the realm of Necessity does the beautiful ordering of the visible world become possible at all. Only because of the cooperation of Necessity is the demiurge able to bring about the ordering of the heavens, i.e., create the gods and order nature on earth. And even more, it should be emphasized that the ordering of reality as that is explicated in the *Timaeus* comes before any and all human possibilities of acting, of any ordering of some thing or ordering of one's own life. This is the express point of the whole narrative. The constitution of the world is meant as the foundation for the possible constituting of human life and human society or, stated more accurately, for the possible realization of an ideal human constitution of the soul and of the state. One hears again and again in the narrative of the *Timaeus* that human beings should learn to order the motions of their own soul while regarding the order of the cosmos. To be sure, what is said in the *Timaeus* to hold for the action of the gods holds no less for the action of men. Even when the god does his best, does the best thing possible, he is dependent upon the Necessary. It may well be that his actions are aimed per se at achieving orderliness, but even so his ordering activity is not given unlimited possibilities but instead pre-determined ones. He is given a field of open possibilities in which his attempt to order and arrange may be played out. It is no different in human practice. In the competition with Philebus Socrates fights to win only the second prize for phronēsis. And things look the same for the "ideal state." The utopian vision which functions in Plato as the overall framework for inquiry does not claim in any way to escape the real preconditions and necessities of the human political and social task. After the *Republic* comes the *Timaeus*.

8

Amicus Plato Magis Amica Veritas

The formulation, "amicus Plato magis amica veritas," in precisely those words can be traced directly only to the high Middle Ages, but ultimately it goes back to Aristotle's biographers, and for their part the latter may be said to have drawn upon that passage in book 1 of the *Nicomachean Ethics* where Aristotle in introducing his critique of Plato's idea of the Good says something quite similar.[1] Even beyond that, if analyzed by type, so to speak, the passage in the *Ethics* could be said to go back to many utterances which Plato puts in the mouth of Socrates, such as "To refute me is not difficult, to refute the *logos*, however, most difficult" and so forth. The biographies of Aristotle, from which the formulation stems, reflect the dispute between the schools and the situation of the late centuries of ancient philosophy. At that time it was evidently the task of the defenders of the Peripatetic school and the supporters of Aristotle to portray him—despite his criticism of Plato and in opposition to the august tradition of the academy—as a legitimate intellectual confederate of Plato's. This is of no small interest since we need to be clear about the basic intention of the later Peripatetic commentators, who draw upon so many Neoplatonic concepts and interpretations. We can say, in fact, that in spite of Aristotle's critique of the doctrine of ideas, on the whole the tendency to *harmonize* Plato and Aristotle predominated overwhelmingly in ancient times. The same may also be said of the Middle Ages despite all the disputes among schools which pervade that period. Quite recently it has been established that Augustine, the

---

1. *Vita Aristoteles Marciana*, in Düring, *Aristotle in the Ancient Biographical Tradition* (Goteburg, 1957), pp. 94–119.

Christian Platonist, had a healthy dose of Aristotle in him.[2] And
the same point is made in the reverse way insofar as the tradition
of Augustinian Platonism was entirely capable of preserving itself during the time when acceptance of Aristotle was gradually
growing in the high Middle Ages. Consequently we can speak of
a sharpening of the opposition between Plato and Aristotle only
once the modern era had begun. Because of its investigative
mentality the modern era could see in Aristotle only the teacher
whose authority was supposed to protect an out-of-date science
against a mathematically founded physics, a physics which dared
through obsevation of nature, contrived experiment, and mathematical hypothesis to arrive at conclusions contradicting
Aristotle's doctrines on nature. Galileo, for instance, went so far
as to caricature Simplicius, the learned, venerable exegete of
Aristotle to whom we owe so much, by naming the disputant
who refuses to deviate from Aristotle and whom the natural scientist must combat, Simplicio. This, of course, is not only an allusion to Simplicius but also to the supposed simplemindedness of
such book learning as his. Here for the first time one becomes
conscious of a real opposition between Plato and Aristotle:
Plato's extended application of the mathematical, hypothetical
procedure to dialectic could serve to legitimize Galileo's physics
whereas Aristotle's authority only stood in the way of unpreju-
diced inquiry into nature.

Nevertheless along with the Platonism of the modern mathematical method, the attempt to perpetuate the Aristotelian doctrine of substantial forms, the entelechies, continues through the
whole recent history of the modern sciences and the assimilation
of these sciences in philosophy up through Hegel. Leibniz in
particular, that great harmonizer and synthesizer, sought a path
between Aristotle and modern science, and Leibniz's contribution was surpassed by German Idealism as that developed from
Kant to Hegel. Thus only the victorious thrust of natural science
in the nineteenth century (together with the emergence of the
historical consciousness) may be said to have put an end to the

2. Rudolf Schneider, *Seele und Sein. Ontologie bei Augustin und Aristoteles* (Frankfurt,
1937).

influence of a tradition which had unified the Platonic and Aristotelian logos philosophy. Guided by the methodological principle of modern science, i.e., that all dogmatic preconceptions and
expectations should be strictly excluded, scholarship went back
directly to the sources and devoted itself to interpretation of the
Greek texts. Only then did the problem of Aristotle's critique of
Plato become an issue, which at the same time was somewhat dif-
fused, to be sure, by the new historical attitude. For now the
problem itself became a historical, genetic one. The question of
how Aristotle's flat, obviously inappropriate and almost sarcastic
critique of Plato's doctrine of ideas was to be reconciled with
Aristotle's genius, with his twenty years of continued study under Plato, with the perspecuity and depth of his own metaphysical teachings, was put historically, which is to say, biographically
and psychologically.

The variety of answers which modern research has given to
the question raised by Aristotle's critique of Plato wavers between establishing with regret that Aristotle did not grasp the
idea of "critical" philosophy and taking refuge in some sort of
historical, genetic account. In the later case, for example, a late
phase in Plato is constructed which is said to be the real object of
Aristotle's critique. Or it is said that Aristotle did not have Plato
in mind so much as the Platonists of the academy. In recent decades there followed upon that strategy the reverse approach,
which attempted to analyze Aristotle's writings genetically and,
as Werner Jaeger did, for instance, to posit an affinity between
the early Aristotle and Plato. A gradual departure from Plato's
doctrine of ideas and a shift to the empirical standpoint are then
said to characterize the development in Aristotle's own thinking.
To be sure, Aristotle's critique of the doctrine of ideas remained
exceedingly difficult to comprehend from this perspective, and
consequently this most recent philological theory has become
suspect. A closer inspection reveals too many grounds for thinking that such a "development" in Aristotle from metaphysician to
empiricist is incompatible with the tradition as we know it and
even more incompatible with our present conception of an empirical science—which, although Jaeger does not admit it, underlies his hypothesis.

I myself sought at one time to make some sense of this disquieting mystery, for I could not be content with the theory being proffered by neo-Kantians to account for the inappropriateness of many of Aristotle's criticisms, i.e., that Aristotle remained trapped in "dogmatic" thinking and consequently was unable to grasp the "critical" intent of Plato's philosophy. At the very least such a theory, it seemed to me, did not do justice to Aristotle's critique of the idea of the Good in the *Nichomachean Ethics*. But beyond that, how was one to come to grips with such a curious argument as Aristotle's critique of the ideas in the *Metaphysics*? A possible solution seemed to be that of making Plato's dialectical way of putting things responsible for the distortions which his doctrine suffers in Aristotle's critique of it. If today, after Robin, Natorp, and Stenzel, we raise the issue again, that solution seems even more justified, especially since we realize that we possess only literary works from Plato and have knowledge of his doctrines only through them and through reflections of these doctrines in Aristotle's critique, while conversely we possess Aristotle's doctrinal treatises but only fragments of his artful literary works. This fact presents a difficulty for any methodical investigation of our problem, which, as I see it, sets limits to any *philological* approach to it. The attempt to deduce the development of Plato's philosophical doctrines from his dialogues—an undertaking with which modern philologians and historians of philosophy have been struggling for a century and a half—is almost as risky and methodologically overextended as the brilliant but nevertheless fruitless reconstruction of Aristotle's lost writings which we owe to Werner Jaeger. Our situation in respect to the tradition demands that we give philosophy and not philology methodological priority when it comes to uncovering the subject matter at issue behind the different literary forms in which the tradition is given to us and when it comes to orienting ourselves in terms of that subject matter. And was it perhaps not the case that if one wanted to read Plato's actual philosophy—which was never put down in writing—into the dialogues, i.e., if one wanted to translate it into the language of unambiguous concepts, one had to proceed to Aristotle and in passing through him, as it were, produce the philosophy of Plato's which he criticizes? It seemed so.

In this vein I tried some decades ago to circumvent the problem by establishing that one first finds a definite, fully developed awareness of what a concept is as such, only in Aristotle. At that time I was strongly influenced by Heidegger's interpretation of Aristotle, the real intention of which was still not completely evident, namely, its critique of ontology, and which in essence repeated Aristotle's critique of Plato in the form of an existential, situation-oriented, philosophical critique of the idealist tradition. But does that suffice?

It seems to me now that any interpretation which properly adheres to the subject matter under investigation here must start with the assumption that Aristotle's critique of Plato relies on something essential which he has *in common* with Plato. And that common ground is the "turn" to the logoi known to us from its literary formulation in the *Phaedo*. By this I mean the rejection in principle of naive, unreflective methods of investigating and explaining natural events, a rejection which is full fledged in the form in which it is expressed by the Socrates of the *Phaedo*. Indeed those whom we call pre-Socratics can be classed together precisely because of their failure to make the transition to reflection. Plato has Socrates relate that, having failed in his attempt to understand the ancient thinkers, he set out on a "second best journey." Instead of attempting to look at the sun directly (something which would damage the eyes and ultimately cause blindness) he sought to investigate the truth as it is mirrored in the logoi. An ironic passage indeed! In my *Platos dialektische Ethik* I worked out to what extent this investigation of reality as it is present in the logoi provides access to the truth of what is, and how it serves in uncovering the true order of the cosmos. I also showed that investigation of the logoi is the actual task which the whole tradition of early Greek philosophy set for itself, and how Plato, in building upon this tradition, approaches this task mythologically in his *Timaeus*. Unquestionably Plato is indicating in the *Phaedo* that seeking the truth in the logoi is not at all a second best way but in fact the only way to true insight. *And on precisely this point Aristotle is a true Platonist.* Recent research, all of which is indebted to Heidegger's powers of phenomenological intuition in matters of most decisive importance, has brought this foundation of the logoi to everyone's attention, and we now find it quite amateurish when someone juxtaposes the "idealist" Plato to the "realist" Aristotle, thereby applying epistemological categories which have become suspect generally, not just in their application here. When he asks about the being of what is, Aristotle begins with the question of how we speak about it (πῶς λέγεται). This is no propaedeutic, preliminary question concerning usage which he might be raising in order to establish a specific meaning of his own. Rather he takes usage as a basis upon which he stands in seeking to comprehend all the conceptual aspects implied in a way of speaking and to systematize them in a clear explication of their meaning. Thus the "mirror" of the logoi per se is by no means the object to which one restricts one's thinking. That may be said as well in regard to what is in fact the central question of the *Metaphysics*, i.e., that of the ὄν ᾗ ὄν (Being as Being), the logos which states the being of something.[3] One tends to think that at this point Aristotle abandons the sphere of the logos insofar as he views the *tode ti*, the "this here," as the thing that really is and grants the eidos, that which answers the question, *ti esti*, only the function of a δευτέρα οὐσία, a secondary substance. But in putting the matter this way one has improperly applied the distinction between primary and secondary substance. The actual truth implied in this distinction is, as a matter of fact, the truth of the logos. When asked the question what "this here" is, we give the answer by stating its "what," its essence, its *ti ēn einai*. In short the distinction between tode ti and ti esti or eidos, which Aristotle is the first to make, reveals the ultimate meaning and structure of all speaking. This is self-evident, and hence Plato too in no way disputes that all speaking is ultimately speaking about some *thing* which is, except that Plato, insofar as he analyzes the logos as the koinōnia of ideas, does not reflect upon this fact.[4] In Plato the

3. Cf. chap. 6 above on Heidegger's explication of the hermeneutic "as" (ᾗ) in the logos. For Gadamer, who follows Heidegger here, the phenomenal object of any descriptive phenomenology can be described only insofar as it is constituted in language and displays itself therein "as" what it is. (Translator)

4. So it happens that in a most puzzling fashion the *Sophist* gives as an example of a false judgment of perception, a conceptual impossibility: "Theaetetus flies," which in fact

pseudos problem raises the issue of the "thing" spoken of but not the problem of the ti esti, what it means to be (*der Sinn von Sein*).

If we begin by establishing this common basis in Plato and Aristotle—which, moreover, makes understandable how Aristotle, in spite of his critique of Plato's doctrine of ideas, could blend into the essentially unified intellectual influence of Platonic philosophy and thereby become the founder of Western metaphysics—then and precisely then, it no longer makes any sense to reduce the difference between the two to a difference in the forms of their literary production, as I had attempted to do previously. To be specific, one must ask instead whether the structure of synthesis, or symplokē, which Plato sees in the logos in fact does justice to its actual structure and whether Aristotle's distinction between "what" a thing is and the "this-here" is not a superior way of stating the truth of the matter.[5] Whatever the answer may be, our first task must be to establish the perspective from which Plato's doctrine of ideas and Aristotle's critique of it may be understood: *whereas in Plato it is obviously the insight into the nature of number which supports and directs his thinking and conceptualization, in Aristotle it is the insight into the nature of what lives.*

Let us start with Plato. My point of departure is that Plato has very clearly told us, both in his literary works and in the *Seventh Letter* (which I presume to be authentic), that it is his encounter with Socrates which got him started on the way of thinking, an encounter with a man of inconceivable rectitude in the

---

has no bearing on the problem of a false judgment of perception. This has been correctly emphasized by many recently (Kamlah, Marten, Lorenz, and Mittelstrass). Nevertheless this passage does reflect how the logos, as the fitting together of essences in what is stated, asserts itself in Plato over a speaking of some presently given existent. [In this respect Aristotle may be said to be an "earlier" (*ursprünglicher*) thinker than Plato, as will also become evident in the treatment of pseudos below. Cf. chap. 6 above on the inadequacy of Plato's treatment of pseudos and on the problem of "Theaetetus flies." (Translator)]

5. Here too we have an indication of Aristotle's being an "earlier" thinker than Plato. Cf. in this regard Gadamer's translation and commentary, *Aristoteles: Metaphysik XII* (Frankfurt, 1948), where Aristotle is shown to be closer than Plato to the original phenomenon of *alētheia*, or disclosure of Being in the existent thing: "It is evident that Aristotle wants to defend an older understanding of being here against the Platonists" (p. 46). (Translator)

midst of a world which no longer had the slightest inkling of what such rectitude is. The most important testimony here is Plato's *Crito*, in which Socrates' rectitude is displayed in its most radical form. There, despite all the arrangements which had been made and all the political justifications which Crito gives, Socrates refuses to flee prison and escape execution. The question which Socrates' action poses for Plato is this: how is it possible for someone to be so detached from everything which surrounds him that his behavior could differ so radically from the norm—a norm which, as we see, for the most part amounts to adapting to those natural and social conditions of life which determine our existence. How could someone break out of the mold so utterly and hold to the idea of what is right in total disregard of what 'everybody' does and what 'everybody' says. What must this idea be? For one thing, it must be clearly and indisputably present before the eyes of one who lives in this way and decides so unerringly. And for another, it is plain that he who thus sees what is right with his own eyes, as it were, cannot really be said to have to make choices. For one cannot deny what one sees with one's own eyes anymore than one can deliberately miss what one is trying to grab hold of. This is the meaning of Socrates' famous "οὐδεὶς ἑκὼν ἁμαρτάνει" (no one voluntarily does what is wrong), which is to be complemented with the correlative assertion that aretē is knowledge. This implies something with regard to the thing which one knows here, namely, that it is as rock solid and certain as only something can be which is seen with one's own eyes and known for sure. Plato's first writings are plainly devoted to introducing his readers to the ontological sphere of the idea of the Good and he crowns these first writings with a wonderful extrapolation from the undeniable, truly real idea of the Good—an extrapolation which takes the form of a political utopia. In this extrapolation an entire republic, an entire city, an entire political constitution, is thought out and organized in such a way that the puzzlement at Socrates' existence is transposed, so to speak, into marveling at the reality of the true state. In this state the very thing which made Socrates appear such an absurd exception in the Athens of his time becomes constitutive of its citizenry as a whole.

Now it is true that in working out this utopia Plato relies upon mathematics, which according to even his own depiction of Socrates does not fall within the field of Socratic knowing and ignorance. However, all of us can see that mathematics deals with a reality which, to use Aristotle's language, is παρὰ ταῦτα, a reality alongside and beyond the visible world—and it is considerably easier for us to understand that fact than for us to understand the unerring way Socrates sees what is right. Mathematics provides the prime example of the being of that which is in essence supersensible. Like Plato we refer to this mode of being as noetic or intelligible. Mathematics, accordingly, has a significant function in Plato's philosophy and teaching to the extent that it serves as a propaedeutic exercise. And furthermore it is important that mathematical disciplines can be systematized. Number, line, plane, and solid, each of which depends upon the previous one, have a natural order which gives a sequential structure to the mathematical sciences. This is stressed by Plato himself on occasion, and quite often by Aristotle in respect to Plato.[6] Even so, if I am correct, that sequence remains primarily a mere model of systematic deduction in general, just as the number serves only as a model for the task of ascertaining the logos ousias, i.e., in defining the essence of something. In my view this is the conclusion which must be drawn from the decades of debate on the doctrine of ideal numbers. For it is evident that Plato takes the number as his guide in his inquiry into the logos ousias. Obviously this can be understood in the sense that the eidos proves to be the ἕν εἶδος for the πολλά, the one form or unity of the Many, which in its varying multiplicity makes up the world of Becoming. But it has a much deeper meaning too. The very logos of the eidos, in other words, the very attempt to say what the unitary essence of any given thing is, leads necessarily to a systematic combination of many eidetic determinations (definitions by essence) in the unity of a defining statement. This fact too, indeed this fact especially, implies a unity of many. And in the concluding passages of the *Sophist* and *Statesman*, for in-

6. This was made the central point in Konrad Gaiser's recent reconstruction of Plato's doctrine—not, I believe, without placing more weight on this thought than it is able to bear.

stance, the stages in the essential determination which is being sought for the subject of the discussion, for the sophist or the statesman respectively, are *counted*; thus the definition of the essence finally arrived at has the structure of the number as a sum. This can be seen in the highly ironic way in which Plato repeats the enumeration of the determinations arrived at. In the *Sophist* and *Statesman* especially, the definitions derived in dihairesis are not without a certain gratuitousness insofar as the aspect of something which one takes to begin the division has no inherent necessity to it. And observe too that even Plato himself plays a delightful, ironic game with this gratuitousness in these dialogues. Consider further that exactly as Aristotle has critically noted, the result arrived at in any such mode of division is in fact anticipated in the steps of the division. These things having been established, we can only conclude that the whole procedure is not intended to arrive at a rigid systematization, a pyramid of ideas. What *is* revealed is that the number as the unity of many is the ontological paradigm. These dihairetical classifications point to a whole of explications, as it were, a whole which is incapable of ever being completed. And precisely in that fact we have perhaps the most important analogy between idea and number.[7] One must consider Plato's real insight to be that there is no collected whole of possible explications either for a single eidos or for the totality of the eidē.[8] Moreover, the either/or here is only a pseudo alternative, for if one really wanted to complete the demarcation of an eidos on all sides, one would have to mark it off from all other eidē as well, which is to say that one finds oneself in the situation—the situation on which I base my interpretation—where only the assembled whole of all possible explications would make the full truth possible.[9] This is the teaching implied in the *Parmenides*. It is my belief that Plato's doctrine of

7. Cf. chap. 6 above on the unendingness of numbers. (Translator)

8. Cf. Speusippus, frag. 31 a–e (Lang), who draws from this fact conclusions in opposition to, and critical of, the doctrine of ideas.

9. In this argument Gadamer's own divergence from Hegel and from systematic philosophy's contention that the "truth is the whole" is evident (cf. *Hegel's Dialectic*). The truth is indeed the whole, but since the whole always exceeds the horizons of what can be present to us at any given time we have only partial truths, glimpses of the truth, as it displays aspects of itself in human discourse. Cf. chap. 5 above. (Translator)

the One and the indeterminate Two as Aristotle and others have transmitted it to us is intended above all to make clear that in every seeing of a unity and saying it the infinity of possible explications afforded by the logos can never be closed off.

The significance of this point, it seems to me, can be grasped only against the background of Pythagoreanism. There, although it is left completely unaccounted for, all thinking is guided by the basic conviction that despite the boundless and confusing variety of appearances, astonishingly precise, pure mathematical relationships exist in these appearances, such as those which are particularly evident in harmonies, be they harmonies of sounds or those of the cosmic order. To this extent harmony is a fundamental constituent of the world, and thus it makes sense to say that things "consist" of numbers and numerical relationships. Harmonies are instances of compatibility, dissonances, instances of incompatibility; Plato remains a Pythagorean insofar as he carries precisely this conception of harmony over into the realm of reflection and the logos. Plato always has in mind the compatibility and incompatibility of ideas. That is already evident in the *Phaedo* in the argument founded on the incompatibility of Death and Soul. In the *Sophist* this same theme emerges explicitly as the koinōnia of the highest genera, and there, as in the *Philebus* as well, it is illustrated by special phonemes which can combine with all other phonemes, the "vowels" which hold everything together, as opposed to the "consonants" which are limited in their ability to combine with one another. That, unquestionably, is an ingenious choice with which to illustrate the transposition of the Pythagorean idea of harmony to the sphere of the logos, and it provides an indication of how numbers and numerical relationships function as the model for the configuration of the ideas.

Having pointed out these aspects of Plato's assimilation and transformation of the Pythagorean doctrine of the peras and the apeiron, it seems logical for me to rework what I had indicated in my *Philebus* interpretation of 1931. For there the method used was more that of phenomenological description than interpretation within a historical context. There I elaborated on the curious persistence of indeterminacy in the effect of the peras on the

being of what is limited by it. There is something specifically
Platonic about that indeterminacy (despite Philolaos, frag. 2).
For in Plato's *Philebus* the determination by the peras is spoken
of as a "letting go" into the apeiron, and that way of putting the
matter gives the old Pythagorean pair of concepts, peras and
apeiron, a new meaning which ultimately relates them to the
logos. Not a new meaning, however, in any neo-Kantian sense of
determining the indeterminate by an external act or "positing"
of thought. In the *Philebus* we find the phrase, εὑρήσειν γὰρ
ἐνοῦσαν (for we would find it existing therein) (16 d).[10] Rather
what is meant is that the intelligible order of number and measure in the world of "sense" phenomena is always actualized *only
approximately*. Plato is thus reflecting upon the ontological difference between idea and phenomenon, and for him the phenomenon's falling short of ideal exactitude is to be thought of as
a diminution of Being or reality. The being of what has "become," which constitutes the third genus, is precisely not "pure"
Being but a mixture of Being with Not-being and Becoming.
When Plato then refers to it as γένεσις εἰς οὐσίαν (coming into
being) it sounds more Aristotelian than it is supposed to. For
there is no reference here to a natural process in which something develops into its essence, i.e., to the *entelecheia*. Instead
what is meant is the approximation of the phenomena to their
ideal numbers and measures. Now Aristotle's ti ēn einai certainly
takes this element of indeterminacy into account. Whoever
speaks of the eidos must speak as well of the limitations and contingency in its appearances. But for Aristotle the emphasis is on
determinacy and not indeterminacy. In spite of all ineradicable
contingency, existent things in nature display a determinacy in
becoming what they are. And it makes quite a difference if one
thinks of Not-being as the "not-yet" hidden in the seed, i.e., as a
potentiality and possibility for eventual determination or as the
ineradicable adulteration of the essence by an "Erdenrest" (rem-
nant of earth) (Goethe's *Faust*, 11954).

Thus in teaching that his dialectic could never be brought to

10. Cf. Natorp's astonishingly bold reinterpretation of this turn of speech in *Platos
Ideenlehre*, pp. 321 ff.

a completion Plato seems to have drawn the appropriate conclusion from the fundamental experience of the early Greek thinkers. The doctrine of the indeterminate Two is a doctrine of the primordial discrepancy between essence and phenomenon, a discrepancy which is as inchoately expressed in the *Timaeus* as it is in Parmenides' doctrinal poem, a poem which appends a description of the dual world of oppositions to the Eleatic teaching on unity, without clarifying the connection between its first and second parts.[11]

Let us turn now to Aristotle's critique of Plato's doctrine of ideas. That critique, I submit, must be seen against the background of the following question. Is Being pure numerical harmony? And correspondingly, is the logos, with which we grasp what truly is, an intertwining of eidetic determinations? Put another way, is the logos properly understood when it is taken to be a reflection or repetition of the intelligible sort of being characteristic of the number? Can the eidos really be a kind of paradigmatic cause (αἰτία παραδειγματική) if, as Plato's Pythagoreanizing disciples have evidently taught, it is the true reality? Does the order of our world derive from the pure harmonic relationships among the ideas? How are we supposed to think of its deriving from the ideas? How would that be possible? If one should not be satisfied with the mere metaphors of the *Timaeus* (the manufacturing of the All by a demiurge), how is one supposed to conceive of the idea's really being παρὰ ταῦτα, "alongside" the things here, and of its developing an efficacy of its own? Where do we see something of that sort? It really does appear that in nature a primordial form of the genus existing by it-

11. It would be worthwhile to inquire whether the existence side by side of unrelated doctrines, such as occurs here, seems improper only if measured against *our* standard of theoretical coherence. Such an inquiry would not only shed light upon the aporiai in the teaching of Empedocles and Anaxagoras, and not only upon the insolubility of the methexis problem in Plato, but perhaps also upon the heretofore irresolvable age-old dispute between realists and nominalists concerning just who is the true Aristotle. Indeed one might chance the suggestion that Greek thought was susceptible to being absorbed into the Judeo-Christian theory of creation precisely because of its acceptance of what to us is a theoretical deficiency and because of its abjuring of any requirement of systematic coherence. It does indeed appear that the question of existence versus essence became crucial only in the Christian era. And in this respect Gilson's interpretation of Aquinas does in fact have something to be said for it.

self reproduces the cycles of life in its mysterious way. Thus *if* the doctrine of the eidos has any ontological significance, *if* the eidos were actually an effective reality, then it would have to be that most of all in the realm of nature and life.

In departing from this assumption, it seems to me, I can successfully resolve a problem which heretofore has remained totally irresolvable in the tradition, viz., where did Plato get the ideas? Research until now has told us roughly the following. To begin with, Plato took the ideas from the aretai and from mathematical entities, and did so for reasons which I too included in my own account of Plato's development: because here something permanently fixed and stable "beyond" the flood of appearances comes into plain view. And consequently his thinking necessarily led him to conclude that whenever we use words we are envisioning the inner aspect of a thing in a similar fashion, i.e., looking beyond the sense-perceived. We are, so to speak, already "intending" something else, the pure genus, the pure meaning, or however one might choose to explain the "universal" in modern concepts. Thus it is inevitable that ultimately the doctrine of ideas would extend to all things which one can talk about, all things for which one can find words. This argument is quite convincing in precisely the form Plato himself has the old Parmenides state it in the latter's discussion with the still all-too-young Socrates. Accordingly the summary found in the disputed *Seventh Letter* of all those things for which there are ideas cannot be all that astonishing. Now Aristotle's critique of Plato opposes exactly this extension of the ideas. In the first book of the *Metaphysics* one finds in several places—always in the "we" form—that the argument for the hypothesis of the ideas requires one to accept more ideas than "we" do. "We" Platonists, evidently, or as I would prefer to understand it, "we" who are attempting to interpret Plato's doctrine of the ideas *in optimam partem* and to justify it. Plainly Aristotle has every right to speak of "we." For even the statement of Xenocrates cited above restricts the αἰτία παραδειγματική to φύσει συνεστῶτα (what is composed by nature) since the idea was not to be transcended by some creative power prior to it: αὐτῷ τῷ εἶναι λέγωμεν αὐτὴν δρᾶν καὶ τέλος εἶναι τῶν γιγνομένων τὴν πρὸς αὐτὴν ὁμοίωσιν (Let us say that it [the idea] acts by its own being alone and that the end of becoming is to be like the idea) (Proclus, *in Parm.* 136, Stallbaum). Evidently the efforts of the academy were entirely devoted to proving that this mathematical order of Being, structured like the lattice of a crystal, is the true content of the doctrine of ideas. And in seeking such a proof, one will obviously not begin with man-made things, for here it is clearly our own technical intelligence which designs and determines ahead of time the appearance of the thing to be produced. Here one could not just assume that the ideas are there "by themselves." Nor are there ideas of negations which result solely from *our* saying "no." Nor of relationships, for relationships do not exist in such a way that one could name an existent "by itself" by virtue of which the relationship occurs. The relationship can change relative to an individual existent without this individual existent itself changing; for instance, the friend himself is not changed by the relationship of friendship. My thesis then is this: Aristotle reduces the problem of the ideas to that one instance where, given the ontological presuppositions entailed in it, it is most likely to be resolved—to the case of the *physei on*. And, as we know, he then shows that even in this most promising case one cannot speak of ideas existing "by themselves."[12] The arguments which Aristotle applies shed light in several respects on Plato's way of formulating the problem of the ideas. To begin with there is the curious beginning of Aristotle's critique of the doctrine of ideas in which he declares that the hypothesis of the ideas ultimately leads to accepting twice as much to be real as is necessary, and that it thus leads to a doubling of the world. This, he tells us, would be just as senseless as trying to make a task of counting a sum of things which one finds too difficult easier by positing an even larger number. Such an argument is provocative precisely because it is so silly. What is significant about it is that it contains the idea of *counting*. First the ideas are counted; then the things are counted, and that yields double the number. As absurd as that may sound it is not nonsensical. It seems obvious to me that

---

12. The *locus classicus* for the formulation of this theme is the *Metaphysics* Λ3. And as a whole this twelfth book seems to stand in close relationship to the discussion of the ideas in the academy.

Aristotle could justifiably, and in genuinely Platonic fashion, conceive of the being of the ideas as I think Plato meant them to be conceived, i.e., as a sum number, and that accordingly he could speak of a sum of all ideas.[13] As a matter of fact Plato attributes no further sense of cause to the ideas besides parousia, methexis, and koinōnia; consequently, the logos is the total computation and "account" constituted by "counting" its coexistent contents. Another example occurs when Aristotle refers to the awkward fact that the eidos (species) is in fact not always an eidos and the genos (genus) not always a genos. Sometimes the latter is a species of the next highest genus. In that case, both the species and the genus appear as "causative" in the logos. But in which does the individual participate? Evidently in both. This too is an argument which makes sense only if one counts the eidos and genos together in the same 'computation' being carried out in a logos, i.e., in the sum counted up as a number. Cf., for example, the ironically pedantic summations at the end of the *Sophist* and the *Statesman*. I conclude, therefore, that Aristotle's actual critique of the doctrine of ideas turns to the physei onta because in essence physis is where the doctrine of the ideas seems most likely to be exemplified (cf. *Metaphysics* 1070 a 18).

And Aristotle now shows why even there it will not work. He sees in Plato's thinking a mathematization of nature and develops—in opposition to Plato, although not in opposition to him alone—the doctrine of the four causes, a doctrine based on the model of technē. There must be an existent which figures as the mover, just as there must be *hylē* in order for a new existent with the same eidos to be created. The biological genus per se does not propagate itself as some kind of mysterious "self"—be that self unchangeable selfsameness or be that self the cause of the continuing reproduction of itself. No, it is *the* man who engenders man. This means, however, that the eidos does not exist "by itself." The presumed existence by itself of the eidos is a false disengagement from what actually is. What is, is always an *enhylon eidos*.

The first book of the *Physics* shows us how much that argu-

---

13. Cf. chap. 6 on the sum number (*Anzahl*, arithmos). (Translator)

ment is intended in opposition to Plato. There the seminal observation is made that what Plato refers to as Not-being actually can
be said to have two meanings. Not-being is not simply and unequivocally the not-being of heterotēs in the eidos, i.e., that
which in any given eidetic determination excludes all other determinations. There is a not-being in the eidos which has to do
not with its relationship to other eidē but with existence itself or,
in Aristotle's forceful way of putting it, with being deprived of
something, *sterēsis*. Every natural process runs its course between
sterēsis and eidos, Not-being and Being. Such not-being of the
existent thing is dependent upon its eidetic determination *insofar*
as the latter is missing in it. To this extent it is indeed defined by
the eidos. It is, exists, as lacking the eidos, as the absence of itself, so to speak. Thus it contains within itself all Being-not-yet
which ultimately becomes something. The living thing which
emerges from the seed does not simply assume another eidetic
determination and it is not simply something "different," something defined by essentially different determinations, though if
viewed *mathematically* it would be. On the contrary, it is the same,
identical being which passes from the state of still lacking determination in itself to the state of fulfilled determinacy; it is an existent which still lacks complete determinacy. *Hence, it cannot be*
described as a combination of different eidetic determinations; rather it is
the transition and ascendance of the immature to the ripe. Here there is
always an existent which is "not yet" its form, and accordingly it
may be called hylē, the ὑποκειμένη φύσις (underlying nature) insofar as it underlies whatever changes in form occur. Consequently every such determination of form is an enhylon eidos.
The thought here is modeled on technē to the extent that the
technē-concepts of *morphē*, hylē, kinēsis, and telos or οὗ ἕνεκα
(that for the sake of which) may be applied. However, many distinctions from technē are evident as well. One of the most obvious of these is that in the case of the artwork clearly only the
finished product is what we could say constitutes its eidos. An
unfinished artwork is not at all that which it is supposed to represent. A natural being, on the other hand, which is not yet
finished, not yet grown, is in spite of that fact, already that
which it will be. The essential structure of physis is that it is al-

ways an ὁδὸς ἐκ φύσεως εἰς φύσιν (a path out of a nature into a nature). That is the sense of the *dynamis* concept, which is obviously to be applied specifically in the realm of natural things, and which points up how untenable the assumption of the eidos existing by itself is. In nature the eidos exists only as the enhylon eidos.

The significance of this anti-Platonic thesis can be illuminated in reference to a small philological point regarding a minor problem in Aristotle, a point, however, which in my view has not yet been properly explained. Aristotle is fond of illustrating the doctrine of the enhylon eidos with a particular language usage, that of the words σιμός and σιμότης, which is to say, "snubnosedness." We have no real expression for it, and in Greek too, as far as I know, it is not a common word but one which has achieved a measure of immortality only through Aristotle. This word is of such a sort that it can be used only in reference to noses with a hollow form. Nothing else can be said to be σιμόν. Σιμός thus means *a nose* which has "snubnosedness," or σιμότης. (If we want to characterize the mere form here abstractly and mathematically, we would say κοιλότης.) Now what kind of an example is that! There are, to be sure, words the use of which is so limited that they resist any extension to other spheres, such as, for instance, the German *schielen* (to look askance) which can be said only of the eyes. Thus σιμότης seems to be best rendered by "snubness" assuming that we could use this word "snub" as a pure adjective without "nosed" too, although only in reference to a nose. But does the example not have a special point beyond this? We must remember after all that Socrates had such a nose. And if we examine what Aristotle has to say about Socrates, we find the following: In *Metaphysics* M 4 Aristotle describes Socrates' significance for the development of definition. Democritus and the Pythagoreans had touched upon the matter of definition only from afar. Socrates, however, was quite properly attempting to determine the "what," for as we know, he sought to develop syllogisms, and the basis of all syllogisms is the "what." But then Aristotle adds that Socrates made neither the universal itself nor the defined concept a separate reality; but others, he says, did separate uni-

versals and concepts and then named such things "ideas."
Socrates, in other words, did not do that. For him the universal
was still immanent in the existent thing. Since he did not make
the chōrismos mistake, the mistake of separating the eidos from
that which has it and in which it is, he remained close to the
truth for which his own face was the guarantor. Something of
this sort seems to have been intended by Aristotle's witty example of σιμότης. The point would not be lost on anyone, for similarity to Socrates was something which even a complete novice in
the sciences would be proud of. Theaetetus was proud of it and
was praised for having a Socratic nose, and Aristotle's choice of
this example demonstrates that Socrates' nose was well known to
later generations as well. In any case it seems clear to me that
Socrates is being alluded to here in order to illustrate the superiority of his metaphysics over Plato's with one of the former's
physiognomical characteristics. (Cf. Plato's *Theaetetus*, 143 e, 209 c.)

More important, however, is the way in which Aristotle's basic critique of the contention that only the ideas are true Being
affects his own doctrines and especially that of the logos ousias,
which is just as much a λόγος τοῦ εἴδους (statement of the form).
Here, if I view things correctly, Aristotle penetrates to the root
of the insoluble difficulties to which the grounding of Plato's
doctrine of the ideas in the logos had led. We have seen that, for
Aristotle, the ontological claim that the eidos is true Being or reality finds its most convincing substantiation in the realm of nature, i.e., in the physei onta. On the other hand, it is undeniably
the *logical*, not physical, aspect of the eidos which gives it its
claim to ontological universality. The question of the ti esti can
be limited neither to those (mathematical) realities which actually
do exist "by themselves" nor to the ideas, to which one—in following Plato—might be willing to attribute true being "by itself."
*The extension of the concept of the idea to all that can be said and meant
is an inescapable consequence of orienting one's thought to the logos, a
consequence which Plato himself saw clearly enough (cf. the* Parmenides). This extension is plainly the task which Aristotle sets
for himself. He must strip away the appearance of ontological
supremacy deriving from the logical universality of the "idea"
while at the same time providing new legitimation of the primacy

of ousia. And that he must do, not in turning away from the
logos but by making distinctions which illuminate it. For in a
strange way Plato's thinking on the eidos tends to obscure the actual sense of the logos insofar as he conceives of it as the combination of ideas with one another. For the logos itself implies
more than a fitting together, more than a sum of essences. It is
always a reference to something, to something which is here and
now, a "this here" (todi ti), of which not only its essential
definition may be expressed but to which much else besides may
be attributed which is precisely not constitutive of its permanent
essence. The forms of this further attribution are highly differentiated within themselves. They are the σχήματα τῆς
κατηγορίας (categoreal schemata).

The point of departure of Aristotle's doctrine of categories
appears to have been a matter of logic, *logic* however, not in the
sense that the original point of it was to avoid equivocations and
sophistic arguments.[14] On the contrary, there is more than likely
a real connection between the categorial differentiation of the
various senses of "to be" and the priority in being which Aristotle
assigns to that which is "by nature" and which he makes the
standard for every thing that one could claim "is" really. The
doctrine of categories may be said to originate in a "logical" concern only in the sense that within the universality of the logos
which Plato uncovers, within the possibility of applying the ti esti
question to everything which can be meant in discourse, Aristotle
perceives distinctions in the senses of *is* which can be given in answer to that question. Thus in what is probably the earliest mention of the ten categories (in the *Topics*) the differentiation of the
categories is undertaken with no apparent difficulties emerging.
The question of what something "is" provides the theme
throughout all the categories. Within that question the different
senses of "to be," ousia, *poion*, *poson*, and so on can be distinguished. They all arise in the same way, one alongside the other,
so to speak. On the other hand, they diverge from one another

14. Kurt von Fritz has quite properly pointed out that the sophistic paralogisms
which play on Being as existence and Being as the copula are not eliminated at all in the
exposition of the categories, because Being is never treated there as an assertion of something's existence (*Archiv für Geschichte der Philosophie* 40 (1931): 453 ff.).

when one does not ask about what they are in themselves but
about what they may be attributed to. Then it becomes evident
that the essence is distinct from all the other predications which
can be attributed to an existent thing. For everything besides the
essence has the changing character of inessentiality, of "this way
or that." This distinction between the essential (ousia) and inessential (poion) is already presupposed in Plato's dihairetical
definitional logic. But Aristotle recognizes that incidentals too,
the συμβεβηκότα, may be said of the existent thing in very different senses and that they refer to its being, even if in diverse
ways, and not at all to some sort of not-being or irreality.

The concern here nevertheless is with the priority which the
eidos has over the other categories insofar as it is not just an attribute of the existent thing but that which constitutes its reality.
The priority of the eidos derives from the fact that it makes possible the basic ontological articulation of reality given in any valid
logos, i.e., that it gives existences of all sorts their initial stamp.
But it is not the koinōnia of eidetic determinations existing *in
general* which the logos provides, rather the *particular* contents of
an assertion, contents which are encountered in the logos, which
"are" in it different ways. Heading the list of these contents is the
"what" of the existent thing, its essential determination, which is
to say, that which constitutes its lasting essence. What fundamentally distinguishes the other categories from the essential "what"
is the fact that the content of what they state can exist only in
something else, the essence of which has already been determined. Their content can never exist by itself. Now of course the
essential determination of the existent thing cannot have an independent being by itself either, but in its case this is only because it is completely absorbed in the thing of which it is said:
Its sense or meaning can only be to mean this being. Since essential determinations make no claim to be "by themselves" but only
to express the being of existent things (*das Sein des Seienden*), they
are not "there" in the way the existent thing is there; they do not
belong to the same rank, are not ὁμοταγές, as Proclus puts it.[15]

15. Proclus *in Parm*.

And the same may be said of all the generic determinations included in the essence: eidos and genos are not what they appear to be in Plato, i.e., eidetic "items" or units, the sum of which is the logos. Their function is only that of designating the existent thing itself, which nevertheless can be pointed to (δείκνυσθαι) in a way which ultimately remains inaccessible to the logos. The essential determination is indeed a manifold which explicates itself in the logos ousias, from which explication the logos ousias then collects itself into a unitary essence. But *that* manifold is entirely different from the manifold of those determinations, the attribution or nonattribution of which constitutes the true or false statement about some thing.

Thus the decisive insight in Aristotle, the one which provides the basis for his entire doctrine of categories, is that the unitary nature of the essence which is delimited and comprehended by the logos of the ti ēn einai is not a being by itself at all; *rather it constitutes the being by itself of the existent thing.* If one were to look for a single motif in the so-called substance books of the *Metaphysics*, whose subtle intricacies are wont to divert one from the point, it must surely be to establish a unitary nature of the essence which belongs indissolubly to a particular existent thing as its property. It is no mere logic chopping or extreme formalism when, in a limited sense at least, Aristotle admits the question of essence even in regard to what is of composite form, e.g., the "white man" (Z 4,5). Here he is only countering the tendency to universalize and abstract in answering the "what" question whenever this question is taken to be merely a question of logic. He intends the precise opposite. He wishes to fend off the groundless ontological assumptions which result from that tendency and to isolate that special intertwining of unity and multiplicity which is the primary characteristic of the logos ousias. The multiplicity of the latter is not a multiplicity of separable determinations existing in itself. Or put another way, "what" an existing thing is in essence is not a fitting together of genus and specific difference. These two only serve to delimit the "what" as the one, unitary (ἁπλοῦν [simple], ἀσύνθετον [noncomposite]) essence which constitutes the being of the exist-

ent thing immediately (εὐθύς), i.e., quite apart from any form of
mediation (methexis, symplokē, koinōnia, and so on) (*Metaphysics*
Ēta 6, 1045 b 3 ff.).

Thus it is not a matter here of some mysterious "inverting of
the pyramid of being" (Stenzel) which Aristotle undertakes in di-
verging from Plato but of drawing the consequences of a question raised by Plato, the question, that is, of what we actually
mean when we imprint the seal of "ἔστι" ("is") on something. To
be sure, Plato nowhere gives an answer to this question in clear
and precise words, but his answer is sketched in in his doctrine
of the eidos. And it is constantly tossed back and forth, as it
were, in the aporiai of the doctrine of ideas, aporiai which far
from forcing Plato to abandon that doctrine, allow him to unfold
it in all its consequences: "That is the one and the many, which
creates the problem here . . . the cause of all *aporia* if it is not
properly allowed for, and of all *euporia*, if it is" (*Philebus* 15 c).
Contained in the aporia is not only an inevitable cul de sac to
which the doctrine of ideas leads but also the way out, the way to
all discourse which discloses a thing under discussion. One must
assume in principle that no turning away from Plato results if
one immerses oneself in these aporiai. It is evident that the diverse problems in the doctrine of ideas generated the most diverse attempts to solve them among Plato's successors. It would
be arbitrary indeed to select any particular one of these as genuinely Platonic from among the variations of the doctrine of ideas
advocated by Eudoxos, Speusippus, Xenocrates, and many others, some of whose names we scarcely know, e.g., Hestiaios. Of
these Aristotle alone rejected the paradigm role assigned to the
eidos in a doctrine which would make it merely an εἶδος κατὰ
τὸν λόγον (eidos of the logos), and in so doing, he placed
himself in opposition to the other Platonists—not by his objections to the doctrine of ideas as such but by the new ontological
foundation which he gives to the eidos as the ti ēn einai of the
tode ti.

It is a reasonable assumption from which to proceed that the
conceptual formulas which are to provide the new foundation
for Aristotle's position are precisely those which most of all originate with him. It is not the ti as such in distinction from what is

inessential (ποιόν, συμβεβηκός) which provides this foundation but more probably the persistence of the essence through the phases of its self-realization, the ti ēn einai, and above all the definition of this realization of being as *energeia* and entelecheia, respectively, and the "analogical" determination of the sense of these concepts in correlation to dynamis.[16] To be sure, these concepts, like the categories, are formed at first in regard to kinēsis, to the movement of the physei onta. But ultimately it is they alone which succeed in expressing the unified essence of the logos ousias. Even though the pair of concepts, energeia and dynamis, appear typically and regularly *along with* the categories as an appendix to them—a fact which Paul Gohlke[17] and Max Wundt[18] have made much of—in essence it is only these two that fully articulate the new sense of the category of substance and do what the latter was intended to do: express the being of the existent thing itself. For the "analogical" application of δυνάμει (in potential) and ἐνεργείᾳ (in actuality) makes it possible to grasp the essential unity of all things so conceived. Just as in the process of production the material which is δυνάμει is not combined with a "form," but instead becomes in the process of formation that which it "not yet" was, so the determination of the simple essence of a thing is not a *combination* of separately existing determinations; rather it is a bringing to the fore of an essential unity, the ἄτομον εἶδος (indivisible eidos), the "what" content of that unity.

To this extent Aristotle's metaphysics may be said to culminate in the recognition that in the seeing of the essence (nous) a

16. In commenting on Aristotle's *Metaphysics* 12. 4, Gadamer suggests that it is in response to Plato's doctrine of the One and the indeterminate Two that the question is raised concerning whether the principles for all things are the same. In defending his own point of view against Plato's doctrine, Aristotle relies on the categorial differentiation of Being: "Neither is there a common being above the categories nor is any one category contained in another" (Gadamer: *Aristoteles: Metaphysik XII*, 49). What emerges here is the Aristotelian doctrine of the *analogia entis*. It is the *analogy* structure of being which refutes Plato: "One can speak of identical principles only insofar as the same relationship obtains in each case" (idem), i.e., the same analogous relationship of energeia, dynamis, and hylē in the structure of any given thing. (Translator)

17. P. Gohlke, *Die Entstehung der aristotelischen Prinzipienlehre* (Tübingen, 1954).

18. M. Wundt, *Untersuchungen zur Metaphysik des Aristoteles* (Stuttgart, 1953), pp. 79 ff.

meaning of noncomposite (ἀσύνθετον) truth and disconcealedness is realized which precedes all Plato's synthetic or "additive" assertions and their possible truth or falsity.[19] Such a prior disclosedness of the essence occurs in *noein*. And insofar as thought (nous)
is aware of what it is thinking (noein) it is aware of itself. In this
way the disclosedness of the essence points beyond itself to a highest awareness of self which makes the former possible just as light
makes it possible to see things. Any disclosedness of the essence
is possible only when there exists that which is aware of itself. In
this insight we have the highest principle of Aristotle's metaphysics,
which allows him to explicate the traditional concept of the divine philosophically. What is ultimately open to the human being
looking ahead to his highest possibilities, the possible human existence to which finally all else must be subordinated, is the pure
viewing of the truth, i.e., wakefulness of mind, *theoria*. The mind's
living existence, its energeia, is the nearest thing to the all-pres-
ent wakefulness of the divine, to being purely present with what
is purely thought (*noēsis noēseōs*). And so despite all criticism regard
ing this or that point, Aristotle agrees with Plato on the tenability
of the so-called doctrine of ideas. Even in Aristotle there still
persists an element of Pythagoreanism: The highest is the pure.
Hence when all is said and done, nothing has changed concerning
that which Aristotle himself acknowledges when, despite all his objections and criticisms, he characterizes Plato as his friend. Between
him and Plato an ultimate common ground remains. But to pursue this transition into philosophical theology would involve going beyond the confines of this study, for its theme would then
be shortened to *amicus Plato*.

19. The point here is one Gadamer made in his Heidegger lectures in Heidelberg.
From Heidegger's standpoint it is Aristotle who has the "earlier" sense of alētheia and,
correlatively, of pseudos insofar as in Aristotle the eidos is experienced in the
disconcealment of the thing and not, as in Plato, in reflection. In Plato what is in truth
reduces to a proper combining of compatible eidē. Cf. nn. 4 and 5 above. (Translator)

Index

academy, 52, 94, 97*n*, 98, 111, 120, 124, 140, 196, 208
aesthetic consciousness, 65 and *n*, 86*n*
anamnēsis, 26–27, 31 *See also* recollection
anankē, 120, 160, 170–172, 177. *See also* Necessity
Anaxagoras, 43, 141, 145, 171, 206*n*
Anaximander, 185
apeiron, 154–55, 191, 204–05
Apology, 23, 41
Aristophanes, 40, 44, 114, 134
Aristotle: on logic, 5–6, 111, 148; on ethics, 8, 10, 89; account and critique of Plato, 94–95, 118, 126, 130, 132, 140–41, 150–51, 156–59 passim, 174, 180*n*, 183, 188, 194–218; on mathematics, 101*n*, 106n, 107 and *n*; on time, 146; unity with Plato, 194–96, 198–200, 217–18; understanding of Being, 210–17
arithmos. *See* number
Augustine, 91*n*, 194–95

Beautiful, the, 27, 133–34, 161, 163, 187
Being, 12, 27, 28, 32, 57*n*, 90–92, 110, 120, 143, 149, 151, 153 and *n*, 161, 165, 172, 175, 199, 205, 208; Aristotle's understanding of, 210–17

Callicles, 50, 116
Charmides, 2, 7, 84
chōra, 174–76, 179, 186, 188
chōrismos, 140, 157*n*, 212
Christianity, 21, 158, 206*n*
copy, 59, 112, 162, 164–65, 174–75. *See also* imitation
Cornford, F., 162*n*, 163*n*, 165, 167, 175, 176, 177, 178*n*, 180*n*, 190
Cratylus, 105, 107
Critias, 3
Crito, 3, 201
Crombie, I. M., 160*n*, 177, 182

Democritus, 107*n*, 184–85, 211
dialectic, 1*n*, 3, 67, 92, 93–123, 124–25 passim, 157, 158, 190, 195
dialogue, 2, 93, 125. *See also* discussion
dihairēsis, 93, 102, 110*n*, 122, 129, 149, 151, 153, 203, 214
dikaiosynē, 76–77. *See also* justice
discussion, 1–6, 21, 70, 112, 117, 119, 123, 126, 128, 154, 190. *See also* dialogue

education, 47–72 passim, 73–92, 118. See also *paideia*
eidos: hypothesis of, 33–35. *See also* ideas
Eleatic thought, 93, 135, 165, 175, 207
Empedocles, 12, 182, 187
Epinomis, 141*n*, 178
Euclid, 99, 141
Eudoxos, 140, 216
Euthydemus, 84

Fichte, J. G., 138, 157
Friedlander, P., 61*n*, 95
friendship, 7–20 passim, 56, 86

Gaiser, K., 95*n*, 127, 129, 140, 150, 157, 168*n*, 202*n*
Galileo, 158, 195
Goethe, J. W. von, 39, 205
Good, the, 27, 79, 92, 98, 110, 111, 115, 118, 120, 130–31, 133, 154, 191–92, 194, 197, 201
Gorgias, 30*n*, 175

Hartmann, N., 138, 157*n*
Hegel, G. W. F., 1*n*, 53*n*, 86*n*, 87, 93, 98*n*, 120, 133*n*, 138, 153*n*, 195, 203*n*
Heidegger, M., 19*n*, 32*n*, 57*n*, 86*n*, 91*n*, 103*n*, 114*n*, 152, 153*n*, 198, 199*n*, 218*n*
Heraclitus, 43, 145
hermeneutics, 5, 97*n*, 127, 156, 160*n*
Hesiod, 13, 57